T0346765

the FARMER and the CHEF

Farm Fresh
MINNESOTA
Recipes
and Stories

minnesota **cooks**™

MINNESOTA FARMERS UNION • BRUCE MILLER
CLAUDINE ARNDT • KATIE CANNON

Globe Pequot

Guilford, Connecticut

Globe
Pequot

An imprint of The Rowman & Littlefield Publishing
Group, Inc.
4501 Forbes Blvd., Ste. 200
Lanham, MD 20706
www.rowman.com

Distributed by NATIONAL BOOK NETWORK

British Library Cataloguing in Publication
Information available

Library of Congress Cataloging-in-Publication
Data available

ISBN 978-1-4930-4658-4 (cloth : alk. paper)
ISBN 978-1-4930-4659-1 (electronic)

∞™ The paper used in this publication
meets the minimum requirements of American
National Standard for Information Sciences—
Permanence of Paper for Printed Library
Materials, ANSI/NISO Z39. 48-1992.

*For Bruce, for staying true to his rural roots
and always advocating for the farmer.*

Contents

Forewords

The Road to Farm Fresh Food

—Mary Lahammer, Anchor, Reporter, Producer Twin Cities PBS

Finding farm fresh food changed my life: what I eat, how I live, where I shop, who grows my food, and why I care.

I grew up in the 1970s and '80s in the suburbs. Our food was fast, convenient, processed and, well, terrible. My roots are on the farm. My parents grew up on farms as did their parents before them. I am even part owner of our family farm. Yet it has always amazed me how quickly we lost our connection to the land. Sure, we visited the farm and it was a fun place to play as a kid, but I didn't actually understand the value of farms for some time. As a television anchor and reporter in Minnesota, North Dakota, and Wisconsin, I worked in rural areas, covering agriculture as a news topic. Then came the day when everything changed and the issues I was covering surrounding agriculture would get personal.

My path to reconnecting to the land began when I was pregnant with my daughter. Growing another human being encouraged me to monitor more closely what I was putting into my body. I starting buying much more local and organic food. It tasted better and made me feel better. Yes, it was often more expensive but I figured it was worth it. Farmers' markets, CSAs, and my local co-op provided prolific resources and offered me an easy path into a food world I would go on to fully embrace.

My infant daughter was by my side when I first appeared as a celebrity taster for Minnesota Farmers Union's local foods program, Minnesota Cooks, at the State Fair. It was eye-opening to hear farmers and chefs talk about working together while chefs demonstrated cooking techniques

for the audience. The flavors in the food we sampled were fantastic. We learned not just about the quality of the food, but the positive effects local food has on the environment and economy. Chef Andrew Zimmern, Minnesota Cooks' original emcee, would eventually pass the baton to me as I became a host of the not-to-miss annual event at the Great Minnesota Get-Together.

Then, while covering a governor's inaugural for Twin Cities PBS, I encountered Minnesota Farmers Union visionaries President Doug Peterson and Bruce Miller. I shared what a meaningful experience it is to participate in their Minnesota Cooks event and suggested trying to help more people understand the local food movement by making a television show that would reach a larger audience. That's where our first collaboration was born, called "Farmers & Chefs of Minnesota," produced in 2012 for public television in which we traveled to farms and cooked outdoors with chefs.

On an ideal day in Minnesota, cooking and filming outdoors is a great idea; however, the reality of hosting and producing an outdoor cooking show proved difficult. Yet despite our challenges something remarkable did happen during this production—I ate meat.

For decades I had eaten little or no meat. Growing up with poorly processed foods and meats, I didn't think I liked it. As a competitive athlete and avowed healthy eater, I thought not eating much meat was a good decision. I had never liked or really eaten a pork chop. But it turns out high-quality heritage-breed, free-range pigs—yep, pigs who prowl the woods and gobble up grass—taste different. The difference is delicious. During production, I tasted a small bite of a sweet nutty pork chop, and then another bite, and another. Soon I was officially eating meat. Locally, ethically raised meat changed my entire attitude toward animal protein. As one of the featured chefs said, "When you care that much, you can taste it." Now it's an important part of my nationally ranked athlete daughter's daily fuel—the baby who originally inspired my renewed interest in locally and sustainably grown foods.

As we learned from the challenges of cooking outdoors, we decided to move the show indoors and add the precise food photography of Katie Cannon whose work you'll enjoy in this book. "Farm Fresh Road Trip" is part cooking show, part travel show, and part public affairs show. The first program aired in 2013 and featured local fare in food trucks, cafes, and restaurants across the state. We added local wine, beer, and spirits, which were quickly emerging along with local food. It proved a winning combination. "Farm Fresh Road Trip" earned the Regional Emmy Award for Lifestyle Program in 2014. More programs and Emmy nominations would follow. The formula continues to delight audiences who can watch it on Twin Cities PBS or online anytime. This show, along with the book you're about to enjoy, is part of Miller's legacy that will live on long after his passing in 2019.

Connection — A Farmer's Perspective

—Jodi Ohlsen Read, Shepherd's Way Farms

As sheep dairy farmers and cheesemakers, my husband Steven and I cherish our connections with people who love food. All along, chefs have been crucial connectors for us, bridging the gap between farm and plate.

When we began making sheep milk cheese in 1998, we met Lucia Watson, a leader in the Minnesota farm-to-table movement. Lucia was the first chef to use our Friesago, highlighting it at Lucia's, her Minneapolis local foods restaurant. When she included our cheese on her table, the farm named on the menu, our food circle began to grow. With every meal, more folks were introduced to our cheese, to our farm.

Including a local, artisan product regularly on a restaurant's menu is a commitment. Price, seasonality, and availability can all be challenges, but as Chef Julie Bloor of Lucia's taught me, with determination and creativity it can work well. In the early days, I delivered cheese with my four young sons in tow, with Lucia's as my last stop of the day. Julie welcomed the boys with fruit or freshly baked cookies, and we paused to talk a minute about the farm, the foods in season, and her menu plans. She talked of her commitment to local products and producers, how she built her menu, balancing select higher priced pieces with lower cost ingredients, all based on seasonal availability. In turn, I told her about the seasonality of sheep milk, the nuance of changes in the milk, all reflected in the cheese.

This was just the beginning of a beautiful web of food and farming connections, which has enriched and sustained us over the years.

How exciting it has been watching the hunger for local foods grow, seeing more restaurants dedicated to farm fresh food thrive. We've been so fortunate to have many talented, dedicated chefs include our cheese on their menus, valuing the work behind it, honoring it, and elevating the cheeses far beyond their first incarnation.

In the midst of day-to-day work, the depth of these connections isn't always apparent. But, at one farm-to-table dinner, I was reminded how the work we do ripples outward. During a course that featured one of our Shepherd's Way Farm cheeses, a guest across from me paused mid-bite, looked around the room, and leaned forward. "Isn't this cool? Everyone here is, right now, eating something you created! You are connected to everyone in the room!" I was stunned. And honored to be part of this beautiful circle.

Minnesota Cooks, and now *The Farmer and the Chef*, celebrates this connection of farmers and chefs, our mutual admiration, and the dedication to good food that ties us all. We invite you to join this celebration of all of those who work endlessly to produce, create, and share our local foods.

Fellowship — A Chef's Perspective

—Chef JD Fratzke

I was nervous as hell the first time I loaded up my daughter's wagon with hanger steaks, heirloom tomatoes, Faribault bleu cheese, and a swiss chard and barley salad in the parking lot of the Minnesota State Fairgrounds in Saint Paul. My watch read that it wasn't quite eleven. I wasn't scheduled to take the stage until one in the afternoon, but the last thing in the world I wanted to be that day was unprepared or late.

It was 2006 and I had been the Executive Chef at Muffuletta in the Park for a little over a year, and though we were in the throes of patio season, I'd been given permission to accept an invitation from the Minnesota Farmers Union to represent our little neighborhood bistro on stage during their Minnesota Cooks program. My nerves were jangled because I'd been placed in the middle of a roster studded with superstar local chefs whom I'd admired, pursued, and emulated for years. Included was Lenny Russo of WA Frost, who would later go on to open Heartland, arguably one of the most influential restaurants in the history of Minnesota. Lucia Watson of the eponymous Lucia's—an Uptown Minneapolis institution of French-influenced fine dining that changed its menu monthly and relied almost exclusively on locally sourced, sustainably raised agriculture—was there as well. Alex Roberts of Restaurant Alma would be there, too. For my money, his kitchen was, and still is, the gold standard for culinary technique and broad, deep flavors created with Minnesota ingredients—many of which were delivered to the walk-in cooler door straight from his father's farm.

Moreover, when I took the stage I would be introduced and interviewed by Andrew Zimmern, who rumor had it, had just begun development of an adventurous gastronomic television series, one that would have him globe-trotting and devouring foods most Minnesotans had never heard of.

I arrived at the event pale and wide-eyed, looking for any familiar face. A giant hand clapped down on my shoulder and I wheeled around to the wide mustachioed grin of the one and only Bruce Miller, membership director, and MFU's President Doug Peterson. Within ten minutes I had shaken a dozen hands, been given a cup of watermelon salad and assigned a Le Cordon Bleu student as a prep assistant. My stress sank away, and though I was still intimidated, I was astonished to feel as if I were being treated as a peer, as a welcome friend. Unlike the normally intense atmosphere of a restaurant kitchen, where professionalism and precision were the rule and a tight lid was kept on chaos, the chefs around me, my heroes included, were carrying themselves with ease and laughter. The whole scene felt like a family reunion or a church picnic.

It was a stifling, wet-blanket hot day in late August, but Alex sidled up to me and grinned, remarking how good it felt to get out of the four walls and fluorescent lights of his kitchen and cook outside for a change, to cook for people from Minnesota who had never heard of our restaurants, but after today, with the help of the photos and recipes in the Minnesota Cooks calendar, wouldn't be able to forget them.

That afternoon put the hook in me—into my devotion to the Minnesota Cooks program and the gospel of our great state's dedication to sustainable agriculture, healthy soil, clean air, and fresh water—if for no other reason than the fellowship I experienced. The farmers, ranchers, cooks, and facilitators took off their labels and celebrated not only the newly burgeoning farm-to-table movement but the reality of our grand interdependence.

That day shifted my perspective immensely, showing me that food and where it comes from can be far more than expression, recreation or commerce. It was my introduction to a family of growers and producers who love to nourish Minnesota in a way that surpasses appetites satisfied on a plate or in a bowl.

Minnesota Cooks introduced me to the idea that a life in food can be a true spiritual endeavor—a vocation—and that by taking great care of our water and our soil, we in turn take care of one another for far longer than our time on Earth.

In the following years the memories and friendships I accumulated while participating in the program piled like treasure: Claudine Arndt's laughter from the staff tent, Bruce Miller shading himself with an umbrella, Doug Peterson's straw hat, Katie Cannon smiling behind her ever-present camera, JP Samuelson and I sharing an inside joke together, Senator Al Franken comparing my butchery skills to the classic Dan-Ackroyd-as-Julia-Child-bloodbath skit he wrote for *Saturday Night Live* in 1978, a conversation with Don Shelby about Mark Twain's perfect meal, a power outage that killed the PA system and left all of us shouting from the stage like nineteenth-century carnival barkers, and the immense flavors created by chefs from every corner of Minnesota, each bite celebrating summer sunshine in our Land of 10,000 Lakes.

It is my greatest wish that anyone who reads this book and explores the recipes found in the following pages will quickly discover the kind of laughter, deliciousness and fellowship we celebrate with one another in the caring, tight-knit food and farming communities of Minnesota.

Introduction

This is a book about farmers and what is possible because of them. There is an increasing hunger among consumers to know and connect with the people responsible for growing and raising the food we eat. Consider *The Farmer and the Chef* an invitation to spend some time with farmers—to experience the day-to-day rhythms alongside the unpredictable adventure of farming, to delve into the struggles and triumphs alike. Woven throughout this book's collection of chef-driven recipes, you'll find stories depicting the effort, mentality, and support needed from sunup to sundown, in sunshine and in rain, to make it as a farmer. Beyond just names and faces, these pages hold real stories about farmers' lives.

Minnesota is a great agricultural state, and it's the rare person here who doesn't have familial roots in farming. Perhaps these deep roots are responsible for the nostalgia, admiration, and sincere love Minnesotans possess for farmers. In farmers we see our fathers, grandfathers, uncles, mothers, grandmothers, and aunties and their strong ties to the land—even if our own families moved off the farm generations ago. Despite the fact that everyone eats, currently less than 2 percent of the population farms; therefore, everyone has a stake in the success and future of family farms and vibrant, rural communities, each of which cannot survive without the other.

In the early 2000s, a local food movement was building in Minnesota as farmers and chefs began cultivating powerful relationships with one another. The idea that farm-restaurant partnerships could become another viable market for farmers was far from mainstream, but it was gaining a foothold. Thanks to a small group of visionaries within Minnesota's food and farming communities, this emerging market steadily grew stronger, forming both a tangible farm-to-table network and also a widespread field-to-plate mentality, first in the Twin Cities of Minneapolis and St. Paul, then radiating outward across the state.

It was only natural that Minnesota Farmers Union (MFU), an organization founded to support farmers, would take this trend to heart and encourage its growth. For 100 years MFU has been the voice of agriculture at the Minnesota legislature, in the media, and with the citizens of Minnesota, helping influence farm prices and policies to benefit family farmers and rural communities. MFU is rooted in the concept that a group of farmers working collectively has a stronger voice than an individual and builds its strength on three pillars: education, cooperation, and legislation.

In 2003, then MFU president, Doug Peterson, collaborated with hometown-turned-celebrity chef, Andrew Zimmern, to create Minnesota Cooks, MFU's local food program devoted to highlighting and fostering farm-restaurant partnerships. MFU saw the burgeoning interest in local food as a meaningful opportunity to engage consumers about where their food comes from.

The program started out small and has steadily expanded over the last eighteen years to feature twelve exemplary partnerships annually. Selected participants are featured in the stunning Minnesota Cooks calendar and at Minnesota Cooks Day at the Minnesota State Fair, an annual, all-day celebration showcasing farmers alongside chefs demonstrating the use of their locally grown and raised foods. Harnessing the momentum of Minnesota Cooks, MFU went on to partner with Twin Cities Public Television to create *Farm Fresh Road Trip*, a Midwest Emmy Award-winning program which introduces viewers to farms and restaurants across the state. Whereas *Farm Fresh Road Trip* took us farther into restaurant kitchens, *The Farmer and The Chef* explores farmers' fields and lives more deeply while bringing chefs' recipes to the home cook.

Throughout the years Minnesota Cooks has highlighted growers yielding impressive harvests off of small, vacant city lots, as well as large, established dairy and grain farmsteads. We've celebrated bustling restaurants that almost single handedly keep nearby farmers afloat with their purchasing power, as well as small rural cafes that buy what they can to support their neighbors. Everybody wins in the local food model.

The life of a farmer is often one of struggle, yet despite how bleak the future can look when the numbers don't make sense on paper—which they often don't—farmers head back to their fields, pastures, and barns day after day, a testament of their unwavering commitment. Ambitious people continue to rise to the challenge and show an interest in continuing the family farm, moving back to the farm, or building farms from scratch, oftentimes trading city living and high incomes for work that feels honest and meaningful. No one should have to settle for simply eking out a living, whether working at a desk or working the land. Farmers need health insurance for their families and a decent vehicle. They want to send their children to college, too.

So what can each of us do? Change happens through commerce. Every time we eat we're voting with our fork and food dollars. If we want our local farmers and rural communities to survive, we need to vote accordingly and choose local products whenever possible. Eating locally changes your routine and nudges you out of your comfort zone, but it also sparks curiosity and fosters a reverence for the people who poured their sweat and tears into their crops and livestock.

It's time to take collective action. Share what you know with others by bringing friends and family along to shop at farmers markets. Join a CSA, buy your meat or cheese directly from a local farmer, or simply visit a nearby farm and start building a connection to the source of food. Try a new vegetable, learn some cooking skills. The food you buy and bring into your home matters. Please choose carefully and support a food system that keeps local farmers farming.

—Gary Wertish, President, Minnesota Farmers Union
with the MFU Executive Committee
and Claudine Arndt & Katie Cannon

A Note About the Recipes

The *Farmer and The Chef* is a curated collection of chef-driven recipes created using farm fresh ingredients. The chefs and restaurant cooks whose recipes lie herein value and support farmers and respectfully honor their hard work through careful attention in the preparation of their food. They recognize how much better food tastes when it arrives straight from the farm.

Because these recipes were developed by chefs and professional cooks, they range widely from simple and straightforward to complex and challenging. *The Farmer and The Chef* has something for everyone—easy, quick recipes for the busy home cook and more complicated recipes for those wanting a more complex culinary endeavor. Every recipe was tested by our trustworthy recipe testers and adapted for the home cook, when necessary. Unless noted otherwise, assume herbs listed are meant to be fresh and kosher salt is preferred.

For those familiar with Minnesota's food and farm scene, the book will also be a walk down memory lane. The recipes and partnerships included in this book are snapshots in time, reflected by the year accompanying each which indicates when they appeared in the Minnesota Cooks calendar. These recipes span the rich history of the Minnesota Cooks program and include dishes from some influential restaurants that closed years ago but played an important role in shaping the strong farm-to-table culture in Minnesota's dining scene. These restaurants remain etched in our minds.

To cook is to be creative. Though the recipes inside these pages come from professional chefs and cooks, many of whom have been recognized both locally and nationally for their talents, don't be intimidated. Quality ingredients are hard to screw up, which is part of the beauty of local foods. Fresh, seasonal foods translate into utterly delicious meals, often with little effort. Embrace the experience of cooking and allow your own creativity to shine. Improvise, play, relax, and enjoy the process.

Welcome to Minnesota's food world. We're proud of what we have here.

Daybreak

Daybreak on the farm is a moment ripe with anticipation and possibility. As the sun breathes life into another day, farmers usher in the sunrise with chores that have been trailing them their whole lives and will continue to wait for them every day that follows. Many farmers are heading into their fields to inspect their crops or fences as the sun comes up, others are in their barns feeding chickens, milking cows, or changing animals' bedding. Some are en route to deliveries already. They harness the morning's first light with determination and purpose, beginning their workday knowing that it will be long but rewarding because they're doing one of the most important jobs in the world—providing food.

Sunrise on Ben Penner Farms

There's nothing quite like the sight of the sun quietly, steadily rising over wheat fields.

Ben Penner of Ben Penner Farms frequently witnesses the summer sunrise from the edge of his fields or his tractor seat, arriving early enough to observe the transition from the predawn dark to the day's first hint of light. As the sun begins its daily ascent, he pauses to soak in the pink and orange hues melting together, feeling privileged to witness something so spectacular and a bit wistful he's not sharing it with anybody. It is a sacred time.

Ben, his wife, Anna, and three young daughters live in St. Peter, a charming town roughly sixty miles southwest of Minneapolis and St. Paul in the scenic Minnesota River Valley. They moved from Kansas in 2008 in support of Anna's career and soon thereafter, Ben found an opportunity to farm some land nearby. In a bold move, he gave up his career in academic publishing and returned to his wheat farming roots. It is often said how when you grow up on a farm, the yearning to farm never fully leaves you; it stays in your blood and haunts you until you find your way back. This has certainly been true for Ben, whose passion for agriculture is evident after a single conversation.

Since Ben and his family live in town and not on the land he farms, he can't just look out the window or step out the door to assess his fields. He has to drive to his land to check on his crops, which isn't ideal, as he farms a total of seventy-three acres divided over three locations. He would rather live on the farm, but the economics are such that it's not a possibility right now.

Once spring arrives, most mornings Ben hops in his truck and sets out to see what's happening in his fields, curious whether it will align with his intuition and what he believes will be true that day. He's interested in the moisture level of the soil, weed pressure, crop growth, and whatever else his fields have to tell him. Sometimes a quick drive-by suffices, but if it's dry enough he likes to stop and walk through the fields, carefully surveying the smallest details. Often, without thinking about it, he instinctively digs into the soil, sinking his fingers into the ground to physically feel the temperature and texture of the earth.

The relationship between a farmer and his or her land is intimate. Ben has walked his fields hundreds of times. He knows them by heart, how they look and sound different from one hour, day, or season to the next. Life as a farmer has cultivated within him a hyper-awareness, tuning him in to the smallest details of the natural world easily missed by the average eye. This ability allows him to see, feel, and sense everything happening in his fields—how the soil on a dewy morning differs from the feel of soil later in the day, how the symphony of insects grows louder each hour as the day wakes up, how the rustle of wheat shifts with the winds and how his crops have changed since the day before. He marvels at how the bare fields of spring suddenly explode into an expanse of wheat with summer's arrival, and how in a single day his fields become home to an army of beneficial insects who've mobilized and moved in overnight. The intensity of life never ceases to surprise and inspire.

Ben is a farmer, but first and foremost, Ben is a father. Everything he does—the early mornings, long laborious days, the calculated risks he takes—is for his family. Whenever possible, mornings involve quiet, quality time with his daughters, readying them for their days while they tease him about his uncompromising need for coffee. While these morning family rituals unfold, Ben notices how his mind automatically starts "operating in the background," just like anybody fulfilling a calling. He begins running through the day ahead, planning, getting a sense of the weather and the season, and trying to zero in on the five, ten, or fifteen different things that could happen. Many mornings, especially during the school year, Ben uses his own freshly milled flour to make pancakes or crepes for his daughters before he sends them on their way.

Ben feels driven to help fill what he sees as a large gap in sustainable and localized grain production. He approaches this through his roots as a Mennonite, a community known for its strong ties to wheat farming dating back at least two hundred and fifty years. Ukrainian Mennonites began moving to the United States in great numbers beginning in 1873, seeking both religious freedom and economic opportunities. Many settled in Kansas and became wheat farmers, including Ben's ancestors. They focused on growing a winter wheat brought from the Ukraine called Turkey Red, which became one of the more popular varieties of wheat until the 1940s when higher-yield crops overtook it. It is now considered a heritage grain, sometimes called a "boutique wheat." Ben's mission is to inspire human flourishing through agriculture, and he's committed to carrying on his family's legacy and the Mennonite tradition of growing this wheat even if its days in the limelight seem to be over. Turkey Red is noted for its "unique, rich and complex flavor and excellent baking qualities," according to Slow Food USA. It grows well in climates similar to the Ukraine's, requiring long winters, dry summers, and rainy spring and fall seasons to thrive. Ben also grows spring wheat and food-grade soybeans.

Ben's Organic Brown Bread

**2019: Chef Owner Christine "Montana" Rasmussen,
River Rock Kitchen & Bakery
in partnership with Ben Penner Farms**

In the early morning hours at River Rock Kitchen & Bakery in St. Peter, the ancient bond between a farmer and a baker springs to life. Skilled hands transform Ben Penner's artisanal, freshly milled flour into bread and other artful pastries. Ben's wheat possesses distinct flavors and milling characteristics pleasing to discerning consumers. Owner of River Rock Kitchen & Bakery, Montana Rasmussen, says simply, "Ben's flour makes our products come alive."

YIELD: 2 LOAVES

- 5¾ cups Ben Penner's* organic whole wheat flour
- 1¾ cups bread flour
- 3½ cups water (90–95°F), divided
- ¾ teaspoon instant dried yeast
- 1 tablespoon plus 1 teaspoon kosher sea salt

In a large bowl mix together both flours by hand. Add 3 cups water and mix by hand until incorporated. Cover and let rest 20–30 minutes.

Sprinkle yeast over top of dough and mix by hand, squeezing and pinching dough until yeast disappears. Dissolve kosher salt in remaining ½ cup water and pour over top of dough. Using both hands, squeeze and pinch dough until it absorbs the salt water and becomes a cohesive mass. Be sure to wet hands so dough does not stick. Cover bowl with plastic wrap or a clean towel and let rise. Set a timer for 30 minutes.

This dough needs 3 folds, each 30 minutes apart. At the end of 30 minutes, pull side of dough closest to you up and toward you. Only pull as far as it will go without ripping, then fold it over the top of itself. Do this with all 4 sides of dough, then flip it upside down so all seams are now on the bottom of the bowl. Do this twice more, 30 minutes apart each time.

After the final fold, let dough rise for 2 hours or until it is triple its original volume. Dust work surface liberally with either type of flour and tip dough out. Using a dough knife or plastic dough scraper, cut dough into two equal pieces. Line two proofing baskets or bowls with clean cotton towels, then dust with flour. Shape each piece into a tight ball and place seam side down in its proofing basket. Cover with a kitchen towel and set aside to rise for 1–1¼ hours.

At least 45 minutes before baking, put a rack in the middle of the oven and place 2 dutch ovens on rack with their lids on. Preheat oven to 475°F.

Carefully remove heated dutch oven from oven and place one proofed loaf inside, making sure that the seam side is up. Replace lid and put dutch oven into oven. Bake for 30 minutes, then carefully remove lid and bake another 20 minutes, or until loaf is dark brown all over. Remove from dutch oven and let cool on a cooling rack.

If you don't have access to Ben's flour, another freshly milled flour from your natural foods co-op can be substituted.

Minnesota Raspberry Jam

2019: Chef Owner Christine "Montana" Rasmussen, River Rock Kitchen & Bakery

The goods produced at River Rock Kitchen & Bakery are inextricably tied to the surrounding land, seasons, and farmers. Owner Montana Rasmussen and her team endeavor to nourish people, communities, and the earth through their work. They support friends and neighbors by buying quality ingredients they believe in and then proudly creating food they believe in. Organic berries, plucked at their peak moment of greatness from a nearby farm, are folded into batters or transformed into luscious jams like this one.

YIELD: 1¼ CUPS

5 cups fresh organic raspberries

½ teaspoon kosher salt

¾ cup organic sugar

2 teaspoons organic lemon juice

½ cup water

Place a plate with 3 metal spoons in the freezer for testing the jam later.

Combine everything in a medium sauce pot and heat over medium low heat. Cook, stirring and mashing constantly with a heatproof rubber spatula until juice begins to run from the berries. As soon as sugar dissolves, increase heat to medium-high. Stirring constantly to avoid scorching, cook jam until it becomes thick. If jam is sticking to the bottom of the pan, turn heat down. To test for doneness, carefully transfer a small amount to one of the frozen spoons. Place spoon back in freezer for 3 minutes (it should be neither hot nor cold). Tilt spoon vertically to see whether jam runs. If it doesn't run, the jam is ready. If it does, cook for another couple of minutes and test again. Repeat as needed until desired consistency is reached. Refrigerate and use within 2 weeks.

Variation: To make Raspberry Mint Jam, after sugar dissolves, add 8 sprigs of mint to sauce pot. Proceed with recipe as written, trying not to break apart mint from stems. Let jam cool with mint in it. Once cool, remove mint stems and leaves, scraping off any excess jam before discarding them.

Swedish Pancakes with Lingonberry Sauce

2020: Owner Lisa Lindberg, Amboy Cottage Cafe
in partnership with Whole Grain Milling

It all began when an abandoned 1928 cottage-style gas station, slated to be demolished, captured the heart of Lisa Lindberg. Unable to bear the thought of her town losing the quaint, historical building, Lisa laid claim to the building just moments before the wrecking began, surprising even herself. As one of the only gathering places nearby, Lisa's eatery plays a critical role in her community's well-being and vibrancy.

Swedish Pancakes are a weekend treat at Amboy Cottage Cafe. Although the batter whips up quickly and easily, the assembly takes extra care. Each plate is artfully arranged, then brought out one at a time to the anxiously awaiting guests. Beautiful and delicious, these pancakes are showstoppers and crowd pleasers every time.

YIELD: 6 PANCAKES

For pancakes:

4 eggs

1 cup full fat milk

1 cup unbleached flour

2 tablespoons sugar

¾ teaspoon sea salt

1 teaspoon vanilla
    extract

For lingonberry sauce:

lingonberries (or
    cranberries)

water

sugar

For serving:

whipped cream

blueberries or
    strawberries

powdered sugar

lingonberry sauce

Combine eggs, milk, and flour in a blender. Twirl briefly. Add sugar, sea salt, and vanilla, and blend just until a smooth, "thick cream" consistency is achieved. Let rest for 30 minutes.

To make the lingonberry sauce, mix 1 part berries, 1 part water, and 1 part sugar in sauce pot and simmer for 5 minutes. The berries will pop and thicken into a sauce as it cools. This is less sweet and a bit thinner than a jam.

Pour ½ cup batter onto a hot buttered griddle or into a cast iron pan and rotate to spread and evenly cover bottom of pan. Bake until dry on top, then flip with help of a lefsa stick or long thin spatula. Brown well on both sides. Crispy edges are lovely and tasty! If batter has thickened add a little milk.

Transfer to your favorite old platter and fill with homemade whipped cream, lingonberry sauce, blueberries, strawberries, powdered sugar, or all of the above.

Serve immediately and individually, one at a time as you get them done.

Possibly the World's Best Cinnamon Rolls

2018: Owner Alicia Hinze, The Buttered Tin
in partnership with Hope Creamery

The Buttered Tin in St. Paul exists thanks to owner Alicia Hinze's love of brunching. Growing up, Saturdays were spent sharing the ups and downs of life with family and friends over brunch, a ritual rarely missed. Baking is Alicia's forte, a passion she shared with her paternal grandmother, and since really good butter and eggs are key ingredients in most baked goods Alicia won't settle for anything less than the butter from Hope Creamery in Hope, MN.

For sweet dough:

2 teaspoons active dry yeast

1 cup plus 2 tablespoons warm milk

3¼ cups sifted bread flour

¼ cup white sugar

2¼ teaspoons salt

5 tablespoons softened, unsalted butter

1 egg

For filling:

3 sticks softened, unsalted butter

¼ cup dark brown sugar

½ cup cinnamon

Preheat oven to 350°F.

Add yeast to milk, then combine all dough ingredients into the bowl of a mixer fitted with a dough hook. Mix until smooth, then cover dough with plastic wrap or double towel and let dough rise on warm stovetop until doubled in size—at least an hour. Alternatively, wrap dough in plastic and proof overnight in the refrigerator.

Once dough has doubled in size, roll out onto a floured surface into a rectangle about 1½ feet x 1 foot. Spread butter all over dough. Combine cinnamon and brown sugar in a small bowl then sprinkle on top of butter, making sure to cover the whole surface.

Starting from the long side of the rectangle, roll dough into a log. Using a sharp knife, cut log into 8 pinwheels, 1½–2 inches wide. Place pinwheels into greased 9 x 13-inch baking pan, cover with plastic wrap or a double towel, and proof on warm stovetop until nearly double in size and rolls are soft and sticky.

Bake for about 20 minutes until they are browned. When rolls are done, pull from the oven and let rest in pan for 5 minutes. Then turn rolls over onto another pan and serve hot.

Note: To make this recipe ahead of time, complete the recipe until unbaked rolls are in the baking pan, then refrigerate overnight. The next morning, remove from fridge and put in a warm place until dough has warmed and rolls have risen a little. You can set the oven on a low setting such as 175°F to speed up this process. Continue with recipe as written.

Chorizo Biscuits and Gravy

2019: Chef Jillian Forte, At Sara's Table Chester Creek Cafe
in partnership with Yker Acres

YIELD: 10–12 SERVINGS

For biscuit mix:

YIELD: 20 BISCUITS

4½ cups all-purpose
   flour

2 tablespoons baking
   powder

2 teaspoons baking
   soda

4 teaspoons salt

¾ cup shortening

For biscuits:

4 cups biscuit mix

1 cup buttermilk

For gravy:

1 tablespoon canola oil

2 onions, diced small

3 tablespoons garlic,
   6–8 large cloves,
   peeled and minced

2 pounds ground
   chorizo sausage

1 pound ground pork

¾ cup flour

6 cups chicken stock

1½ cups heavy cream

1½ teaspoons salt

1 teaspoon smoked
   paprika

1½ cup roasted red
   peppers, diced

To make biscuit mix: Place dry ingredients in bowl of a large mixer; mix until combined. Add shortening and mix until it looks like coarse meal. Store in covered container at room temperature for up to three months.

To make biscuits: Preheat oven to 450°F.

Place biscuit mix in a bowl. Make a well in center and add buttermilk. Mix vigorously with a fork until dough comes together. Do not over mix!

Turn dough out onto lightly floured surface; pat or roll out to ½-inch thickness. Cut with a circular biscuit cutter or juice glass. Place biscuits on ungreased sheet pan; prick tops with fork.

Bake for 10–15 minutes until golden brown.

To make gravy: In a heavy-bottomed pot, heat oil over medium heat and sauté onions and garlic until translucent, stirring occasionally.

Add chorizo and pork to pan. Using the back of a spoon, break into small pieces. Cook until done.

Sprinkle flour over everything in pan and stir to combine flour with sausage. Cook 2–3 minutes, stirring so mixture doesn't stick. Whisk in chicken stock and heavy cream and bring to a gentle simmer; cook until mixture thickens.

Add salt, smoked paprika, and diced roasted red peppers. Taste gravy for seasoning, adding more salt and paprika as desired. Serve over buttermilk biscuits.

The Forecast at Blue Fruit Farm

In no uncertain terms, the weather shapes a farmer's day. Despite loving to complain about the weather, Minnesotans relish talking about it. Our location in the Upper Midwest causes Minnesota to experience some of the most widely varied and dramatic weather in the US, which may sound like an exaggeration to someone who has never experienced four seasons with such distinct personalities. Clinging to Canada in the north, Minnesota winters often mimic those of our neighbor, bringing heavy, quieting snowfalls and weeks of cruel below-zero temperatures and bitter, breath-stealing winds. The transition seasons, spring and fall, can be tricksters, surprising us with late or early frosts, sudden snowstorms or tornadoes, and relentless winds. And then there's summer, brimming at times with heat and humidity so intense and suffocating you might mistakenly think you're in the South. For farmers everywhere, the weather is perhaps the most formidable challenge they endure; if you're a farmer in Minnesota, the weather can feel like a veritable nemesis.

For Jim Riddle, co-owner of Blue Fruit Farm along with Joyce Ford, checking the weather forecast is one of the first things he does in the morning—second only to brewing a pot of organic coffee. His morning routine rarely wavers: wake up, grind and brew the coffee, then hop online and see what the weather will dictate—taking stock of both the day's forecast and the extended radar conditions to evaluate what Mother Nature has in store. Spring through fall, he likes to step outside and feel the weather for himself, listening to the songbirds welcoming the day while soaking in the surroundings. Like it or not, the weather is every farmer's boss.

Mornings at the farm feel peaceful and deliberative. Jim and Joyce wake up early and ease into the day, feeling gratitude for the work they do and the people who work alongside them. During harvest season, the air hangs with anticipation as Jim and Joyce look forward to the flavors that lie ahead, to the interesting conversations that will be shared by the harvest crew, and to how many pounds of fruit will be harvested.

As Jim drinks his coffee and considers what kind of work the weather will permit, he starts drafting a list. As only an experienced farmer can, he envisions which tasks he and Joyce and their team will be able to successfully tackle in a single day. Jim and Joyce are avid list makers, operating off both a finely tuned, three-page seasonal work list built through years of experience, as well as a daily list organized around what's most pressing on the farm at that moment. If it's raining, they will defer to their always-handy "Plan B Rainy Day List," which includes duties like updating the website, tweaking their new online ordering system, or making sure the receiving area for freshly picked fruit is clean and orderly. If the weather is cooperating, the daily list will reflect the highest priority outdoor tasks: pruning, weeding, repairing irrigation lines or the bird exclusion system, harvesting, packing fruit, or any other number of farm-related chores. Yet even the most thoughtfully crafted list can be thwarted by unforeseen and inopportune curveballs, such as a key piece of equipment breaking down and halting everything until it's back up and running. Farming is an ongoing dance between anticipating how a day will unfold and reacting to what is actually true—a balancing act between careful planning and sheer luck.

Located in the picturesque bluff country of southeastern Minnesota, Blue Fruit Farm is home to five acres of certified organic blueberries, elderberries, aronia berries, black currants, honeyberries, juneberries, and plums. Though many of their fruits are still somewhat mysterious to the average consumer, Joyce and Jim specifically settled on growing "blue" fruit because of the high antioxidant values and powerful health benefits attributed to fruits with deep blue-purple hues. Plus, there weren't any other blue fruit farmers nearby, ensuring a unique niche for themselves.

The farm overlooks a microclimate known as Wiscoy Valley and sits swaddled by forest or native prairie on all sides. This diverse landscape is home to a robust population of beneficial insects and pollinators who gracefully and efficiently pollinate the nearby fruit. Far from the nearest freeway, railroad, or chemically sprayed farm, Blue Fruit Farm experiences very little man-made noise but teems with the sounds of nature, which can get pretty raucous at times, an indication of the immense volume of life on the farm. When some of their fruits are pollinating, there's a constant buzzing in the air, like a super highway of insects as the purposeful pollinators go about their own work.

From June through September, daybreak at Blue Fruit Farm can be a dazzling sight as blueberries, currants, and elderberries glisten with dew, thousands of mini prisms sparkling seductively in the morning light. Enticing as they may be, the hard and fast rule during this time is "look but don't touch." Until the morning dew has completely dried off, it's critical to leave the glistening globes alone; picking wet fruit can damage its integrity, spread diseases, and destroy a plant's ability to produce fruit. During harvest season, this means the beginning of the workday at Blue Fruit Farm is spent labeling and packing already-picked fruit for sale. While this is happening the crew is entertained listening to an eclectic mix of bluegrass, rock, and reggae tunes. Once the dew has dried, it's safe to move into the fields and start hand-harvesting whatever is at peak ripeness that day: honeyberries in June, blueberries and black currants in July, elderberries in September through the first frost. For the rest of the day until suppertime, that's where they'll be—lost amongst the many rows of blue fruit; hour by hour, plant by plant, hand-picking the literal fruits of their labor.

Jim and Joyce began farming organic produce together in the early 1980s, a time when the term organic *was often misunderstood and confusing due to a lack of uniform national standards for organic farming. This immense need for standardization—combined with their own drive and passion for organics—prompted them to form the International Organic Inspectors Association (IOIA) in 1991, an organization responsible for training organic inspectors and committed to consistency and integrity in the organic certification process. Over the next twenty years, their work as trainers, inspectors, and educators through IOIA consumed them, temporarily interrupting their work as farmers as they traveled the world. "I certainly missed it when we set our farming enterprise aside," Jim remarks, reflecting on the decades spent advocating for organics. Jim and Joyce found their way back to farming in 2009, but rather than attempt to join a now-crowded organic vegetable market in Winona, they brainstormed their new niche and entered the world of blue fruits. The IOIA continues to thrive today, training hundreds of inspectors annually and collaborating with the organic sectors of governmental agencies to ensure uniform organic integrity.*

Loaded Local Oatmeal

2015: Chef Marshall Paulsen and Owner Tracy Singleton, Birchwood Cafe
in partnership with Blue Fruit Farm

Six Minnesota farmers are represented in this loaded, hyper-local oatmeal. Everything from the oats to the maple syrup come from Birchwood's farmer friends, including blueberries and black currants from Blue Fruit Farm.

YIELD: 4–6 SERVINGS

For black currant blueberry jam:

YIELD: ABOUT 4 CUPS

2 teaspoons Pomona pectin, available online or at your local natural foods coop

¾ cup cane sugar

1 cup black currants,* mashed

3 cups blueberries, mashed

2 teaspoons calcium water (comes with Pomona pectin)

Any soft berry can be substituted if fresh currants are not available in your area.

Chef's note: The black currant blueberry jam, bacon, and sambal maple syrup are meant to be prepared in advance and stored. Prepare and then use whatever quantities you desire on your steel cut oatmeal with charred sweet corn.

To make jam: In a small mixing bowl, whisk pectin into sugar. In a heavy-bottomed pan, bring berries to a gentle simmer. Add calcium water, then whisk pectin/sugar mixture into berry mixture until sugar and pectin are dissolved. Stir often to avoid scorching. Transfer to jars for water processing if canning, or store refrigerated.

To make homemade sambal: Put peppers, garlic, and lime juice and zest into a heavy-bottomed pan. Cook on low heat for about 15 minutes to soften and sweat. Add vinegar and slightly increase heat. Cook gently for 8–10 minutes.

Remove from heat, add salt and sugar. Cool to room temperature and process in Robot Coupe or home blender. Transfer to jars for water processing, or store refrigerated.

To make sambal maple syrup: In a small bowl or jar mix together sambal and maple syrup.

To make oats: Freeze and then finely mince bacon. At very low heat, stirring often, render fat from bacon until very crunchy. Strain through a fine-mesh chinois or folded paper towel. Store at room temperature.

Cook oats in water with pinch of salt according to package directions until soft but toothsome. Keep warm.

For homemade sambal*:

1 pound red fresno peppers, stemmed (or any spicy red pepper available at the farmers' market)

2 cloves garlic, peeled

juice and zest of ½ lime

⅓ cup rice wine vinegar

pinch of salt

1 tablespoon cane sugar

*Sambal is also readily available in the ethnic condiment area of your local grocery store.

For sambal maple syrup:

1 tablespoon sambal*

4 tablespoons maple syrup

For oats:

4–6 strips of bacon

steel cut oats

3–4 ears of corn

3–4 tablespoons chia seeds

fresh blueberries to top

While oats are cooking, grill or roast corn. Place shucked and cleaned corn directly over a very hot grill, turning occasionally, until charred and cooked through—about 10 minutes. Shucked and cleaned sweet corn can also be prepared indoors, roasted naked in a hot oven or over an open flame on the stovetop until nicely charred. When cool enough to handle, place ears of corn into a deep bowl tip down. Using a sharp paring knife, remove kernels from cob. The depth of the bowl will keep mess to a minimum.

Mix 2 cups of corn into oats.

To assemble: Place warm steel cut oats with charred sweet corn into individual bowls. Each guest can personalize with desired amounts of bacon, black currant blueberry jam, fresh blueberries, and sambal maple syrup. Finish with a sprinkle of chia seeds.

Easy Being Green Juice

2017: Owner Nicci Sylvester, Tonic Local Kitchen & Juice Bar in partnership with Pine Creek Organics

The inspiration for Tonic Local Kitchen & Juice Bar in Rochester hit creator Nicci Sylvester one day while she was out running errands with her kids. Far too hungry and disgusted with the surrounding fast food and chain restaurants, she wondered, "Why isn't there a place in this town where I can get a fresh juice, homemade wrap, or something healthy for my family?" That frustration, coupled with some serious drive, inspired her to open Tonic, where neighborhood regulars and international visitors to the world-famous Mayo Clinic alike now enjoy locally sourced, organic food one expects in a renowned medical community.

The bright, refreshing flavors in Easy Being Green will kick off your day with a nutrient-dense energy boost, but it also makes for a healthy late afternoon pick-me-up when hunger starts to creep in.

YIELD: 2 SERVINGS

2 cups packed spinach leaves

2 cups packed lacinato kale

¼ cup packed mint

1½-inch chunk ginger with peel

2 whole green apples, such as Granny Smith, quartered

½ small lemon

Run all ingredients through a juicer. Enjoy.

Morning Chores on Braucher's Sunshine Harvest Farm

Perhaps there really is no typical morning on the farm. Surprises happen often enough to break up any monotony that threatens to settle in, and seasonal transitions ensure a constant rotation of duties. At Sunshine Harvest Farm, as on most farms, daily routines are consistently counterbalanced with exceptions and the unexpected. Still, there is an overarching, familiar rhythm to most farmers' days, and this rhythm steadies the unpredictable.

It's a widely held belief that all farmers are natural early morning risers. Mike Braucher from Sunshine Harvest Farm dismisses this notion with the heartiest of chuckles, then quips that the real reason his internal alarm clock wakes him up by four-thirty every morning has less to do with being a farmer and more to do with simply getting old. Since Mike is only in his mid-fifties, his joke is instantly laughable—especially given his youthful, charismatic energy. Mike is the definition of a morning person. Experiencing the early morning quietude on his farm is something he savors: the hours when an air of calm blankets his land, before any sense of urgency or being overwhelmed has had a chance to sneak in. Most days Mike wakes up with a clear mind and an optimistic attitude, and despite decades of demanding physical labor as a farmer, his body still feels strong (aside from a stiff back now and then).

In the predawn darkness, Mike harnesses his clear mind and bank of morning energy to tackle Sunshine Harvest Farm office tasks first thing—bookwork, entering deposits into the accounting software, and endeavoring to answer the endless stream of emails from both customers and curious potential customers. Computers aren't typically the first tool that comes to mind when thinking about a farmer's extensive tool kit, yet Mike could—and often does—spend hours each day at his computer, thoughtfully responding to as many emails as he can. When asked what people write to him about, he responds simply, "Anything and everything you can think of related to food." Some customers are placing orders or arranging pick-up times, usually loyal fans familiar with the farm's products. Others email because they found Sunshine Harvest Farm in an online search and want to know more before buying: *What do the animals eat? What are their living conditions like? In short: do they live a good life?* And then there are the lengthy, heartfelt stories people share about their health concerns, describing in detail the reasons they've embarked on a quest for quality food. Mike does his best to respond to everybody; understanding that people reach out because they're craving a connection with their farmer, and he's committed to providing that connection.

As greater numbers of people express concern for and interest in how their food is grown and raised, the attraction to family farmers does seem real, signaling a vital and positive trend for farmers like Mike who depend on conscientious consumers to survive. Since Sunshine Harvest Farm is a relatively small farm that direct markets their meat and eggs (meaning they don't count on a distributor or "middleman" to sell their products for them) Mike and his family know most of their patrons by name. They've watched couples get married, grow their families, and navigate big life transitions. Every correspondence, every relationship, is important. Nevertheless, the emails are time-consuming. Mike never really catches up, and in the back of his mind he knows more will be waiting for him tomorrow.

Once the sun begins to rise it's time to transition to morning chores. Stepping away from his computer, leaving any remaining unanswered messages until after sundown or the following morning, he makes his way outside, usually witnessing the sunrise on the way to the chicken barn or on his walk out to the pastures. The freshness and newness of this moment—the beginning of another day—is Mike's favorite thing about morning on the farm. He can't remember the last time he missed a sunrise.

Of all the animals, the chickens are the most needy and must be tended to first. The cows and lambs grazing out on pasture are largely self-sufficient—the lambs might even ignore him if they're too busy frolicking or eating—but the chickens depend on Mike or his son to show up like clockwork. Each morning they seem to be awaiting his arrival with curiosity and impatience, chattering loudly at his appearance and creating a loud hum as they gather around, eager for their chicken feed and the opportunity to go outside and forage. Some greet Mike by pecking at his feet. He gives them fresh water and a mixture of oats, barley, alfalfa, peas, corn, beans, and minerals, then leaves them to eat, quibble over nesting boxes, and go about their business for a few hours. Eventually they'll settle down to lay their eggs, but they're pretty leisurely about it—often taking a full day to get the job done. Mike won't return to gather eggs until after ten, then he'll have to make a second pass to pick the rest in the afternoon.

Part of Mike's morning is devoted to walking his property and checking fences. While doing this, he is making sure both the electric and barbed wire fences are secure in an effort to avoid the dreaded "your cows are on the road" call from a neighbor later in the day. Visually he looks for strands that are broken or have popped off the fence post. He also uses a "fence tester," a hand held device that measures volts in the electric fences. All sorts of things can happen unexpectedly that will damage or take down a fence—storms, bounding deer, fallen trees—each of which can result in an entire afternoon spent rounding up cows that have wandered onto a neighbor's property. It's a morning ritual Mike can't afford to skip, but it's also a highlight because it will eventually bring him around to his favorite animal on the farm—the cows, who are waiting to move to a pasture with fresh grass.

The day is still fresh with cool, comfortable temperatures, and the air might even be a bit foggy. As he nears them Mike calls out to his cows, "Come boss, come boss!" a phrase he's been saying as long as he can remember, one he learned from his dad, who learned it from his dad. Mike isn't actually sure how many generations back in his family that phrase might stretch, but it's been with him his whole life. "Come boss, come boss!" Most likely these words come from the Latin name for cow, "Bos Taurus," but the cows themselves understand simply that it means they get to move to another pasture. They respond by walking toward Mike, sometimes emerging out of the morning fog, happy and ready to move to the next fresh paddock.

Bacon Jam Slam Breakfast Pizza

2014: Chef Owner Steve Lott, Big River Pizza
in partnership with Braucher's Sunshine Harvest Farm

Sunshine Harvest Farm sells meat and eggs at two weekly farmers' markets in the Twin Cities, an hour's drive from home. Farmers' market mornings have their own feel, a bustling energy and some mild chaos, a stark contradiction to the solitude and steadiness of the farm. Faithful customers excitedly greet them each week, and it becomes a social event for everyone.

YIELD: 1 PIZZA

For pizza dough:

YIELD: 4 PIZZA DOUGH BALLS

1¼ cups beer (or water)

2¼ teaspoons active dry yeast (one packet)

8 tablespoons olive oil

1 egg

¼ teaspoon salt

4 cups unbleached all-purpose white flour

To make pizza dough: Heat beer (or water) to 110° F. Add yeast and wait 5 minutes to be sure it's activated (foamed). Add olive oil, egg, and salt. Mix with spoon or whisk.

Place flour in bowl of kitchen mixer fitted with a dough hook and add liquid ingredients on top. Mix on lowest speed for 6 minutes. Increase speed one level and mix for another 2 minutes. Place mixed dough in lightly oiled bowl and cover with plastic wrap for 2 hours or until doubled in size.

Remove from bowl and cut into 4 equal pieces. Form dough into balls, and place on lightly oiled tray. Cover with plastic wrap and refrigerate until ready to use. Dough will keep for 2 days in the refrigerator or 3 months in the freezer.

Each dough ball yields a 14-inch pizza.

Chef's note: Beer makes the dough flakier and lighter, but water can be used, if you prefer.

recipe continues . . .

For bacon jam:

1½ pounds sliced bacon, cut crosswise into 1-inch pieces

2 medium yellow onions, diced small

3 garlic cloves, peeled and smashed

2 ounces Makers Mark Whiskey or your favorite brand

½ cup cider vinegar

½ cup packed dark-brown sugar

¼ cup pure maple syrup

¾ cup brewed coffee

For pizza:

1 pizza dough ball

3 tablespoons bacon jam

¼ pound cooked sausage

6 ounces mozzarella, grated

½ cup tomato sauce, Muir Glenn suggested

1 large handful fresh arugula

½ cup white onion, diced

2 ounces pecorino/romano cheese

2 eggs

a small bowl of olive oil

To make the bacon jam: In large skillet, cook bacon over medium heat, stirring occasionally, until fat is rendered and bacon lightly browned and lightly crispy, 10–15 minutes. Transfer bacon to 6-quart slow cooker with slotted spoon. Pour off all but 1 tablespoon fat from skillet (reserve for another use). Add onions to skillet and cook until caramelized, about 6 minutes. Add garlic after onions are caramelized.

Deglaze pan with whiskey; add vinegar, brown sugar, maple syrup, and coffee and bring to a boil, stirring and scraping up browned bits from skillet with a wooden spoon for about 2 minutes.

Transfer mixture to slow cooker and mix to combine with bacon. Cook on high, uncovered, until liquid is syrupy, 3½–4 hours. Transfer to food processor; pulse until coarsely chopped. Let cool and refrigerate in airtight containers, up to 4 weeks.

To make the pizza: Prepare grill for direct medium-high heat.

On a lightly floured surface, flatten one pizza dough ball with the heel of your hand. Use fingers to stretch dough out, or hold up edges of dough with your fingers and let it hang and stretch while moving it in a circle. Once dough is stretched into a circle, let it sit for 5 minutes then push out the edges of the dough with your fingers again, until it is a circle approximately 10–12 inches in diameter. Do not make a raised rim; it will interfere with the grilling process. If dough is too soft to properly complete the process, put in the refrigerator for 5–6 minutes and try again.

The grilling process will move quickly, so as the pizza dough rests, gather your grilling set up, which includes a pizza peel or a rimless cookie sheet dusted with flour (semolina works well), paper towel saturated with olive oil, tongs, a small bowl of olive oil, a ladle, a pastry brush, and prepared toppings.

Once grill is hot (it is ready when you can hold your hand an inch over the grate for no more than 2 seconds), use tongs to rub grates with olive oil paper towel. Place pizza dough round on pizza peel or cookie sheet to transfer, then slide dough off the peel onto the grill grates. Close grill lid and cook for 2 minutes.

Open grill and check underneath dough to see if it is browning. If the bottom is not browning evenly, use a spatula or tongs to rotate dough 90 degrees and cook another minute. If it is not beginning to brown, cover grill and continue cooking a minute at a time until bottom has begun to brown. It should only take a couple minutes if the grill is hot. The top of pizza dough will start bubbling up with air pockets.

Once bottom of pizza dough has browned lightly, use cookie sheet or pizza peel to remove from grill. Use spatula to flip dough so grilled side is up. Keep grill covered so it retains its heat.

Brush grilled surface of pizza with a little olive oil, then cover with 1 ladle of sauce, sausage, onions, and mozzarella cheese. Add dabs of bacon jam randomly on top of pizza. Dust lightly with pecorino/romano cheese blend then add arugula. Top with eggs last. Remember to go light on the toppings or the pizza will be heavy and soggy. Add salt to taste.

Slide topped pizza back onto grill. If using a gas grill, reduce heat. If working with a charcoal grill, close vents on cover almost entirely. Close lid and cook 2–3 more minutes, or until bottom begins to char, cheese is bubbly, and egg whites have set. Pull off grate with a spatula onto a cutting board or other flat surface and let rest for a couple minutes before cutting into slices.

Steve's notes: Dough stretching can be done with either traditional hand stretching method or with a rolling pin. If dough is too soft, put in freezer for 5 minutes and let set up. For larger parties, pre-stretch dough and separate with oiled parchment paper in the fridge.

Foxy Falafel Shakshuka

2013: Chef Owner Erica Strait, Foxy Falafel in partnership with Minnesota Peach

Erica Strait, owner of Foxy Falafel in St. Paul, learned how food is grown and meant to taste on her family's farm. Working in the fields and cooking alongside her mother and grandmother, she inherited a love of pickling, a kinship with farmers, and a strong work ethic.

Drawn to Middle Eastern and Mediterranean flavors, Erica has a reputation for serving the best-tasting falafel this side of Israel. She uses as much local, seasonal produce as possible to bring dishes like her shakshuka to life. While delicious for breakfast, shakshuka can be served any time. It's lovely served with a simple side salad.

YIELD: 4 SERVINGS

- 1 tablespoon olive oil
- 1 large onion, peeled and diced
- 1 red or yellow pepper, cored and diced
- 1 teaspoon ground cumin
- 7 ripe Roma tomatoes, roughly chopped
- 1 pinch saffron strands
- 1 teaspoon red pepper flakes
- 1 bay leaf
- 6 sprigs thyme, picked and chopped
- 2 tablespoons fresh flat-leaf parsley, chopped
- 2 tablespoons cilantro, chopped
- salt and pepper, to taste
- 4 duck or chicken eggs
- 2 tablespoons crumbled feta or goat cheese
- 1 tablespoon chives, chopped
- thick slices of sourdough bread

Preheat oven 350°F.

In a large cast-iron pan, add olive oil, onion, and peppers, and sauté over medium heat for 2–3 minutes. Add cumin and sauté until fragrant for an additional 1–2 minutes. Add tomatoes, saffron, pepper flakes, bay leaf, thyme, parsley, cilantro, and salt and pepper. Cook over low heat for 20–30 minutes until tomatoes are cooked down to a sauce consistency. Remove bay leaf, taste and adjust seasonings. Sauce may be prepared in advance and reheated in a saucepan before adding eggs.

Use the back of a spoon to create 4 wells in sauce. Carefully break 1 egg into each well. Cover and bake in oven for 20 minutes until eggs are just set. Sprinkle with cheese and chives. Serve with sourdough bread or Cottage Bread on page 45.

Savory Morning Crepes

2014: Chef Helen Walden & Owner Theresa Cook, Anodyne Coffeehouse in partnership with Bossy Acres

YIELD: 5-7 CREPES

For chickpea crepes:

1 cup chickpea flour

1⅓ cups water

pinch of salt

pinch of pepper

1 tablespoon oil

For roasted squash:

1 medium-sized butternut squash, peeled, seeded, and diced in ½-inch cubes

1-2 tablespoons oil

salt and freshly ground pepper, to taste

For vinaigrette

YIELD: ABOUT A CUP

¼ cup balsamic vinegar

1 tablespoon Dijon mustard

1 teaspoon white sugar, plus a pinch more

dash salt and pepper

¼ cup equal parts extra-virgin olive oil and sunflower oil

For plating:

1 cup goat cheese, crumbled

roasted squash

2 cups microgreens

5-7 eggs, fried

balsamic vinaigrette, to taste

To make the chickpea crepes: In a medium bowl, gradually stir water into chickpea flour—a fork or whisk is best for this in order to avoid lumps. The batter should be the consistency of heavy cream. Season with salt and pepper. It will thicken as it sits, so add more water as needed.

Heat oil in a nonstick pan over medium-high heat. Test pan with a few drops of batter. It is ready when it sizzles. Give batter one more stir to recombine and, using a circular motion, pour enough batter into the pan to form about a 5-inch circle. Using a rubber or silicone spatula, gently push batter outwards from center to thin and increase size of circle to about a 6-inch crepe. When bubbles form and edges crisp, carefully flip crepe and cook other side. Store crepes on a plate with waxed paper between each—they reheat well.

To make the roasted squash: Toss squash pieces with a little oil, salt, and pepper and roast at 400°F for about 25 minutes until fork tender, checking on them after 20 minutes.

To make the balsamic vinaigrette: Combine first 4 ingredients in a medium mixing bowl. Slowly whisk in oil, pouring it in a steady, thin stream.

To plate: Place one crepe on a plate. Top with roasted squash, microgreens, and goat cheese. Top with fried egg and drizzle with balsamic vinaigrette.

Reflections from Dutch Fury Farm

A farmer's land is often a living memory of a family's history—the sweat, struggles, triumphs, and stories. For Josephine Rapatz, these memories fill her with a sense of determination and purpose. When facing setbacks or feeling disgusted by the aches and pains that have started to settle in her body and limit her activity, these memories fuel her to keep going.

There is a room in the back of Jo's converted barn house with three walls of windows, facing north, east, and west. She has claimed this room as her home office, and it's where she begins each morning. In the middle of Jo's office sits a desk, angled slightly to the east, where she spends an hour or so paying bills, reviewing orders, reading ag papers, and perusing cookbooks while she watches the day awaken. She can view all of her fields from this room, and it also overlooks her grandfather's property, the original farmstead adjoining hers. Mornings are pleasant here, no matter what season it is or how the weather is behaving that particular day. Hawks, coyotes, geese, and deer wander by like characters on a stage, and Jo has a front row seat for whatever show happens to be playing on her farmland each morning.

The early hours spent in this room are also a time for reflection. Jo has dedicated her life to caring for the land surrounding her, land her grandfather homesteaded and her father helped develop. There's a rich family history here, and the farm brims with stories. As she gazes out the windows, drinking her tea, she's often reflecting on the heritage of the farm, her father working alongside her grandparents, and all they endured to pave the way for her as the proprietress of her fifty-eight acre, organic, self-sustaining Dutch Fury Farm.

Jo's grandfather on her dad's side of the family was the son of bakers in Holland. He didn't like the early hours required of bakers and dreamt of a different, better life for himself. At the same time, Roman Catholic Crosier Fathers were spreading promises of rich, abundant farmland in the US' Midwest, hoping to entice Dutch Catholics to immigrate to Minnesota in order to grow their religious community. Jo's grandfather decided to follow these promises of land and the possibility of a new beginning to escape his destiny as a baker. On the boat over he met his future wife, and together they settled near Onamia in Central Minnesota.

Unfortunately, the promise of idyllic farmland wasn't totally accurate. Upon arrival they discovered that the land they were chasing was actually a newly logged white pine forest, and the supposedly fertile fields were littered with enormous stumps and rocks. Nothing had been tilled, and nothing could be planted until the land was properly cleared. They persevered, and over time her grandparents did successfully transform the property into the farmland they had been seeking, using dynamite to blow up the stumps and horses to haul out the debris, but Jo thinks back on what that must have been like for them: new to the country, lonely pioneers trying to create a new life together, doggedly building a farm from the ground up. Eventually Jo's dad was born and would become an integral part of developing the farmstead as a young adult. After serving in World War II, he returned and bought property adjacent to Jo's grandfather's farm; the land she farms today.

To understand the name *Dutch Fury Farm*, it's helpful to understand Jo's family a bit. "Fury" is typically defined as rage or madness, but in this context "fury" represents the singular passion and zeal everyone in her family—grandparents, parents, sisters, her brother—has possessed for growing and eating exceptionally good food. And while it's safe to say that most family farmers share a passion for good food, Jo's family elevates that passion to a level bordering on obsession—in the most positive sense possible.

Jo's interest in food began as a young girl thanks to her Grandpa Baert, who had a habit of giving freshly dug vegetables a quick dust and swipe on his pant leg before handing them to her and saying simply, "Here, taste this. Now taste this. And now taste this one." From one day to the next she eagerly followed her grandfather around the farm, eating slightly dirty garden produce as they worked side by side, and slowly training her taste buds to appreciate and delight in all the fresh flavors of the foods they grew and raised themselves.

On holidays the extended family had a tradition of getting together—sharing meals and animated conversations, most of which predictably revolved around the subject of growing, cooking, or preserving food. Recipes were analyzed and dissected with an enthusiasm that could be off-putting to outsiders who sometimes mistook the passionate exchanges as heated or excessive. The family came to understand that what was normal to them wasn't the case with everybody; other households didn't seem to fixate on food like they did. So when it came time to officially name the farm that had always unofficially been known as "Blomer's Farm," Jo's son suggested melding their Dutch heritage with the one word that perhaps best encompasses the passion, resoluteness, and whirlwind nature that makes Jo the force that she is: fury. Dutch Fury Farm.

As if subconsciously proving just how deep this cord of Dutch fury runs, Jo has not just one, but two kitchens on her farm. One is in her converted barn house, which is still being renovated and sits off her office, and she also has her "summer kitchen" located a few strides from the high tunnel on the other end of the property. Both are filled to the brim with antique and modern cookware, shelves of mason jars containing dried spices, herbs and teas, and enough dishware for a good-sized family reunion. Jo is drawn to anything utilitarian. Chances are good she could equip a small commercial kitchen with all the measuring cups, sheet pans, and ladles she's collected. Hanging from the sides of her cupboards are recipes printed on index cards and protected in plastic sleeves, favorites she wants to keep handy. Her cookbook collection is vast, some dating back decades, and she can't always remember which recipe came from which book. She laments having too many books to read and no time to read them.

Jo also has seven freezers on her property with enough food stored away to last two years, just in case there's a bad harvest one year. Growing up as her dad's "right-hand man" on the farm, Jo adopted his philosophies around the importance of being a self-sustaining farmer to ensure food security for oneself, beliefs shaped by The Great Depression and worldwide famines. There are fewer than a dozen items she routinely buys from the store because she doesn't grow or raise them herself. Most of the things on this list are cooking oils, but she also treats herself to peanut butter, avocados, and an organic banana every once in a while.

Every day is a juggling act for farmers. In every field, around every corner, behind every door there is a project waiting for attention—projects fit for every season and every type of weather: transplanting, watering, weeding, pruning, harvesting, haying, fence repair, equipment repair, roadside sales, and much more. For Jo, cooking, fermenting, freezing, drying, and canning food are additional projects of equal importance. Each morning over her standard breakfast of eggs with veggies, sprouted grain bread, milk, and coffee, Jo pores over recipes and plans the daily and weekly meals, thankful for the few minutes to savor a cookbook and the land that feeds her.

Rhubarb Wild Rice Scones with Raspberry Rhubarb Compote

2017: Pat Root & Barb Eller, Farm Market Cafe
in partnership with Dutch Fury Farm

Rhubarb, an early perennial vegetable, unofficially but triumphantly announces spring's arrival in Minnesota. Bakers and cooks look forward to its emergence with impatience and enthusiasm, as it signals the much-anticipated beginning of another growing season. The lush Dutch Fury Farm rhubarb patch is visible from the nearby highway, enticing passersby to stop and collect some of the tart, ruby stalks for themselves. If customers can't find owner Jo Rapatz working in her fields, most know to leave their money in a big purple jar on her porch just around the corner.

For the scones:

3 cups flour

1 tablespoon plus 1 teaspoon baking powder

⅔ cup sugar

½ teaspoon cardamom

¼ teaspoon anise

1 cup cooked wild rice

8 tablespoons very cold unsalted butter, cut into pieces

2 cups fresh or frozen rhubarb, chopped into ¼-inch pieces (if frozen, do not thaw)

¾ cup milk

1 large duck egg

For the raspberry rhubarb compote:

2 cups raspberries

2 cups chopped rhubarb

1 tablespoon plus 1 teaspoon chocolate balsamic vinegar

⅛–¼ teaspoon ground anise

¼ cup honey

4 tablespoons sugar

1 medium firm, sweet apple such as Prairie Spy or Pink Lady, peeled, cored, and diced

To make the scones: Preheat oven to 400°F.

Mix first 6 ingredients together in a large bowl. Using a pastry cutter, cut butter into flour until the size of peas. Add chopped rhubarb to flour mixture. In a medium bowl, whisk together milk and duck egg.

Add wet ingredients to dry ingredients and mix together gently. Once all the flour is incorporated, gently pull together using a large spoon or your hands. Do not over-mix.

Lightly flour a large cutting board. Place scone mixture onto board; pat into a circle about 10 inches round and 1 inch high. Cut into wedges or circles and arrange about an inch apart on a baking sheet lined with parchment paper. Bake for 15–17 minutes on the middle rack.

To make the compote: Combine all ingredients in a large saucepan and cook slowly over medium heat, stirring frequently to prevent burning. Simmer until fruit is cooked and sauce is thickened, about 30 minutes. Serve with scones.

Breakfast Potatoes

2007: Chef Owner Nathalie Johnson, Signature Cafe & Catering in partnership with Northwoods Organic Produce

These breakfast potatoes have all the sizzle and flavor you could ask for, but it's also an easy dish to experiment with and make your own. Consider adding ham (or sausage) for brunch or serve with over easy eggs for a complete breakfast. These potatoes also pair well with a sharp, crisp salad.

YIELD: 12 SERVINGS

- 6 large white russet or red potatoes, about 3 pounds, peeled and left whole
- 2 tablespoons extra-virgin olive oil, plus 1 tablespoon for casserole dish
- 4 cups fresh spinach, chard leaves, arugula, or dark greens washed well and torn coarsely
- salt and pepper, to taste
- 3 garlic cloves, peeled and minced
- 1½ cups high-quality dry-aged cheese; Parmesan or a local hard cheese, divided
- 2 cups heavy whipping cream

Preheat oven to 400°F.

Bring a large pot of salted water to boil and add potatoes. Reduce temperature to a heavy simmer and cook until fork tender. Your boiling time will depend on the size and type of potato.

While potatoes cook, heat 2 tablespoons of olive oil in a sauté pan and add greens by the handful. Lightly season greens with salt and pepper and cook until softened.

When potatoes are fork tender, cool quickly by placing in an ice bath, then place on a towel and pat dry. Using a grater, shred potatoes into hash brown consistency into a large bowl.

Add cooked greens, garlic, and 1 cup of cheese to bowl. Add cream by the quarter cup to potatoes and combine, continuing until cream is incorporated and potatoes are well coated. The mixture should be very moist.

Oil a 3-quart casserole dish with remaining 1 tablespoon olive oil. Sprinkle ¼ cup cheese in the dish until bottom is coated. Add potatoes and spread evenly. Sprinkle remaining ¼ cup cheese on top of potatoes.

Bake, uncovered for 40 minutes until lightly browned on top. Cool 15 minutes before serving.

Red Flannel Hash

2020: Duluth Grill, Owners Tom & Jaima Hanson in partnership with Food Farm

Duluth Grill's Red Flannel Hash has been a staple side dish at the diner for over fifteen years. Owners Tom and Jaima Hanson added the hash to their menu after noticing guests' tastes were evolving and gravitating toward flavorsome comfort foods that were also more nutritious. Tom says, "We wanted to offer a breakfast option that would satisfy the soul and also fuel folks up for the day; there's no better combination than roasted root veggies." This hash is now the most requested recipe in Duluth Grill's history. The name Red Flannel Hash reflects the "Up North" feel that embodies time spent in Duluth.

YIELD: 4–6 SERVINGS

- 2–3 beets
- 4 cups 1-inch diced sweet potatoes, about 2 large sweet potatoes
- 1½ cups carrots, diced small
- 1 cup onions, diced small
- 2 cups bell peppers, diced small
- 1 teaspoon pepper
- 2½ teaspoons salt
- 1½ teaspoons fresh garden herbs or dried herbs of choice, such as fresh, flat-leaf parsley, chives, and basil
- ½ cup olive oil

Wrap beets in foil and roast for 30–45 minutes in a 350°F oven.

Toss diced vegetables together in a large mixing bowl with remaining ingredients. Set aside. Remove beets from oven when easily pierced with a paring knife. Cool. Remove skin, and dice into 1-inch pieces (this should yield about 2 cups).

Increase oven temperature to 450°F. Place diced beets on a baking sheet. Add bowl of mixed diced vegetables to a second baking sheet. Roast at 450°F for 25 minutes or until the mix is nice and tender with some caramelization.

Chef's note: To make this into a complete meal, serve with your favorite grain, greens, and eggs as a breakfast bowl. To make for a speedy breakfast, consider roasting the vegetables the night before. Crisp the vegetables in a pan with a little oil just in time for breakfast.

Quiche Lorraine with Potato Crust

2019: Chef Beth Fisher, French Meadow Cafe & Bakery
in partnership with Larry Schultz Farms

YIELD: 8-10 SERVINGS

For potato crust:

6 large russet potatoes

1 cup yellow onions, diced small

½ cup olive oil

1 tablespoon sea salt

2 teaspoons black pepper

For custard:

12 eggs

2½ cups heavy cream

1 teaspoon salt

For filling:

2 cups Gruyere cheese (not packed), shredded

1 cup crispy cooked bacon, rough-chopped

½ cup green onions, diced

2 tablespoons flat-leaf parsley, rough chopped

sprinkle of paprika

To make the potato crust: Preheat oven to 350°F.

Wash potatoes and poke a couple holes in the skin. Bake whole potatoes 45 minutes; allow to cool, then shred and toss with remaining ingredients.

Increase oven temperature to 400°F. Spread potato mixture out onto a sheet pan and bake, uncovered until golden brown, 20–25 minutes. Cool.

Press cooked mixture into a 10 x 2-inch cake pan (this is a deep-dish quiche). Pre-bake potato crust until golden brown and crispy, 20–25 minutes. Once the crust is filled, it won't get much crispier, so it needs to be crispy before being filled.

To make the custard: Whisk ingredients together until well blended. No need to over whisk—we don't want air bubbles.

To assemble the quiche: Preheat oven to 400°F.

Distribute Gruyere in bottom of pre-baked potato crust. Sprinkle bacon pieces, sliced green onion, and parsley over cheese. Pour custard mixture into pan, leaving ½ inch from top of pan. Sprinkle top with paprika.

Bake for 20 minutes, then reduce heat to 300°F and bake another 30–40 minutes. Quiche is done when top springs back when gently pushed. Allow quiche to rest at least 30 minutes before cutting and serving.

Tractor Meals

A farmer's office is wherever the farmer happens to be: the milking parlor, the kitchen table, under a high tunnel, inside the farm pick-up truck, or on a tractor. Twenty-first-century farmers spend as much time studying spreadsheets as they do with their animals or crops, running complex businesses requiring them to be experts across an array of subjects: soil science, livestock, pest management, machinery repair, accounting and finance, marketing, and sales. Despite the workload and hefty contributions they make to the US economy, farmers routinely struggle to stay afloat. To survive, farmers are forced to innovate, walking a tightrope between the tried-and-true and the path unknown. Everyone knows farmers are hard workers; equally important, they're creative, savvy entrepreneurs. Some days there's little time to eat, even for a farmer, whose lives revolve around food. Every day is a hustle.

The Rebels of Whole Grain Milling

Among farmers, there's a widespread belief that if you're not acquiring more land and actively striving to grow bigger, you're going backwards. To think otherwise is somewhat rebellious. Doug Hilgendorf, farmer and co-owner of Whole Grain Milling in Welcome, Minnesota, has always disagreed with this belief. Call him a rebel, but he just never understood the point in getting bigger if you could figure out a way to earn a living with what you already have. Sometimes all it takes is a little tenacity and ingenuity.

Doug and his wife Lin, along with several family members, farm less than five hundred acres in southwest Minnesota—a small farm by modern standards. During the 1980s, farms were disappearing at an alarming rate, leaving many farm families in financial ruin. The Hilgendorfs certainly weren't exempt from the economic crisis and were among those forced to take an honest, wide-eyed look at whether they could continue to farm for a living. Struggling to stay viable, their livelihood felt tenuous and hinged on figuring out how to generate additional income in order to stay on the farm without simply subscribing to the mainstream mindset of buying more land and incurring more debt.

Rather than just acting to survive, Doug and Lin also seized this time of uncertainty as an opportunity to re-evaluate and course-correct some past actions. If they were going to continue farming, they wanted to do it in a way that felt true to their values and sustainable to their lifestyle. This meant questioning and abandoning the conventional farming methods they had adopted for a short time. Chemicals left them both feeling uneasy, as did the undesirable decline clearly visible in the health of their soil and livestock. Staying true to themselves, they began transitioning their farm back to organic production, becoming certified organic in 1989. Once back on course, however, they were faced with yet another harsh reality: the demand for organics was still in its infancy and didn't have a solid market, leaving them to sell their hard-fought organic corn and organic oats at disheartening, conventional prices. Though surrounded by a sea of other farmers, the Hilgendorfs were essentially lone rangers in their dedication to organic production. They needed a better market, or they weren't going to make it, and there was no roadmap available for how to tackle this challenge.

Watchful of emerging trends, they brainstormed possible solutions for adding value to their farm and the clever idea to build a mill rose to the surface. If they could process their organic grains themselves and then seek a fair price for the products created—essentially taking control of their own market—perhaps the farm could survive. It was a bold, untraditional leap, but the Hilgendorfs were not strangers to risk and with familial and institutional financial support, they took it. By 1990 Whole Grain Milling was up and running.

The Hilgendorfs' uncompromising commitment from the get-go was to produce clean, nutritious food. This was ingrained in everything they did, fueled in part by the memory of Doug's dad who died from cancer in 1978. It was at this time they were becoming increasingly aware of how quickly food was changing and how common it was to see unpronounceable additives on food labels. They narrowed their focus on growing nutrient-dense organic grains: oats, buckwheat, rye, and their main crop, a non-GMO, high-lysine corn with nearly double the protein of other corn varieties. Then they revved up their new custom-built facilities and began producing minimally processed oatmeal and assorted flours.

Although they knew their products had more integrity than they were finding on most grocery store shelves, their initial entry into the market was riddled with challenges. Being their own distributors, they found themselves in the dual role of producers and advocates, sometimes facing large distribution channels with deep roots in the supply chain. Not one to shy away from a challenge, they kept knocking on doors and explaining why their products deserved a chance. Soon they gained some traction and successfully broke into the Twin Cities' market, building a solid foundation that still supports them today. The timing was exquisite. While the network of co-ops around Minnesota was still somewhat small, it was positioned for exponential growth. So, too, was the demand for organics. The future began to look promising.

Demand supported growth, and Whole Grain Milling started buying and processing certified organic products from other growers in Minnesota and the Dakotas. One step at a time, one hurdle at a time, their product line expanded to include a variety of bread and pancake mixes and other goods, including their exceedingly popular Whole Grain Milling Tortilla Chips, which exude the taste of real corn and garnered a large enough fan base to justify building their own chip plant, too. As the saying goes, word of mouth advertising is the best form of advertising, and word spread fast about Whole Grain Milling.

The income Doug and Lin earn from farming varies widely every year. It doesn't pay to figure out what the income per acre is because even their most deliberate predictions would be unreliable. Their land is low and has always been susceptible to crop losses from standing water, but increasingly unpredictable weather patterns bringing extreme rains have only made it more vulnerable in recent years. Amidst all the uncertainty, there is one thing Doug and Lin are certain about—their farm, and their lives as organic farmers, would not have been sustainable without Whole Grain Milling.

Instead, on that small parcel of land many would say is too small to survive, the Hilgendorfs' farm and Whole Grain Milling now support twelve people, including Doug and Lin's sons, Ross and Jeff, and other family and community members. Ever humble and grounded, Doug and Lin might not be seen as unwavering and determined, but make no mistake about it—they weren't going down without a fight. As Doug says, they still may not be millionaires, but they earn enough to pay their bills, live comfortably, and pursue work that matters. Their land, which has been in Doug's family since 1948, is rich and healthy. Their banker is happy and they feel proud employing and contributing to others' livelihoods. All this on less than five hundred acres.

Sometimes farming requires the farmer to be a maverick, to go against the grain and design his own unorthodox path forward. Equally important, it takes support. Every farmer Doug knows has received some kind of financial help at some point—parents, a sibling, a neighbor or friend, or a courageous banker willing to take a chance. Somewhere along the line, someone gave a successful farmer a deal on rent, a low-interest loan, a generous donation of capital, or free labor. Everybody, he says, needs a hand up sometimes—even when you're the lone man in the room, raising your hand, wild and willing to stand up and fight for what you feel is right.

Cottage Bread

2016: Owner Lisa Lindberg, Amboy Cottage Cafe
in partnership with Whole Grain Milling

Bake this dough as is or treat it as a canvas for vegetables, meats, herbs, and cheese before shaping and baking. An Amboy Cottage Cafe favorite includes red onion, cheddar cheese, and plenty of oregano. Sausage can be added to make it a full meal. For a hearty roll or bun, the dough can be pinched into rounds and baked.

YIELD: 4 LOAVES

1 cup mashed potato or sweet potato

3 cups water

2 cups milk

3 tablespoons local honey

2 cups old-fashioned rolled oats

2 tablespoons dry yeast

6 cups wheat bread flour, divided

1 cup pumpernickel rye flour

1½ tablespoons sea salt

½ cup unsalted butter, melted, plus more for brushing

3 cups white flour

Preheat oven to 375°F.

Place potato in glass pitcher with water. Microwave 3 minutes. Add milk and honey. In a large bowl combine oats, dry yeast, 4 cups wheat bread flour, and pumpernickel flour in large bowl. Pour water mixture over flour mixture; whisk well.

Allow mixture to rest 10 minutes, then add salt and butter. Stir to combine. Fold in remaining 2 cups wheat flour and add white flour.

Once dough is very stiff, turn onto floured board and knead 400–500 times. Add more flour as needed. Dough should handle well and feel elastic.

Oil a large bowl, turn dough over in bowl to coat. Set in a warm spot to rise until doubled in size, about 1 hour.

Divide dough into 4 equal parts. Shape into 4 oblong loaves (European-style oblong loaves) and place on oiled sheet pans. Using a sharp knife, cut 3 or 4 ½-inch deep slices into the top of dough. Brush loaves with melted butter. Sprinkle with additional oatmeal if desired. Let rest 10 minutes. Bake for 45 minutes until loaves tap hollow. Cool on rack.

For variations: After dividing dough into equal parts, use rolling pin to roll one part into a rectangle about 1 foot x 8 inches. Generously spread additional desired ingredients evenly then roll into an oblong loaf and tuck ends under. Continue with recipe as instructed.

Farmers Sausage

2017: Erik Sather, Lowry Hill Meats
in partnership with Pork & Plants

The base of this sausage is versatile and dependable, leaving plenty of room for the home cook to dress it up with herbs, spices, and produce. Fresh sage, thyme, and finely diced apples create an autumnal sausage. Try crushed red pepper and harissa for an interesting kick. Lowry Hill Meats even adds pickled cabbage to its fermented sausage. If the idea of stuffing sausage scares you, form the mixture into meatballs instead and serve with pasta or shape into patties wrapped in caul fat. Your taste buds won't care about the shape.

2½ tablespoons salt

1½ tablespoons black pepper

3 tablespoons lager

2 teaspoons garlic powder

5 pounds fresh ground pork

5 feet of hog casings, flushed and prepared

Mix salt, pepper, lager, and garlic powder in a bowl to make a slurry. Add pork and mix with hands until combined well. Pinch off a piece and cook it in a skillet. Taste to ensure your flavor is right. Correct seasonings as needed.

Put sausage mix into your preferred sausage stuffer cylinder or hopper, packing it down to remove air pockets. A hand crank stuffer or Kitchen Aid mixer attachment both work well.

Prep casings by running water through to moisten before attaching to the stuffing nozzle, which will prevent the casing from sticking to the nozzle. Tie one end and slip the other end onto the tip of the casing tube. Place sheet pan below the stuffing nozzle. Crank the sausage into the casings or run sausage stuffer on low until all sausage has been stuffed into the casing. If using a hand crank, it may help to have a partner assist in guiding sausage onto sheet pan as it is stuffed.

When all sausage has been stuffed and casing is full, pinch casing off the casing tube, cutting if necessary but leaving several inches of unstuffed casing. Coil sausage into a large circle, nestling it fairly tightly to push out air pockets. Pinch casing where sausage finishes and tie a knot. Using a sterilized needle or pin, starting in the middle and working your way out, poke holes in the casing about every 6 inches to eliminate remaining air pockets.

Starting with the outer edge of sausage coil, measure desired length of sausage and twist entire sausage link 4 or 5 times to create a separate link. Poke link with finger to ensure casing bounces back. If it does not bounce back, then twist the link again, as many times as necessary, until casing is tight and bounces back. The number of twists will vary throughout, depending on how much air is in the casings. Continue linking process until entire coil is separated into sausage links. Cut off non-uniform link at the end of the tube.

Allow sausages to rest in refrigerator overnight. For most cooking methods, rest sausages on sheet pan covered tightly with plastic wrap to hold sausages in place. For smoking sausages, leave uncovered to fully dry casings, which will aid smoke in sticking to sausages. You may also choose to braid sausages together and hang to allow casings to fully dry.

Cook sausages as desired—grill, boil, sauté, or smoke.

Rosemary Focaccia Sandwich with Roasted Sweet Corn and Chevre

2006: Owner Dick Trotter, Trotter's Cafe
in partnership with Whole Farm Cooperative

YIELD: 4–8 SANDWICHES

For rosemary focaccia:

2 tablespoons yeast

2 cups warm water

1 tablespoon fresh
   rosemary, chopped
   plus whole fresh
   leaves and clusters

3 teaspoons Minnesota
   clover honey

3 teaspoons sea salt

¾ cup old-fashioned
   rolled oats, plus
   additional for baking
   sheet

1 cup whole wheat flour

3–4 cups white
   unbleached flour

For spread:

4 fresh ears of corn with
   husks

6 ounces goat cheese

1 cup loosely packed
   fresh cilantro,
   chopped

For balsamic onions:

1 sweet white onion

balsamic vinegar

To assemble:

2 heirloom tomatoes

olive oil

1 head green butterleaf
   lettuce

To make the focaccia: Preheat oven to 350°F.

Dissolve yeast in warm water. Add rosemary, honey, and salt. Add oats, all whole wheat flour, and most of the white flour. Mix until smooth. Add enough remaining flour until it just comes together. Place dough on floured board. Divide into 4 equal parts.

Sprinkle oats on sheet pan. Using floured hands, push each dough into an 8- to 9-inch circle. Let rise approximately 10 minutes. Brush with olive oil and sprinkle with whole fresh rosemary leaves and clusters. Bake for 12–16 minutes, rotating between upper and middle racks.

To make the spread: With husks on, grill corn until tender. Let cool. Remove corn from cob and blend slightly in food processor with goat cheese and cilantro.

To prepare the onions: Slice onions into thick rings and cover with balsamic vinegar for at least 2 hours, up to overnight.

To assemble: Slice ripe tomatoes into ¼-inch thick slices. Slice focaccia horizontally into 2 large rounds ½-inch thick. Brush with olive oil and place on grill for 3–5 minutes or until lightly browned. Spread corn and goat cheese mixture ¼-inch thick on bottom half of bread. Layer onions, tomatoes, and butterleaf greens. Cover with top of focaccia and slice into sandwiches.

Bryant Lake Bowl Meatloaf

2008: Chef Al Potyondy-Smith, Bryant Lake Bowl in partnership with Moonstone Farm

The Sriracha in this recipe makes a fiery meatloaf. If you're not a fan of spice, reduce Sriracha by one-half or less, which will still leave plenty of spice for most Minnesotans. Serve on Cottage Bread for the perfect Tractor Meal sandwich.

YIELD: 6–8 SERVINGS

- 2 pounds ground beef
- ¼ cup diced yellow onions
- ⅓ cup prepared horseradish
- 1 tablespoon finely minced garlic
- ½–1 cup Sriracha chili sauce
- 2 teaspoons sea salt or kosher salt
- 2 teaspoons black pepper (table grind)
- ⅛ cup sour cream
- ¼ cup chopped Italian flat-leaf parsley
- 1 teaspoon dry Italian seasoning
- 1 cup panko (Japanese breadcrumbs)

Preheat oven to 350°F.

Place ground beef in large mixing bowl and add onions, horseradish, garlic, chili sauce, salt, pepper, sour cream, parsley, and Italian seasonings. Mix well by hand. When all ingredients are incorporated throughout, slowly mix in panko until meatloaf holds together.

In a medium to shallow buttered or greased 9 x 13-inch baking dish, form meatloaf by pressing into a 9 x 5-inch loaf. Make sure the meatloaf is at least ½-inch away from all edges of the dish, and pressed tightly with no air holes in the loaf. Cover with aluminum foil and bake for 45 minutes. Remove foil and finish meatloaf uncovered for an additional 20–30 minutes, or until the internal temperature is 160°F or higher. Allow meatloaf to cool slightly and then cut slices to desired thickness.

The Artisanal Life at Capra Nera Creamery

Farmers joke about how they ended up farming by accident, how perhaps they should have thought twice before pursuing such a challenging and financially unrewarding occupation. The drive to be a farmer is often innate and unavoidable, a natural conclusion to one's experiences and inclinations. In Katie Bonow's case, her choice to be a farmer was solidified once she realized she simply may not be suitable for any other way of life.

Growing up on her family's dairy farm near Spring Grove left an enduring impression on Katie: nurturing farm animals, summers spent running around barefoot (so much so that she struggled to put on her shoes again when the school year began), and cultivating a deep respect for the work her parents did as farmers. Looking back, Katie's future as a farmer was set into motion very early in life, but her fate likely was sealed when she was twelve years old thanks to a single, unforgettable goat named Blossom.

Blossom was Katie's first goat, and she was a diva. A loud, needy Nubian goat, Blossom was full of attitude and ruled the farm. But she could also be affectionate, and Katie bonded with her. Within a couple years Blossom was producing too much milk to drink, so with her mother's encouragement and guidance from her 4-H family, Katie began experimenting making simple cheeses in her family's kitchen. The first batch was a dud, but subsequent batches of beginner cheeses were successes, inspiring Katie to master chevre and then tackle harder cheese like cheddar. Some experiments worked; some resulted in hard hockey pucks barely resembling cheese. Regardless, Katie became hooked on the craft.

She became interested enough in cheese making to spend spring break of her sophomore year of college at the Vermont Institute for Artisan Cheese, returning again a few months later to dive deeper into the science of cheese and safety regulations. Simultaneously, Katie found herself gravitating toward the Italian classes she was taking to fulfill her liberal arts degree at the University of Minnesota, prompting her to spend

---

In recent years, the definition of "artisanal" has become blurry. The word artisanal *most accurately describes foods made in small batches in a manner that preserves traditional techniques, such as cheeses, breads, chocolates, cured meats, and even beer. True artisans—or craftsmen—tend to emphasize fresh, local ingredients in their products, often those associated with a certain terroir, and they maintain a sincere focus on quality over quantity. Creating a superior, distinct product is their ultimate goal. Ironically, the labels on their products often don't mention the word* artisanal *at all.*

Conversely, mass-produced foods, especially those produced using automation by large-scale food manufacturers, technically don't qualify as artisanal. Yet because the words artisan *and* artisanal *have no standard or legal definition, these terms have become commodified and are increasingly used to market mainstream, industrialized, mediocre foods.*

A true artisan can tell you the story of his or her product.

a semester abroad studying in Italy and then traveling and working on various organic dairy and vegetable farms throughout the country after classes ended.

Katie is the kind of person who follows her gut and lives life deliberately. She's purposeful and confident without making a big show of it. Though she lightheartedly jokes about the usefulness—or lack thereof—of her Italian Studies major, Katie's time in Italy opened her eyes to possibilities. It showed her a world of successful on-farm production and artisan cheese making and introduced her to a culture that doesn't just like food but *lives* for food. She witnessed how engrained it is in Italian culture to value local farmers and purveyors, how entire festivals are devoted to celebrating hand-crafted foods, and how small farms thrive because they have a robust direct-to-consumer market. It ignited her sense of wonder, causing her to muse whether it might be possible to create this way of life for herself back home in Minnesota.

After college, Katie immersed herself one last time in the Italian farmstead experience in the Lake Como area before returning to Minnesota to make the brave plunge into farming. She grew her herd of sassy goats, invested in a cheese vat, and when her future husband bought a farm, the puzzle was complete. All those years milking goats, conducting cheese experiments, learning Italian, and being wooed by a culture that lives for stellar food finally culminated with the conception of Capra Nera Creamery in Altura, Minnesota, in 2016.

Despite many financial hurdles, Katie jumped in with both feet. Like most entrepreneurs, farmers typically face significant upfront investments to get their businesses up and running, and the return on their investments can be slow and small. Katie managed to wade through the tedious process of securing a low-interest improvement loan through FSA, and she also received a Livestock Investment Grant from the Minnesota Department of Agriculture. Cash flow from these sources early on enabled her to move forward on much-needed renovations to transform their old, dated farm into a functioning food-grade, cheese-making facility. Her family donated capital, hay, hands-on help, and much-needed encouragement. Every bit mattered. It took tenacity, but she patched together enough resources to get a strong start.

In 2019 Katie produced approximately one ton of cheese, her most productive year yet. Her business is young, and she feels optimistic about its potential for growth. She anticipates increasing both her cheese production and sales each year. Still, she's not quite breaking even with her business.

Katie's husband, Ryan, is also a dairy farmer—cow dairy. As milk prices declined in recent years, they needed additional household income in order to make ends meet, so Katie took a position as a backup cook at the nearby school, something she squeezes in alongside farming, making cheese, and caring for their toddler, Oren. This is a truth that is inescapable and real: Most farms—large or small, organic or non-organic—need off-farm employment to survive. Farming alone rarely provides enough income for a family to thrive anymore—let alone feel secure. Many farmers also rely on the support of social services like medical assistance, fuel assistance programs, and property tax refunds. To say it bluntly, because farmers are too often undervalued and undercompensated, they can't support themselves without the assistance of social programs.

There is a story Katie loves to tell to illustrate value, involving her great-grandmother and the eggs she produced on her farm. As the story goes, whenever Katie's great-grandmother went into town to buy groceries, she would tote her fresh eggs along to sell to the grocer. After shopping for her groceries, she would place them on the counter next to her eggs, and then she and the grocer would negotiate a price for her eggs. Most of the time they were able to agree upon a fair price, which would go toward her groceries, and everyone left happy.

But every once in a while the grocer wouldn't give her great-grandmother the price she wanted. When that happened, she would gather up her eggs, leave her groceries sitting on the counter, and exit the store. This story is significant to Katie for two reasons: first, her great-grandmother actually had a voice in how much she got paid—she had negotiating power. Second, her food had value. Katie points out how eggs today might be sold for eighty-nine cents per dozen at a gas station, and of that eighty-nine cents the farmer will only receive twenty or thirty cents—not even enough to buy a cup of coffee.

When farmers and producers sell direct to the consumer, however, they earn a fairer price for their hard work.

It's hard to imagine why a young couple would choose to farm when the odds seem squarely stacked against them, no matter how hard they work. For Katie, she feels a responsibility to keep farming. The average farmer in the US is fifty-eight years old, and currently there are not enough young farmers to replace those retiring. She worries that if they don't do it, no one else will. But more importantly, their commitment to farming, while sometimes financially unstable, ironically translates into their own definition of freedom. They live in the country. They don't have a commute. They raise Oren full time and relish in his squeals of delight when feeding the goats or when he sees his dad driving in from the field on the tractor. They can't imagine creating this lifestyle, one they were born to love, doing anything else.

Minnesota Street Corn

2018: Chef David Bredesen, Forager Brewery in partnership with Capra Nera Creamery

In Italian, Contadina *means "female farmer." In Minnesota's food world,* Contadina *refers to the semi-hard, aged goat cheese produced by Katie Bonow of Capra Nera Creamery, the cheese recommended for Minnesota Street Corn. Aptly named,* Contadina *is a nod to Katie, her mother, and women farmers everywhere, recognizing how female farmers too often don't receive the credit they deserve for their contributions to farming. Though technically not an Italian cheese,* Contadina *is Italian in spirit in that it's an artisan farmstead product made with raw milk. It's aged at least five months and boasts a nuanced nutty, salty flavor reminiscent of Parmesan. If you can't get your hands on* Contadina, *substitute aged white cheddar, cotija, queso fresco, or your favorite hard cheese.*

YIELD: 6–8 SERVINGS

For the beef fat aioli:

1 egg yolk*

2 medium cloves garlic, peeled and smashed

1 teaspoon freshly squeezed lemon juice

¼ cup canola oil

¼ cup beef fat, slightly warmer than room temperature—pourable

⅛ teaspoon salt, or to taste

For the corn:

6–8 ears of corn, in husks

12 ounces Capra Nera Creamery Contadina cheese, shredded, or your favorite aged white cheddar, cotija, queso fresco, or other hard cheese

To prepare the beef fat aioli: Combine egg, garlic, and lemon juice in food processor. With machine running, slowly drizzle in canola oil to emulsify. Add beef fat, drip by drip (fat may need to be warmed slightly to remain as a liquid for dripping). Add a splash of water if aioli is too thick for your liking. Salt, to taste.

To prepare the corn: Heat grill to high heat. Grill corn in husk about 15 minutes, turning occasionally. Remove from grill; allow to sit until cool enough to handle. Remove husks and season corn with salt. To serve, drizzle each cob of corn with aioli and sprinkle with Capra Nera Contadina. Additional optional garnishes include crushed black pepper, paprika, and chives.

Chef's note: For the adventurous cook, Chef Bredesen suggests making homemade roasted beef marrow in place of beef fat for the aioli. Roast 2–3 beef femur bones in an oven preheated to 400°F for 20 minutes. Allow to cool, then remove marrow. Leftover marrow is delicious on toast or grilled cheese, and leftover bone marrow aioli would be excellent on french fries or roasted potatoes.

*To double this recipe for a crowd, use 1 whole egg and double the remaining ingredients.

Collard Wraps with Garden Pesto

2019: Chef Lachelle Cunningham, Breaking Bread Cafe
in partnership with Urban Agriculture

YIELD: 3 SERVINGS

For pesto:

2 cups fresh herbs, tightly packed

½ cup raw and unsalted sunflower seeds

1–2 cloves garlic

½ cup extra-virgin olive oil

sea salt and freshly ground pepper, to taste

1 tablespoon lemon juice

4–6 tablespoons nutritional yeast

For dipping sauce:

¼ cup soy sauce

¼ cup rice vinegar

1 teaspoon sesame oil

To assemble:

6 whole collard or kale leaves, rinsed clean

1 avocado, pitted and mashed

1½ cups vegetables, julienned

broccoli sprouts or other micro sprouts

green onions, sliced thin

To make the pesto: place fresh herbs (basil, green onion, parsley, and cilantro is a good combination), sunflower seeds, and garlic in a blender or food processor fitted with the S blade. Pulse to combine until mixture is coarsely ground.

Turn motor on, and drizzle in olive oil in a thin stream. Add sea salt, pepper, lemon, and yeast; pulse a few more times to combine. Taste and add more seasonings as needed, and set aside.

To make dipping sauce: Mix sauce ingredients together in a small bowl and set aside.

To assemble wraps: Separate each collard leaf into two pieces by cutting lengthwise along stem and removing stem. Kale leaves can be left whole. Spread 1 generous tablespoon pesto inside each green leaf. Spread avocado on top of pesto. Evenly divide vegetables (bell peppers, carrots, cucumbers and/or radishes are good options) among collard or kale leaves and place in middle of each leaf. Roll them up and secure with a toothpick. Serve with dipping sauce.

Heirloom Tomato and Sweet Corn BLT

2019: Chef Marshall Paulsen, Birchwood Cafe
in partnership with Hmong American Farmers Association

The layered flavors in this BLT will knock your socks off. A hit at the Minnesota Farmers Union booth at the Minnesota State Fair, the Heirloom Tomato and Sweet Corn BLT left food critics and state fair goers singing its praises far and wide. The Sweet Corn Chipotle Coulis and Sunny Seed Pesto sauces can be used to jazz up any number of dishes, and both keep well in the fridge. Consider assembling the BLT with either Cottage Bread or Rosemary Focaccia.

For sweet corn chipotle coulis:

3 small ears of corn, grilled and cobbed (2 cups of corn)

⅓ cup heavy cream

⅓ cup coconut milk

2 small dehydrated chipotles, rehydrated in water

salt and pepper, to taste

For sunny seed pesto:

1½ cups rough-chopped basil leaves, packed

zest and juice of ½ lemon

scant 3 tablespoons peeled and rough-chopped garlic

⅓ cup sunflower seeds, toasted and cooled

⅔ cup shredded Parmesan

salt and pepper, to taste

¾ cup sunflower oil

For pesto mayo:

½ cup sunny seed pesto

½ cup mayonnaise

salt and pepper, to taste

To assemble:

16 slices bread

sweet corn chipotle coulis

crisp lettuce leaves

2 pounds thick cut bacon slices, cooked

2–3 heirloom tomatoes, sliced

pesto mayo

For sweet corn chipotle coulis: In a sauce pot mix corn kernels with heavy cream, coconut milk, and chipotles. Heat slowly over low heat; stop cooking when mixture reaches a soft rolling boil. Puree with an immersion wand or food processor until corn mixture is thicker and spoonable. Add salt and pepper to taste.

For sunny seed pesto: Add basil to a food processor or blender and briefly blend with lemon juice, zest, and garlic. Add sunflower seeds, Parmesan, salt, and pepper together until coarsely blended. Stream in oil until pesto is thinned and ingredients are thoroughly combined. Taste and correct seasonings with salt and pepper.

For pesto mayo: Use a whisk to mix ingredients together.

To assemble: Toast bread, then spread a tablespoon of sweet corn chipotle coulis on each of 8 slices. Top each with 2–3 lettuce leaves, 2–3 bacon slices, and 2 slices tomatoes. Spread a tablespoon of pesto mayo on each of the remaining slices of bread and place atop the sandwiches.

Becoming Stony Creek Dairy

"Man, are you a dumbass! What the hell are they teaching you at St. Cloud State?"
Those are the words John Schoenberg playfully fired back at his son, Grant, when Grant asked if he had ever thought about taking the milk produced on their family's dairy farm from start to finish. Grant was in his first year of college, and he couldn't stop thinking about an accounting lecture on manufacturing and vertical integration within companies. Their farm had been weathering some rough patches for a few years, and based on what he was learning Grant wondered whether gaining control over the manufacturing and distribution of their milk might provide some armor against the suppressed milk prices his family was up against. That's when he called his dad and casually ran the idea past him. John, however, had never done business that way. He was a farmer; once the milk left his driveway it was out of his hands. Grant and John shared a friendly, father-son laugh about his wacky idea and moved on.

Grant is the sixth generation of the Schoenberg family to farm land near Melrose in Central Minnesota, dating back to the late 1800's. Before Grant left for college, he told his dad farming wasn't something he was interested in pursuing. He didn't plan on coming back to the farm, so if his dad wanted to sell the cows it was fine with him. John was somewhat disappointed, but he understood. From fifth grade through his junior year of high school, Grant milked cows every day after school and then again from eleven at night until two-thirty in the morning. Long before cell phones were mainstream, Grant carried one with him to school so his dad could reach him if he needed him to come home and help. And when he was sixteen years old, he was already responsible for managing the farm's finances. By the time he left for college, he had already worked a lifetime on the farm, and his parents recognized that. He felt eager to explore new terrain.

But after graduating, Grant soon discovered he didn't fit with corporate environments. Despite some successes, he felt micromanaged, hampered, and under-challenged overall. He felt surprised that he actually missed the responsibility he'd grown up with on the farm. Gradually, he started helping his dad again on weekends, tip-toeing back into the farm's operations.

A year after Grant first opened the conversation about expanding into manufacturing and distribution, it was John who resurrected the idea and asked Grant what exactly he had meant when he'd proposed taking their products from start to finish on the farm. It was 2001, and milk prices had tanked. John was scrambling for ways to expand business and profits; therefore, he was open to expanding the way he *looked* at and ran his business.

In spring of 2003, Grant wrote a forty-page business plan outlining Stony Creek Dairy. He met with seven bankers before he found one willing to work with him, and in 2004 Stony Creek Dairy was officially established. Grant and John built the distribution side of the business first, and once they had established some cash flow from their new direct customer base they launched the second phase of their vision. By June of 2008 they were bottling milk in their new on-farm bottling plant.

Now Stony Creek Dairy manages every detail of its production: Milk from their cows gets pasteurized, bottled, and loaded onto trucks for distribution all on-site. The barn and plant are a mere three hundred feet apart, which means milk that's still in a cow at midnight could be bottled by six o'clock the following morning. That hyper-fresh finished product is something Grant takes great pride in sharing with the world. It represents his family, their toil and sacrifices—including those of the five generations preceding him. Grant and his team aren't shy about emphasizing Grant's family in their marketing. They freely share pictures of Grant, his wife, and their three children, hoping customers will realize and feel good about directly supporting another family when they choose a Stony Creek Dairy product. "From our family farm to your family's table," he says.

Grant doubts whether he would have returned to farming if they hadn't taken the calculated risk of vertically integrating Stony Creek Dairy. The long hours of farming never scared him, but days spent locked in a tractor working in the fields always left him feeling tethered and caged. It was the business side—processing, distribution, marketing, and the potential for innovation—that intrigued and attracted him more than anything else. Grant is the type of guy who, throughout life, often finds himself moving in the opposite direction of the masses. If most people are following a well-worn, predictable course of action, more often than not he'll be on the perimeter, carving out his own niche. With Stony Creek Dairy, Grant seized an idea and an opportunity to take his family's farm to another level. In a time when markets are volatile, milk prices are low, and family farms are dying, Stony Creek Dairy has managed to stay in the black and keep growing. Grant feels strongly that one of the reasons farmers often struggle and feel helpless is because they don't have the ability to control and market their own products. Yet, that's both the beauty and bane of farming; what works at one farm might not work for the next.

Blood, sweat, and tears—it's an oft-used phrase describing anything hard, anything requiring extreme effort. When it comes to farming, this phrase ceases to be figurative. Grant's dad died in a farming accident in 2013. There have been countless tough days on the farm since then, but somehow Grant maintains an infectious positivity and steely determination to keep moving forward. He's driven by the challenge of business, the thrill of marketing, his passion for their products, and a deep sentimentality for his family's storied history. If they hadn't established Stony Creek Dairy, Grant imagines he would have started another business, and the Schoenberg family farm would be gone or in someone else's hands. Instead, he's created an opportunity for his children to follow in the family's footsteps, if they decide it's what will make them happy.

Grant remembers his dad often saying, "No guts, no glory!" Stony Creek Dairy was a risk, but it was a calculated risk. Grant says knowing what he knows now, if he could do it all again with his dad, he would. In a heartbeat.

Jules' Bistro Dill Pickle Soup

2019: Chef Ryan Zerull and Owner Donella Westphal, Jules' Bistro in partnership with Stony Creek Dairy

YIELD: 8-10 SERVINGS

- 1 cup bacon, diced (4–5 strips)
- 2 cups carrots, diced small
- 2 cups celery, diced small
- 2 cups yellow onion, diced small
- ½ cup dill pickles, diced small
- 1½ teaspoons Old Bay seasoning
- ½ teaspoon salt
- ½ teaspoon black pepper
- ¼ teaspoon cayenne
- 1 teaspoon dried dill weed
- 5 cups chicken broth
- 2 pounds Yukon Gold potatoes, diced small
- ¼ cup unsalted butter
- ¼ cup all-purpose flour
- 1 cup sour cream
- 2 cups heavy cream

Heat a large soup pot on medium-high heat and add the bacon. Cook bacon until fat has rendered then add carrots, celery, onion and pickles. Sauté until starting to soften. Add seasonings Old Bay through dill weed and cook briefly. Add broth and bring to a rapid boil. Add potatoes. Cover, reduce heat, and simmer until potatoes are softened.

While vegetables simmer, melt butter in a skillet over medium heat. Gradually add flour to create a roux, stirring constantly. Continue to cook and stir until roux is caramel in color and resembling soft cookie batter.

When the potatoes have softened, add roux to soup, whisking vigorously to incorporate completely. Soup will thicken; vegetables will retain their shape.

Remove soup from heat and let cool to almost room temperature. Whisk sour cream and heavy cream together well and whisk into soup. Bring back up to serving temperature slowly.

North Shore Cider Braised Pulled Pork Sandwiches

2020: Chef Chris Homyak, Lutsen Resort in partnership with Pine Tree Apple Orchard, North Shore Winery, and Yker Acres

Buckle your seatbelts; you're in for a ride. Worth every spice and step, this is anything but your average pulled pork sandwich. Chef Chris recommends Sawtooth Mountain Cider House Herbie's Cider, a favorite North Shore pick, made from apples grown at Pine Tree Apple Orchard

YIELD: 10–12 SANDWICHES

For pulled pork:

3½ pounds whole boneless pork shoulder/butt

pork cure, to taste

24 ounces dry cider beer (for oven/slow cooker method)

2 tablespoons to ½ cup apple cider vinegar, to taste

2 tablespoons to ½ cup ketchup, to taste

4 brioche buns

For cole slaw:

½ cup mayonnaise

¼ cup Dijon mustard

2 tablespoons champagne vinegar

2 tablespoons sugar

salt and pepper, to taste

1 head green cabbage, shredded

½ small head red cabbage, shredded

1 large or 2 medium carrots, shredded

To prepare the pork: Season pork shoulder with about ¼ cup pork cure rub. Let sit 24 hours in refrigerator.

Smoker method: Smoke according to smoker directions 2–4 hours (depending on outside temperature) with Applewood chips until fat starts to render slightly. To prepare pork without a smoker; skip to the next step.

Oven/slow cooker method: If using oven, preheat to 275°F. Place pork into large roasting pan, dutch oven, or slow cooker. Pour cider down alongside of pork shoulder, making sure not to pour over the top. Cover with lid or aluminum foil. Cook until pork is easily pulled apart—about 4½ hours in oven, or if using slow cooker 8 hours on low or 4 hours on high

Remove shoulder from liquid and let sit until cool enough to handle but still warm (pork is easier to pull when warm). Pull meat apart using hands, tongs, or forks. Season to taste with apple cider vinegar, ketchup and pork shoulder cure. Use as much or as little of seasoning ingredients as desired; seasoning is to your taste.

To make the cole slaw: Combine mayonnaise, mustard, vinegar, sugar, salt, and pepper in a large bowl. Mix thoroughly. Toss with shredded vegetables; use as much as needed for desired dressing level.

recipe continues . . .

For bread and butter pickles:

1 English cucumber, sliced

1 cup white vinegar

1 tablespoon turmeric

1 tablespoon whole mustard seed

½ cup sugar

2 tablespoons plus 1½ teaspoons kosher salt

1 yellow onion, julienned

To make the pickles: Place cucumber slices in ice water for 1 hour. Combine vinegar, turmeric, mustard seed, sugar and salt in saucepot and bring to a boil.

Remove cucumbers from ice water and place in a heat resistant container with yellow onion. Pour hot pickling liquid over cucumbers and onion. Place in refrigerator until cool.

To plate: Place a layer of bread and butter pickles on bottom half of brioche bun. Add 4–6 ounces pulled pork on pickles, then top with coleslaw.

To prepare the cure: Mix all ingredients together in a bowl until well incorporated. Store in airtight container until ready to use.

For pork cure:

⅓ cup kosher salt

⅓ cup brown sugar

2 teaspoons honey powder*

2 teaspoons garlic powder

2 teaspoons onion powder

2 teaspoons paprika

1–2 teaspoons cayenne, depending on your level of spice—overall recipe will not be spicy, the rub itself is spicier

1 tablespoon chipotle chili powder

3 tablespoons dark chili powder

1 tablespoon ground cinnamon

Honey powder can be found at most Whole Foods or through Amazon.

Summer Harvest

Long days, short nights, hard work, little sleep—summertime on the farm. Months ago, in the cold wet spring, farmers planted thousands of seeds, then held vigil, hoping they would amount to something. The seeds, warmed and encouraged by the sun, managed to struggle upwards and break ground. Now gardens and fields are the very definition of abundance. Sprawling and overflowing, it's harvest season. Everything is ready. Beans are crisp and snappy. Luscious, perfectly ripe tomatoes explode with tangy flavors. Sweet corn is as sweet as it will ever be. There is no better, more delicious time to eat than right now.

Summer's Heat at Doubting Thomas Farms

There is a farm hugging the western edge of Minnesota that defines summertime. Under high sunny skies and bordered by a disorienting spaciousness, lie expansive fields of oats, barley, wheat, and corn. The crops sway and rustle, tangoing with the breeze, making the best of the blazing heat. Closer to the farmhouse, running parallel to the driveway, sits a bountiful vegetable garden and a tropical high tunnel—a Midwestern jungle—lush intertwining plants with splashes of color. Welcome to Doubting Thomas Farms.

Farmer Noreen Thomas, along with husband Lee, sons Evan and Carsten, daughter Brita, and daughter-in-law Melany run this twelve-hundred-acre certified organic farm in Moorhead—with sporadic help from the rest of the family when needed. Noreen is the local food arm of the business, supplying specialty and heirloom varieties of vegetables and fruits for nearby natural food grocers, farmers markets, and restaurants; Lee manages the large-scale crops, blue and yellow corn for corn chips, barley for breweries, hay for co-ops, and much, much more. Their farm is both a symphony and a circus, a juxtaposition of carefully orchestrated and wildly beautiful crops and the frenzied juggling act each day requires of them.

There's nothing quite like the distinctive smells of summer that wind throughout the farm: the earthy aroma of freshly plowed fields, the sweet heady waft of honeysuckle, fresh cucumbers, uplifting mint, even the stink of dirty shoes. After the tractor fires up, the air fills with diesel. Each smell tells a chapter of the farm's story.

Summertime on the farm is never still. There's always one more job pleading for attention, even after a twelve-hour workday. It doesn't matter if Noreen and Lee are tired, something needs them. Most days Noreen finds herself racing against somebody or something, whether it's the rising summer heat, incoming rains, pests, or the clock. They run at full throttle, doing whatever it takes to capture the season's bounty.

Watering in summer is paramount, a thorough soak of the vegetables and flowers to provide insurance against the sweltering day. Once that's complete, it's time to move on to weeding and harvesting. Noreen's head and back take the brunt of the heat. Weeding can be relaxing, but the majority of the hours labored among her vegetables are focused and intentional. Noreen's mind does not wander. Instead, acutely observant and astute, she stores mental notes about plant and soil health, weed pressure, soil temperature, beneficial insects versus pest issues, tallying it all up and making judgment calls about what needs to happen next.

Working swiftly, Noreen meticulously picks and pulls vegetables for the day's orders, taking her best guess as to how much she'll actually need, especially for farmers markets. As summer progresses, and more and more vegetables are at their peak, the number of hours spent bent over gathering them increases. Orders are reviewed and confirmed, then vegetables and fruits are sorted, washed, and delivered to restaurants and stores—all before lunch time. When Noreen returns to the farm several hours later, chances are good she'll end up back among the rows of vegetables, tending and harvesting again from mid-afternoon until as long as it takes. Chances are equally good she'll get interrupted with another pressing farm chore that takes her in a totally different direction than she'd planned. Or perhaps it's time to lead visitors on a farm tour. Just like seeds scattered in spring, her energy gets scattered here, there, and everywhere.

Though farming and harvesting does feel, at times, wild and chaotic, precision and science guide each decision Noreen makes. With a formal education in the sciences of chemistry, microbiology, and food nutrition, she initially embarked on a career in food science and was working in a lab at North Dakota State University when she met Lee, her future husband and a farmer. Theirs became a love story, one that seduced her into a life of farming alongside him. Naturally, the farm became her new laboratory, her open-field classroom where she could experiment with unusual plant varieties, study the results, and adapt accordingly. Fascinated with seeds—especially heirloom and rare seeds—everything Noreen and Lee grow has been carefully selected for maximum flavor and nutrition. Purple cauliflower, ruby-red corn, chocolate mint, aromatic Mediterranean herbs, fuzzy peach tomatoes, electric pink squash—Noreen's produce is art, especially once it lands in the hands of her chef partners who treasure her unusual, striking varieties. Degree or no degree, to be a farmer is also to be a scientist.

When the sun sets and the day is closing, Noreen tries to balance out summer's madness with deliberate, quiet moments. At nighttime, among the farm's shadows and silhouettes, she'll take a leisurely stroll down their driveway, ambling toward the western horizon. Once she's a little ways out, she'll turn her face straight up toward the northern sky and soak in the dizzying display of stars. Every once in a while she's even treated to northern lights, watching as the sky dances and moves. The night skies restore her.

Then she starts it all over again the next day.

Summer on the farm is simultaneously intense and peaceful, exhausting and restorative. Day after day, week after week, weeding, hauling, and harvesting the earth's jewels brings on a fatigue that settles into one's bones and lingers until winter's arrival. Harvest doesn't stop until the dew falls at night or the frost arrives in fall. When the frost does finally hit and the last day of harvest passes, a feeling of deep relief and joy arises—it's done! Another harvest is behind them. And while the farm never fully sleeps, it is now time to rest.

Given Noreen Thomas's science background and obsession with nutrition, Doubting Thomas Farms is fertile ground for research. Each year the Thomas's host international biochemists from all over the world, visitors to their farm lab interested in the science of antioxidant values, phenol levels, and the overall nutrient density of the plants they grow. Noreen also facilitates studies alongside PhD students from North Dakota State University, tracking, for example, how desirable flavor components may align with higher antioxidant values. Farm-to-table chefs from other states even fly in to visit the farm, eager to see, touch, and taste the abundance of Midwestern agriculture. Noreen's commitment to agricultural education is perhaps most evident in the countless volunteer hours she spends working with children and youth on farm-related projects. Over the last five years, Doubting Thomas Farms has hosted over eight thousand people, eager to provide farm experiences for anyone craving a connection to the earth and the source of their food.

Mushroom Bacon Panzanella

2020: Chef Ryan Nitzsche, Sol Ave Kitchen
in partnership with Doubting Thomas Farms

The term sauce gribiche *sounds fancy and intimidating, but it's actually just a simple and versatile mayonnaise-style sauce. Use it to liven up meat, roasted potatoes, or vegetables, or even as a salad dressing. The flavors in this salad are deeply savory and a little sweet and salty. Simply grilled chicken or pork would be a welcome accompaniment for a full meal.*

YIELD: 4 SMALL SALADS

For mushroom bacon:

1 tablespoon light brown sugar

½ teaspoon kosher salt

1 small garlic clove, peeled, grated or minced fine

1 tablespoon liquid smoke

1½ pounds portobello mushrooms, sliced ½-inch thick

For sauce gribiche:

2 medium eggs, whole

1 tablespoon Dijon mustard

2 teaspoons capers, drained and rinsed

1 teaspoon olive oil

For panzanella:

3 cups seasonal vegetables: corn, zucchini, blanched green beans, etc.

½ cup red onion, diced

1 tablespoon sunflower oil or other neutral oil

½ cup mushroom bacon

To prepare the mushroom bacon: Preheat oven to 350°F. Mix sugar through liquid smoke in a bowl. Add mushrooms and toss gently. Place a baking rack into a sheet pan and lay the mushrooms onto rack, leaving room between each slice. Let mushrooms marinate while oven preheats. Bake about 25 minutes until browned and shrunken, but not yet the texture of a jerky.

To prepare the sauce gribiche: Fill small sauce pot with water and bring to a boil. Add whole eggs and continue to boil for 5 minutes, then remove eggs from pot and place into an ice bath to fully cool, 5–10 minutes. Once cooled, carefully peel eggs and rinse under cold water to remove any small pieces of shell. The egg whites should be fully cooked; the yolk should still be runny. Place peeled, soft-boiled eggs in a mixing bowl and roughly quarter them with a spoon. Gently fold mustard, capers, and olive oil into eggs with spoon. Use immediately or store in refrigerator for up to 24 hours.

To prepare the panzanella: Cut seasonal vegetables to desired size and shape (rough cut for sautéing works well). Preheat large sauté pan over medium-high heat. Add oil followed by onion. Once onion begins to soften add mushroom bacon and remaining vegetables. Cook 2–3 minutes, stirring or tossing occasionally. Reduce heat to medium low and continue to cook for another 2–3 minutes, stirring or tossing occasionally.

1 tablespoon tomato paste

1 tablespoon gochujang paste (or omit and substitute with tomato paste, if desired)

2 slices sourdough bread

kosher salt and black pepper, to taste

½ cup roughly chopped, mixed fresh herbs: dill, parsley, chives, cilantro, mint

egg gribiche

Separately, mix tomato paste and gochujang (if using). Spread tomato paste mix on both sides of bread slices. Place on gas or charcoal grill to toast. Alternatively, toast in an oven set at 350°F for 5–7 minutes. Once grilled, cube bread and add to vegetables. Remove from heat and toss together with salt and pepper to taste.

To plate: Divide and spread gribiche on 4 dishes. Top with mushroom bacon, vegetable and bread mixture, and mixed fresh herbs. Finish with a light drizzle of olive oil.

Corn Chowder

2010: Chef Heather Hartman, Spoonriver
in partnership with Loon Organics

Chef Heather Hartman grew up gardening with her mother and learning how to cook using the produce they cultivated together. This delicate variation of a chowder demonstrates just how flavorful the simplest garden-fresh ingredients can be when used at their peak. In the absence of cream, the "corn milk" from the corn cobs infuses the chowder with a lovely, well-rounded richness.

YIELD: 10 CUPS
(SERVES 6-8)

For the corn stock:

8 ears sweet corn, shucked

2 bay leaves

salt and freshly ground pepper, to taste

For the soup:

4 tablespoons unsalted butter

1 tablespoon fresh rosemary, minced fine

1 tablespoon fresh thyme leaves, minced fine

1 medium onion, chopped

1 medium carrot, diced small

2 stalks celery, diced small

3 medium potatoes, diced small (should yield 3 cups diced)

1 teaspoon chopped fresh, flat-leaf parsley (optional)

To prepare the corn stock: Use two methods to remove kernels from the cobs to create two different textures. Divide corn in half. Cut kernels from four ears. Starting at the tip of each ear, cut straight down, leaving about ⅛-inch of pulp on cobs.

With the remaining 4 ears, use a sharp knife to slice down the center of each row of kernels, from tip to end. Repeat until you have sliced every row of kernels open. Then lay each cob over a bowl and scrape the kernels with the back of a knife, pushing the "milk" from the corn. Rotate each ear completely, extracting as much milk as you can. Combine cut and scraped kernels in a bowl and set aside. Use the cobs to make your stock.

Prepare corn stock by putting all 8 empty cobs in a stock pot. Add bay leaves and salt and pepper. Cover cobs with water; bring to a boil and simmer for an hour. Taste and add salt as necessary. Strain and reserve the corn stock. Stock can be made a day or two before preparing soup.

For soup: Melt butter in a large pot over medium heat. Add herbs and sauté until fragrant. Add onions and sauté until beginning to soften. Add carrots and celery, sauté 4–8 minutes until soft, then add potatoes, reserved corn kernels, and stock. Season with salt and pepper. Simmer 20–30 minutes until potatoes are done. Remove 2–3 cups of soup, puree in a blender, then add back to the pot. Taste and adjust seasonings. Ladle into bowls and stir in parsley if desired.

Garden Gazpacho

2018: Chef Wyatt Evans, Heirloom Kitchen in partnership with Riverbend Farm

This gazpacho is a fun one to play with. The ratios provided by Chef Wyatt are guidelines. He advises the home cook to be creative and use whatever is ripe in the garden, keeping a balance of flavors in mind as you do so, adding more melon for a sweeter flavor profile, more cucumber if you want it more vegetal.

YIELD: 12 SERVINGS

- 2 pounds heirloom tomatoes, blanched, peeled, seeded, and diced
- 1 pound cucumber, peeled, seeded, and chopped
- 1 pound muskmelon or honeydew peeled, seeded, and chopped
- 1 small jalapeño pepper, seeded and chopped
- 1 red bell pepper, seeded and chopped
- 1 teaspoon celery salt
- ¼ cup fresh herbs, chopped (cilantro, dill, etc.)
- ½ cup sunflower or olive oil
- salt and white pepper, to taste
- hot sauce to taste (Tabasco is best here, but use what you like)

Combine chopped vegetables/fruit with celery salt in a large bowl. Leave for 1 hour to pull juices.

Turn vegetable/fruit mixture out into a blender, add chopped herbs, and blend on high. With blender still running, slowly stream in oil to emulsify. Season to taste with salt, pepper, and hot sauce.

Soup can be served right away, but is better after refrigerated for 2–4 hours to allow flavors to develop. Garnish with herbs or croutons or oil or anything fun from the garden.

Chilled Cucumber Soup

2013: Chef Owner Russell Klein, Meritage in partnership with Riverbend Farm

Born and raised in New York, Chef Owner Russell Klein wasn't exposed to many farms growing up and first experienced buying directly from farmers while working in France after culinary school. The practice stuck with him. Today Chef Russell enchants guests at his French brasserie with dishes created primarily from local, in-season ingredients. He and his wife, Desta, even tend their own backyard garden planted with seeds from Greg Reynolds of Riverbend Farm. Russell says, "It used to be that chefs sourced locally grown ingredients to differentiate themselves. Now, if you're not cooking with local ingredients, you're not in the game."

YIELD: ABOUT 5 SERVINGS

2 shallots, sliced

3 small garlic cloves, peeled and chopped

3 tablespoons extra-virgin olive oil

3½ cucumbers, peeled, seeded and sliced (about 5-6 cups)

5 cups cucumber juice*

⅓ cup heavy cream

1 spice sachet: 1 cinnamon stick, 1 clove, 1 juniper berry, 2 teaspoons coriander seeds, 1 whole allspice

½ cup plain yogurt

salt and pepper, to taste

Optional garnishes: chopped dill, smoked fish, or chicken

Sweat shallots and garlic in olive oil until soft, careful not to caramelize or get any color on them. Add cucumbers and sweat for 5 minutes. Again, be careful not to add any color. Add juice, cream, and sachet, and simmer for 20 minutes, or until cucumbers are soft. Remove sachet, and puree soup in a blender. (Be very careful when pureeing hot liquids in a blender jar as there is serious risk of injury. Never fill to more than one-third, and always cover lid with a thick kitchen towel.) Start blender on lowest speed, increasing as soup cools.

Whisk in yogurt. Chill soup in an ice bath as quickly as possible. When soup is cold, season with salt and pepper. Garnish and serve.

To make cucumber juice, juice 8–12 cucumbers in a juicer or run 8–12 cucumbers through a high-powered blender and strain.

Stone's Throw Urban Farm Seasonal Salad

2014: Chef Owner Hai Truong, Ngon Vietnamese Bistro in partnership with Stone's Throw Urban Farm

The green beans and arugula in Chef Owner Hai Truong's seasonal salad are as fresh as fresh can be, served merely hours after being picked from nearby Stone's Throw Urban Farm. The crew at Stone's Throw has just over two acres in cultivation throughout the Twin Cities, an assortment of vacant city lots and larger open parcels that have been transformed into urban farmland. Consider finishing this salad with brown sugar smoked salmon for an extra treat.

YIELD: ABOUT
4 SERVINGS

For dressing:

1 tablespoon soy sauce

2 tablespoons sesame oil

fresh ginger, peeled and grated, to taste

1 tablespoon balsamic vinegar

⅓ cup salad oil

1 teaspoon sea salt, or to taste

dash freshly crushed black pepper

For salad:

filet beans, or Haricot Verts

rice noodles or vermicelli

arugula

gravlax or smoked salmon

To make the dressing: Blend ingredients well.

To make the salad: Gather salad ingredients in desired amounts for about 4 servings. Blanch filet beans by immersing in boiling water for 3 minutes then removing and immediately plunging into ice water to stop the cooking process. Leave in ice water for about 6 minutes before draining. Cook rice noodles according to package instructions; run under cold water and let sit until cool.

To assemble: Toss beans and arugula with dressing. Arrange on plates and top with noodles and gravlax or salmon.

Planning Ahead at Pastures A Plenty

Just as the earth never stops moving, the farm is always in motion, especially so in summer. From sunup until sundown, summer carries an unmistakable rhythm—a steady, unrelenting beat, prodding farmers on. The beat urges, "Go. Move quickly. The time is now."

Jim Van Der Pol was born with the DNA of a farmer—both literally and figuratively. From the time he was quite little, his parents joked how if you couldn't find Jim, all you had to do was locate his dad and look down. There he would be, predictably trailing his hero around the farm, shadowing his every step. Jim remembers his dad repeatedly stressing how extremely fortunate they were to have the opportunity to farm—how not everybody was so lucky and how some would have to settle for doing other work in life. This belief stuck with Jim, becoming his own impenetrable truth, and it's evident in the irrepressible enthusiasm he exudes when talking about farming. After college, when the opportunity arose to take over his parents' farm, his new bride LeeAnn was adventurous enough to take a leap of faith with him and give farm life a shot. Jim brought excitement to the equation, LeeAnn brought patience. Together—and now with their grown family—they've created an honest, rewarding life raising pigs and cattle, growing a meat business, choring, planting, walking pastures, and baling hay.

Jim and LeeAnn farm with their son Josh, daughter-in-law Cindy, and grandson Andrew near Kerkoven. It's a family affair and always a team effort no matter the task at hand. They farm three hundred and twenty acres—small in scope but large on life. Their house is planted in the middle of one of the cow pastures, and they enjoy watching the cattle graze around them, often reveling in the idyllic, meditative surroundings.

The Van Der Pols raise certified organic crops as well as livestock, including a farrow-to-finish pig operation, free-range chickens, and about fifty head of grass fed cattle, supplying most of the animals for their meat business, Pastures A Plenty. Because the Van Der Pols farm organically, emphasize humane husbandry standards, and have decided not to automate their work, many of their farm tasks require more time and patience to get the job done. They're hands-on farmers and spend a big chunk of their time regularly interacting with their hogs and cattle—both because they want to and to ensure every animal they're raising remains healthy. Thanks to their smallish size, maintaining this close interaction with their animals is doable.

Summer. It's a marvel how dramatically the days contract and expand in Minnesota—how daylight vacillates from a skimpy eight hours in wintertime to a robust fifteen hours in the summertime. The Van Der Pols themselves seem to be solar powered, running on the energy of the sun, harnessing its power while the days are long and bright.

The day begins with pig chores, a job that ties up at least one of the Van Der Pols—often two—for nearly half a day. All the pigs get fed by hand, one group at a time. Jim usually tends to the gestating sows and older pigs, while grandson Andrew oversees the younger, smaller pigs, as well as the sows and their litters in the thirty-pen farrowing house. During this time, each group is carefully monitored and tended. Who's pregnant? Is their bedding clean, or did they knock over their water in a playful fit? As the pigs eat, sometimes the Van Der Pols need to referee since not everybody remembers her manners, keeping a watchful eye on bossier pigs who gobble down their food and then try to infringe on their more timid neighbor's ration. Before leaving the barns, the pigs' bedding is refreshed with a blanket of straw to keep them comfortable and also to minimize smells that naturally accompany raising them.

The cattle chores in the summertime involve timing the move just right from one pasture to the next—for the health of both the animals and the land—and then simply dropping gates and letting the cattle wander. For the Van Der Pols the hardest part of raising cattle in the summertime is making enough hay for them to eat in the wintertime. Always conscientious to maximize the potential of their dollars, time, and land, many farmers consider it more cost-effective to make hay themselves rather than hire a custom harvester or simply buy feed for animals. Hay, like any agricultural market, goes up and down in price. Sometimes hay is expensive, and writing out a fat check for cow feed when there's a shortage is no picnic, so they plan ahead carefully for the bleak winter months and bale hay as best they can throughout the summer.

Made from fresh stems, leaves, and seed heads of alfalfa and clover, orchard grass, bromegrass, or fescues, hay is cut and baled when it has the most nutritional value to maximize feed quality, unlike straw, which is made from mature plants whose seed heads were harvested for another purpose.

The key to successful haying is finding the right balance between moisture and timing, otherwise hay can rot—or not get made at all. Many farmers now make both dry hay bales and wet bales (baleage), each of which has advantages and disadvantages. Dry hay, while slightly less nutritious, requires less manpower to make. But it also needs the weather's full cooperation—a string of dry, low-humidity days during which it can lie curing, uninterrupted in the sun. Rain is the enemy of drying hay and increases its chances of spoiling. Wet baleage, on the other hand, can be made even when summertime dew points refuse to drop and rain is in the air. A slightly more nutritious product for their animals because it's fermented, baleage is more expensive and labor intensive to make than dry hay, requiring more equipment and people to get the job done.

It's the quintessential summertime farm scene—hay bales dotted across rural landscapes. Beautiful enough to be the subject of dreamy watercolor paintings, those bales are stoic symbols of preservation, planning, and survival on the farm. And they don't make themselves. Every summer the farm needs to produce about two hundred tons of hay to last through the winter. An additional three hundred small traditional bales of straw are also needed for bedding in the farrowing house. Starting just after Memorial Day and ending in early to mid fall, the family, sometimes with additional help from grandchildren Kirsten and Jacob, spends up to four weeks total of the summer making hay for their farming operation.

Make hay while the sun shines. It sounds simple enough, yet even though making hay is not as physically taxing as it once was thanks to better equipment, it's stressful—even for persistently upbeat people like the Van Der Pols. As farmers wrestle with climate change and increasingly finicky weather patterns, they obsess over forecasts and grapple with the challenging cards Mother Nature deals them, including soaring, unrelenting humidity levels and frequent rainfalls. These factors determine whether they'll be able to make dry hay or will need to turn to wet hay. When all is said and done, the Van Der Pols' goal is to head into winter with nearly an equal amount of each.

The Van Der Pols intentionally wait until after pig chores to begin cutting hay, allowing time for the plant sugars to rise from the roots to the plant itself. When plants boast a higher proportion of sugars, it makes for higher quality, higher energy feed for their animals. Once cutting begins, there's no turning back—they'll spend the whole day mowing their crops, a job Jim thoroughly enjoys when he's lucky enough to win the much jockeyed-for position of driving the tractor. The air fills with the smell of harvest—fresh chlorophyll mixed with subtle floral notes. Then it's time to make the all-important judgment call: dry hay or wet baleage. If it looks like dry hay is possible, there's nothing more to be done at the moment other than let the cut hay lie in the field. In about four days they will return to bale it when the moisture content has dropped to an ideal 15 percent. When the air is humid or the radar shows more rain on the horizon, however, the Van Der Pols have no choice but to commit to wet baling, at which point they need all hands on deck. Once the bales are made, there's a limited amount of time to get them wrapped in plastic, ideally within twenty-four hours, or the hay will start to spoil instead of becoming nutritious, fermented feed. They move quickly and efficiently: baling, collecting, wrapping, and storing hay. Though they started midday, it might very well be midnight before they are finished, working by the glow of headlights for the last few hours.

Many hands make for lighter—but never light—work. When fall arrives and they finish their third cycle of baling, there's a collective sigh of relief and a satisfying feeling of security on the farm. The fruits of summer are stored. They did it. Their animals will eat well this winter.

Pork Belly with Sweet Corn and Heirloom Tomatoes

2015: Chef T. J. Rawitzer, Tiny Diner in partnership with Pastures A Plenty

Hold your horses. This recipe may appear fussy at first glance, but it's off-the-charts delicious and easier than it looks. Whether serving for a dinner party or your family, be prepared for rave reviews.

YIELD: 4 SERVINGS

For pork belly:

½ cup salt

½ cup sugar

2 pounds slab pork belly

1 large white onion, cut into large pieces

2 cloves garlic, peeled and left whole

1 bay leaf

1 sprig thyme

2 cups dry white wine

2 cups water or chicken stock

For corn:

4 ears sweet corn, husked

2 tablespoons butter, cut into small pieces

salt, to taste

fresh lemon juice, to taste

For tomatoes:

½ cup sherry vinegar

½ cup extra-virgin olive oil

To prepare the pork belly: Preheat oven to 325°F.

Mix sugar and salt together and generously rub onto pork belly. Leave uncovered to cure in the refrigerator for at least 24 hours.

After 24 hours, quickly rinse off any visible salt and sugar. Pat belly dry with a paper towel and allow to air dry for about an hour.

In a large heavy bottom sauté or braising pan, sear pork belly fat side down until deep brown. Lower heat and carefully flip the belly. Add onions and sweat until they become aromatic and translucent. Add garlic, bay leaf, and thyme. Deglaze pan with wine. Add water or stock; cover pan with a lid or aluminum foil

Braise pork belly in oven for 3–3½ hours, or until tender but not mushy.

Remove from oven and place belly on a small-rimmed plate or pan. Cover with a flat pan or plate and add weight, two canned goods are sufficient for this. While it cools it should start to have an equal thickness due to the weight. Once cool, portion belly into 4 rashers. Set aside until ready to complete the dish.

To prepare the corn: Remove corn from cob and place in a sturdy blender. Puree on high until very smooth. If needed, add a tablespoon of water to get mixture moving. Strain corn puree through a fine mesh strainer into a

pinch of salt

About 2 pounds mixed heirloom tomatoes, cut and variously sliced to show off their color

Micro greens, chives, or small basil leaves for garnish

small saucepot. Discard chunky pulp. Heat corn liquid over medium low heat and whisk constantly until corn begins to gently simmer. Once corn begins to thicken, slowly add butter piece by piece. Season with salt and a few drops of lemon juice.

To prepare the tomatoes: Whisk together vinegar, oil and salt. Add tomatoes and toss.

To complete dish: On one side only, crisp pork belly in a medium hot pan until deep brown. Once belly is crisp and hot, set on paper towel to drain.

Spoon some corn pudding onto a plate and place pork belly on top. Arrange tomatoes around plates and garnish with micro greens, chives, or small basil leaves

Cauliflower Three Ways

2020: Chef Kyle "Butch" O'Brien, Wise Acre Eatery in partnership with Tangletown Gardens' Farm

This dish takes some advance planning, but once it comes together the often under-estimated and overlooked cauliflower positively shines and will turn everyone into a cauliflower lover. Three heads should be plenty to start with, but don't be afraid to double the recipe. You're definitely going to want extra cauliflower cream.

RECIPE YIELD:
8 SERVINGS

For pickling liquid:

1 cup white distilled vinegar

¾ cup rice wine vinegar

3 tablespoons plus 1 teaspoon kosher salt

4 tablespoons granulated sugar

3 cups water

For purple pickled cauliflower sachet:

½ small red beet, peeled, small diced

¼ yellow or white onion, diced

For white pickled cauliflower sachet:

¼ onion, diced

1½ teaspoons whole black peppercorn

1½ teaspoons caraway seeds, toasted

For the finish:

4 cups cauliflower florets, cut into 1-inch pieces, reserve stems for cauliflower cream

For the pickled cauliflower:

To prepare the pickling liquid: Combine vinegars, salt, sugar, and water in a heavy bottomed pot. Bring to boil. Stir to make sure all solids are dissolved.

To make the purple pickled sachet: Place in cheesecloth and bundle up to form sachet. Tie securely with kitchen twine.

To make the white pickled sachet: Place in cheesecloth and bundle up to form sachet. Tie securely with kitchen twine.

To finish: Divide the cauliflower between two heat-proof quart-sized containers, mason jars work well. Place one sachet in each container on top. Add the liquid, dividing between the two jars, and store in refrigerator 24 hours for optimal color/flavor extraction. Remove sachets when ready to serve.

Note: Leftover pickled cauliflower is great on salads, as a garnish in bloody marys, or added to a charcuterie board.

recipe continues . . .

For the cauliflower cream:

YIELD: 3 PLUS CUPS

3 heaping cups bite-size cauliflower florets and stems (about 1-inch)

olive oil

salt and pepper, to taste

¼ yellow onion, thinly sliced

1 clove garlic, peeled and sliced

3 cups heavy cream

3 tablespoons butter, cut into pieces

For the cauliflower:

1 head cauliflower, broken into bite-size florets

olive oil

salt, to taste

For everything bagel seasoning:

2 tablespoons poppy seeds

2 tablespoons nigella seeds (can be substituted with black sesame seeds)

1 teaspoon caraway seeds

¼ cup sesame seeds

¼ cup pepitas (pumpkin seeds)

2 tablespoons dried onion flakes

2 tablespoons dried garlic flakes

1 tablespoon flaked sea salt

For the cauliflower cream:

Preheat oven to 375°F.

Toss cauliflower with olive oil, salt, and pepper; roast on a baking sheet for 20 minutes, until tender but not browned. Sauté onion and garlic in olive oil in a heavy bottom pot on medium-low heat to soften.

Add roasted cauliflower and cream to pot and simmer 15–20 minutes. Puree contents of pot in blender, slowly adding cold butter pieces to emulsify. Strain. Season with salt and pepper, to taste. Let rest while preparing the rest of the dish to allow the puree to thicken.

For the roasted cauliflower:

To prepare the cauliflower: Place florets on a sheet pan, drizzle with olive oil and roast at 400°F for about 25 minutes until tender and caramelized. Remove from oven and season with salt by tossing in mixing bowl while releasing salt with your other hand to ensure salt is evenly distributed.

To make the seasoning: All seeds toast at different rates and will need to be toasted individually. To toast, place seeds in pan and cook on medium heat, stirring constantly, until fragrant, 1–3 minutes depending on seed. When you can smell them, they are done. Remove from pan quickly to avoid burning and allow to cool completely. Roughly chop toasted pepitas. Combine with the rest of the toasted seeds and onion flakes, garlic flakes, and sea salt in mixing bowl; toss to evenly distribute.

Note: Leftover seasoning is wonderful on eggs, popcorn, avocado toast, or mix into hummus or yogurt for a savory dip.

To assemble Cauliflower Three Ways:

Spread about ¼ cup cauliflower cream on bottom of serving bowl. Place ½ cup roasted cauliflower on top of cauliflower cream. Garnish with 2–4 florets of each of the pickled cauliflower. Sprinkle entire dish with everything bagel seasoning.

Summer Squash Rollatini with Herbed Goat Cheese

2017: Chef Eliot King and Co-owner Jennifer Jackson-King, Prima in partnership with Farm Farm

Owners Jennifer Jackson-King and Eliot King opened their cozy neighborhood eatery, Prima, in 1999—long before local food was the rage. They've been quietly serving loyal guests and friends locavore cuisine ever since, working with over a dozen Minnesota farmers and also supplying the restaurant with food from their own farm.

YIELD: 4 APPETIZER PORTIONS

For heirloom tomato vinaigrette:

2 cups heirloom tomatoes, blanched, peeled, seeded and diced

5 tablespoons extra-virgin olive oil

1 tablespoon balsamic vinegar

2 tablespoons roasted garlic (see instructions, page 224)

2 teaspoons chives, minced

1 heaping tablespoon fresh basil, chopped

2 teaspoons fresh flat-leaf parsley, chopped

1 tablespoon shallots, chopped

salt and pepper, to taste

To prepare the vinaigrette: Mix all ingredients together.

To prepare the herbed goat cheese: Mix together until combined.

To prepare the kale: Sauté kale and garlic in olive oil over medium heat. Deglaze with white wine. Cook until dry. Add chicken stock or water ¼ cup at a time until kale is tender. Season with salt and pepper, taste and adjust seasoning.

To prepare the onions: Preheat oven to 375°F. Toss all ingredients in a bowl, then place in a foil packet. Roast until onions are tender, about 15 minutes.

To prepare the squash: Heat grill to medium-high. Brush squash slices with olive oil; season with salt and pepper. Grill until tender but not falling apart.

To assemble dish: When the squash are cool, roll each slice with 2 tablespoons herbed goat cheese. Place three rollatini on a bed of kale, then spoon vinaigrette around the plate and a little on top. Garnish with cipollini onions and top with extra herbs or a spicy microgreen, such as micro radish.

For herbed goat cheese

½ cup goat cheese, softened

1 teaspoon fresh thyme, chopped

½ teaspoon fresh flat-leaf parsley, chopped

½ teaspoon chives, chopped

1 teaspoon shallot, chopped

zest from ½ lemon

salt and pepper, to taste

For kale:

4 cups lacinato kale, cut into strips

2 tablespoons garlic, slivered

2 cups chicken broth or water

2 tablespoons white wine

1 tablespoon extra-virgin olive oil

For balsamic roasted cipollini onions:

12 peeled cipollini onions

2 tablespoons extra-virgin olive oil

2 tablespoons balsamic vinegar

salt and pepper, to taste

For grilled squash:

12 ⅛-inch-thick slices summer squash (sliced lengthwise)

olive oil

salt and pepper, to taste

Extending the Season at Untiedt's Vegetable Farm

There's a farming revolution happening. Some call it a *climate culture revolution.* Others say it's a wake-up call. Whatever it is, it's dramatically changing the look and productivity of farming around the world, from Italy and France to Britain and China. And now this revolution has arrived in Minnesota, empowering farmers to elongate the growing season and armor up when Mother Nature strikes. We're talking about high tunnels, a tool to bring summertime undercover.

Also called hoop houses, high tunnels are essentially unheated greenhouses in which plants are planted directly into the ground. Convex metal frames are covered with plastic, providing sheltered canopies to protect crops from the angry moods and tantrums of summer—epic rain falls, violent hail storms, sneaky frosts, and other unwelcome curve balls. But they don't just protect, high tunnels also accelerate plant growth, significantly increase crop yields, and extend the growing season on both ends of summer. For these reasons, they are quickly becoming popular assets in local food production systems and are especially helpful in a state like Minnesota, with a short growing season, where farmers are lucky if they get one good production cycle annually. High tunnels can help farmers sculpt two or even three production cycles out of some crops in a single growing season, which feels nothing short of magical. In short, they are changing the landscape of farming.

Leading this farming revolution in Minnesota with their scaled up high tunnel production is the Untiedt family of Untiedt's Vegetable Farm. Their Montrose farm, one of three Untiedt farms, is a veritable sea of white elongated domes in summertime, an expansive high tunnel village spanning about forty acres. Inside each tunnel lie cloistered rows of flourishing vegetables and fruits, orderly, deliciously verdant, and breathtaking in their sheer abundance. Tomatoes, melons, cucumbers, radishes, jicama, strawberries, peppers, raspberries—the list of crops they raise nearly as long as the high tunnel itself. From the right angle, peering down the length of a tunnel, the view can appear never-ending.

The Untiedts' journey to reach the point they're at now happened as all journeys do: one small step at a time. Fifty years ago, husband and wife team Jerry and Sue left city living to follow Jerry's undeniable call to agriculture. As a youngster, Jerry had spent a considerable amount of time on his grandparents' farm and caught the farming fever from his grandfather. Jerry isn't exactly sure whether or not his grandfather was a great farmer, but he does know he was a great observer of nature, instilling many non-monetary values in him, including the value of wildlife, healthy land, and meaningful work. Driven by these principles, Jerry and Sue bought a small thirty-eight acre parcel of land in Waverly, just forty miles west of Minneapolis, where they still live today. Sue, an elementary education teacher, found steady employment in the nearby rural school district, a "real job" for which they often felt deeply grateful when harvests were poor and funds were scarce. Over the years they grew both their family and farming operation, raising four daughters and expanding Untiedt's Vegetable Farm with two additional locations. They also gained two sons-in-law who have become instrumental to the operation along the way. Through trial and error, the Untiedts discovered they were better at retail sales than massive wholesale accounts and decidedly concentrated their efforts on farmers' markets, roadside stands, and individual high-end grocery stores, where their focus remains today. They also added a twelve hundred member community supported agriculture program ten years ago—another revolutionary act aimed at gently educating people about what it actually takes to grow the food they eat.

The Untiedts' adventure into high tunnel production started out thirty years ago, when evidence of climate change had already begun showing up as heavier than normal rainfall and stronger winds and storms. The changes felt ominous, and Jerry and Sue weren't sure what to do about it except educate themselves and stay tuned into the larger agricultural scene around the world for cues to possible solutions. That's when they learned about high tunnels, a newfangled "season enhancement tool" from Western Europe, and figured it was worth a shot. Starting with a single high tunnel, just as an experiment, the results were immediate: earlier crops, substantially higher yields in a given area, and the ability to focus their management on smaller areas with larger production. It looked as if it might be the wave of the future, and they decided to ride it.

It turns out the Untiedts were indeed at the beginning of something big. High tunnels have upped their productivity as much as tenfold as they've become skilled and intricate managers of square footage versus acres, and because high tunnels allow them to extend summer on their farms—sometimes by a month on each end—they've earned a strong competitive edge in the marketplace. When summer kicks off and Minnesotans begin feverishly craving the first real, local tastes of the season, consumers find Untiedt strawberries and tomatoes irresistible.

Even so, high tunnel production isn't without its difficulties. Simply covering and uncovering all the frames with plastic in spring and fall is a major job, taking a full three weeks for each. The infrastructure needed to make it work is quite tremendous, including an elaborate drain tile system underground which diverts water into a wetland. And while plants are generally the picture of health because they're regularly drip irrigated and their leaves never get wet, if a disease or pest does find its way into a tunnel it can be disastrous, spreading like wildfire among the rows. To prevent this, three employees police the rows all day, every day, turning over leaves and inspecting plants to make sure there aren't any surprises. You have to know what you're doing.

Jerry, easy in his skin, is forever modest about the impressive operation his family has built throughout the decades. He jokes about how his neighbors think he's wacky for not farming all of their land, choosing instead to plant cover crops and make hills of compost to enrich the high tunnels' soil. It's obvious he finds their bewilderment amusing. Steadfast and resilient in nature, Jerry insists their failures have far surpassed successes and credits strong mentors, a willingness to learn as you go, and passion for what you do as keys to climbing the proverbial mountain. As he drives from one end of the farm to the other in his dusty, lived-in pick-up truck, his black lab Molly at his side, he greets employees with a genuine, warm smile and pauses to ask how everyone is doing, both personally and professionally.

"Good, better, best. Never let her rest, 'til the good is better and the better is the best." This is the farm motto, their guiding mantra each day. The Untiedt family, along with upwards of ninety employees during the growing season, puts on a dramatic display of endurance from March through October as they move in lockstep with the perpetual momentum of the season. As summer gives everything it has to give, so too does the Untiedt Vegetable Farm crew, harvesting the endless rows of bounty thriving under the canopy of high tunnels. The revolution is underway.

Farmers' Market Vegetable Panzanella

2019: Chef Owner Ann Kim, Young Joni
in partnership with Untiedt's Vegetable Farm

"I depend on farmers so I can make beautiful creations people can enjoy together at my restaurants." – Chef Owner Ann Kim

Chef Owner Ann Kim inherited her love of fresh ingredients and cooking from her mother and grandmother. She remembers gardening with them as a young child, nurturing plants from seeds her grandmother smuggled in her pocket on the journey from Korea to the US, and then eating exclusively scratch-cooked food as a family. When gardens are overflowing with tomatoes, cucumbers, and zucchini, you'll find a tasty home for them in this Farmers' Market Vegetable Panzanella.

YIELD: 8 SERVINGS

For sherry vinaigrette:

1 small shallot, finely minced

3 tablespoons basil, finely chopped

1 teaspoon fresh thyme, chopped

½ tablespoon Dijon mustard

¼ teaspoon kosher salt

⅛ teaspoon black pepper

2 tablespoons sherry vinegar

¾ cup olive oil

For garlic crostini:

1 baguette

olive oil

2 garlic cloves, peeled and slightly crushed

To prepare the vinaigrette: Combine all ingredients except olive oil in a mixing bowl. Slowly drizzle in oil and whisk briskly until dressing starts to emulsify. Adjust salt and pepper to taste; set aside.

To prepare the crostini: Preheat oven to 375°F. Slice baguette into ½-inch thick slices and drizzle with olive oil on baking sheet. Bake crostini until crispy and lightly golden 10–12 minutes, flipping mid-way through cooking. Keep an eye on crostini to prevent burning. Cool to room temperature, then gently rub garlic cloves on each piece.

recipe continues . . .

For summer vegetable & herb panzanella:

2–3 Kirby cucumbers, sliced into ½-inch cubes or 1 English cucumber

2 medium zucchinis, thinly sliced or put through a mandoline for strings of zucchini

¼ cup Castelvetrano olives, pitted and halved

1 small handful dill (about ¼ cup), de-stemmed, roughly torn into bite-size pieces

1 small handful mint (about ¼ cup), de-stemmed, roughly torn into bite-size pieces

1 small handful Thai basil (about ¼ cup), de-stemmed, roughly torn into bite-size pieces

few pinches kosher salt

few pinches black pepper (or to taste)

homemade Sherry Vinaigrette

2 cups heirloom cherry tomatoes

8 homemade garlic crostinis, roughly broken into bite-size pieces

½ cup feta cheese (about 4 ounces)

To prepare the panzanella: Combine cucumbers, zucchini, olives, torn herbs, salt, pepper, and ½ cup vinaigrette in a large bowl. Gently toss until coated. Add tomatoes, crostini, and feta; toss again lightly until dressing is fully incorporated. Crostini bites should be dressed but still have crunch. Top with more broken crostinis and vinaigrette, if desired. Add more or less of the fresh herbs to suit your taste.

Fried Green Tomatoes with Skillet Sweet Corn and Bacon Vinaigrette

2015: Chef Beth Fisher, Wise Acre Eatery
in partnership with Tangletown Gardens' Farm

It's the rare chef with the privilege of having a farm at his or her fingertips, but the chefs at Wise Acre Eatery are among the lucky few who experience this reality. Owners Dean Engelmann and Scott Endres also own Tangletown Gardens' Farm in nearby Plato, resulting in a restaurant-farm relationship that is both intimate and far-reaching. Chefs work directly with farmers on seed selection for the upcoming growing season, giving thoughtful consideration to desired flavors, textures, and varieties of produce they want to highlight on the menu. When green tomatoes are more abundant than red, a platter of these fried green tomatoes easily hold their own against their ripe counterparts.

YIELD: 4 SERVINGS

For skillet sweet corn and bacon vinaigrette:

½ pound (5–6 slices) bacon, cooked crispy and rough chopped

2 tablespoons bacon fat, reserved from cooking bacon

1 cup onion, diced

1 cup sweet corn, fresh off the cob (or frozen)

½ cup cider vinegar

½ cup canola oil

½ cup extra-virgin olive oil

2 teaspoons seeded mustard

⅛ cup honey

½ cup mixed herbs, rough-chopped: chives, basil, tarragon

1 teaspoon salt

1 teaspoon ground fresh pepper

To prepare the vinaigrette: Heat pan with reserved bacon fat over medium heat. Add onion and cook 3–5 minutes until onion softens a bit. Remove pan from heat and stir in remaining ingredients, including bacon.

To prepare the fried green tomatoes: Place oil in a 3-quart saucepan over medium-low heat while you prepare tomatoes and dredging mixtures.

Slice green tomatoes ½-inch thick and set aside. In a shallow bowl combine flour, sea salt, black pepper, and cayenne (if using). Stir to combine well. In another shallow bowl whisk eggs really well. Place cornmeal in yet another shallow bowl.

Begin by dry coating 2–3 slices of tomato in seasoned flour, then move them into the whisked eggs, coating well. Finally, move them into the cornmeal (your fingers will get a bit messy), coating them well here, too. Place triple coated tomato slices onto clean, dry baking sheet. Repeat until all tomato slices have been triple coated and are ready to fry.

For fried green tomatoes:

4 cups sunflower or canola oil

4 large green tomatoes, baseball-size and rock-hard

2 cups all-purpose flour

2 tablespoons sea salt

1 tablespoon black pepper, freshly ground

1 teaspoon cayenne, optional—but tasty!

6 fresh eggs

3 cups cornmeal

Turn heat up under oil to medium-high and wait 3 minutes (oil temp should be 350°F). Start by frying 3–4 slices at a time (be careful adding tomato slices to oil; "slip into oil" to avoid splashing hot oil). Fry until golden brown, 3–5 minutes per side. Remove to paper-lined baking pan. Repeat with remaining tomato slices. Serve immediately or reheat in oven before serving.

Serve on a bed of garden greens with the accompanying vinaigrette.

Summer Pasta

2015: Chef Owner Matthew Jensen, La Ferme in partnership with Sundogs Prairie Farm

Locavore chef Matthew Jensen was one of the first chefs in the Alexandria area of Minnesota to seek out and build relationships with farmers nearby. By the end of his first year in business, he was already working with over a dozen farmers; now 90 percent of the product served at La Ferme comes from within twenty-five miles of the restaurant during the growing season. The pasta itself, which cooks more like a dumpling, is quite sturdy thanks to extra kneading and won't fall apart while the cream is reducing.

YIELD: 4 SERVINGS

For pasta:

1 cup flour

1 egg

2–3 tablespoons cream

For sauce:

2 tablespoons unsalted butter

1 small onion, diced small

3 ears corn, cut off cob

1 zucchini, diced small

1 summer squash, diced small

2 garlic cloves, peeled and minced

¼ cup white wine

1 cup heavy cream

1 tomato, seeded and diced small

1 tablespoon minced fresh tarragon

To make the pasta: Mix all pasta ingredients in a bowl. This is a very sturdy pasta dough. When it becomes stiff, use hands to incorporate fully, kneading in bowl for about 10 minutes. Cover dough and let rest. Bring a large pot of water to a boil. Once water is boiling, roll out dough to about ⅛-inch thick; cut into desired shape. In a couple batches, blanch pasta just until it rises to the top of water. Remove and let cool. Repeat process until all pasta is cooked. Toss cooked pasted with a bit of olive oil to prevent sticking.

To make the sauce: In a sauté pan over medium heat, melt butter. Add onions and cook until translucent. Add corn and cook about 1 minute. Add zucchini, summer squash, and garlic and cook until garlic becomes fragrant, about 30 seconds. Add white wine and simmer until wine is almost gone. Add cream and bring to a simmer. Add cooked pasta and simmer until cream is thick. Toss pasta with tomatoes and tarragon.

Heirloom Tomato Salad with Crispy Ham

2014: Chef Thomas Boemer, Corner Table
in partnership with Two Pony Gardens

Owner Nick Rancone and Chef Thomas Boemer, the dynamic duo who took over Corner Table in 2011, staunchly upheld the legacy of local foods associated with the highly revered restaurant since its inception in 2004. Nick and Thomas share a European mentality about food, focusing on straightforward, simply prepared dishes while highlighting quality ingredients and letting the flavors of each season speak for themselves.

For goat cheese dressing:

2 ounces heavy cream

salt and pepper, to taste

2 ounces goat cheese, crumbled

For crispy ham:

3 ounces ham, thinly sliced

1 teaspoon cooking oil, divided

salt, to taste

2 tablespoons brown sugar

For brioche croutons:

2 slices thick brioche bread, crust removed, cut into 9 pieces

olive oil

kosher salt and freshly ground pepper, to taste

For salad:

4 heirloom tomatoes, quartered

2 tablespoons sherry vinegar

2 tablespoons olive oil

kosher salt and freshly ground pepper, to taste

3 ounces petite mixed greens (a baby green or microgreen mix works well)

crispy ham

goat cheese dressing

brioche croutons

To prepare the goat cheese dressing: Heat heavy cream in a small saucepan over low-medium heat; add salt and pepper to taste. As soon as bubbles start to form in cream, whisk in goat cheese, a few crumbles at a time. Whisk until completely melted. Adjust consistency by either adding more cheese if too runny or more cream if too thick.

To prepare the crispy ham: Heat skillet over medium-high heat, add a drizzle of cooking oil. Add salt and a pinch or two of brown sugar to each slice of ham. Add as many slices of ham to skillet as pan will hold without layering. Cook until crispy and done on both sides, taking care not to burn. Remove and drain on paper towel to maintain texture. Repeat with remaining ham slices.

To prepare the brioche croutons: Heat oven to 350°F. Add bread pieces to small sheet pan. Drizzle with olive oil. Season with salt and pepper. Bake about 10 minutes until just browned.

To make the salad: Toss tomatoes with sherry vinegar, olive oil, salt and pepper. Mix in petite greens and toss again. Transfer to plates. Garnish with more petite greens and crispy ham, then drizzle warm goat cheese dressing over tomatoes and greens. Finish with brioche croutons.

Basil Quinoa and Garden Greens Salad

2013: Chef Christine "Montana" Rasmussen, River Rock Coffee in partnership with Living Land Farm

Owner Tamika Bertram and the devoted staff of River Rock Coffee in charming St. Peter are committed to providing an affordable farm-to-table experience in a welcoming environment that celebrates sustainable food and business practices. They've created a friendly cafe community where countless regulars now rank as friends. In addition to having plenty of buttery pastries and other sweet treats at the ready, daily offerings range from soups and sandwiches to salads like this light but filling quinoa grain dish—a perfect summer lunch.

For basil vinaigrette:

1 medium garlic clove, peeled and sliced thin

¼ cup plus 1 teaspoon red wine vinegar

⅛ teaspoon Maldon salt (or kosher salt)

1 teaspoon local honey

¾ cup extra-virgin olive oil

1 cup fresh basil leaves, loosely packed

For salad:

1½ cups cooked quinoa, cooled

basil puree (reserved from basil vinaigrette)

2 (4-inch) sprigs fresh tarragon, minced

7 fresh garlic chives or 1 small clove garlic, minced

12 fresh chives, minced

2 tablespoons basil vinaigrette plus more for drizzling

kosher salt and freshly ground pepper, to taste

3 cups mixed greens

2 heirloom tomatoes, such as Brandywine or Sungold, halved and quartered

½ cup cherry tomatoes, halved

¼ cup edible flowers, such as bachelor buttons, nasturtiums and chive blossoms (optional)

To prepare the vinaigrette: In a small bowl, combine garlic, red wine vinegar, and salt. Let marinate for a few minutes, then add honey and stir until almost dissolved. Taste and adjust salt if needed. Pour mixture into a blender. Blend on low, slowly adding the olive oil until emulsified. Add basil leaves and pulse briefly. Sieve out basil; reserve for quinoa grain salad. Refrigerate unused portion for up to 1 week.

To prepare the salad: In a large bowl, combine quinoa, basil puree, tarragon, chives, and basil vinaigrette. Gently toss until just combined. Taste and adjust seasonings, as needed.

To serve: Toss mixed greens with a drizzle of basil vinaigrette, salt, and pepper. Add greens to a platter, top with quinoa, then tomatoes. Season with salt and pepper. Garnish with your favorite edible flowers.

Lakes

Fresh water is a basic human necessity. For Minnesotans, our fresh waters are also basic to our identity. We are the Land of the North, but even more than that, we are the Land of 10,000 Lakes, and we love making the most of our fresh, wild-caught, local catch.

The Thread of Water

Be still and listen for a moment. That is the sound of water. You don't have to travel far to find it here—it's everywhere, lapping against rocky shorelines and fishermans' boats, winding through isolated forests, and rushing like a highway through our bustling, most populated city. The sound is primal and meditative, like nature's heartbeat. Let it lull you. Now notice the sunlight dancing across its surface, the clouds bobbing playfully among the waves. Glassy and soft, then rough and threatening, the powerful waters of Minnesota shape our land and our lives as much as anything can. Minnesota simply wouldn't be Minnesota without an abundance of water, one of our greatest glories.

Affectionately referred to as the *Land of 10,000 Lakes*, Minnesota actually has bragging rights to nearly 12,000 lakes, or about 2.6 million acres of water not counting magnificent Lake Superior—more than any other state in the nation, according to the Minnesota Department of Natural Resources (DNR). We're also home to 70,000 miles of rivers and streams, including the mighty Mississippi, whose birthplace lies at Lake Itasca in north central Minnesota. The name Minnesota comes from the Dakota Sioux word *Mnisota*, meaning *sky-tinted water*. Our reflective waters do show us the sky; they also mirror the moods and whims of Mother Nature, sometimes forceful and ominous, other times gentle and soothing. From the window seat on a plane, the aerial view is a mesmerizing, tangled jumble of green and blue, a richly textured and fertile landscape of land and water intermingled.

Just as those living near mountains or the ocean can't imagine life otherwise, it is the rare Minnesotan who doesn't feel an affinity for the water. Its current and ripples influence our traditions, hobbies, and culture throughout each season. A widespread summertime cabin culture is to blame for predictable weekend traffic jams, as folks eager for time in, on, and near the water pack up their cars and head to lakeshore retreats after work each Friday. Winter brings pop-up villages of ice houses, sometimes thousands on a single lake, as undeterred fishing enthusiasts brave Minnesota's snow-blasted elements to drill through frozen surfaces and try their luck at the wintertime sport. Nothing can keep us away. Whether it's sailing in the city, fishing up North, a picnic shore lunch, swimming, kayaking, paddle boarding, or recreational boating, being Minnesotan means being at home with water. We are even the birthplace of water skiing. Minneapolis is the *City of Lakes*. We are the Land of 10,000 Lakes.

Water is life, and besides simply entertaining us, Minnesota's fish-filled rivers and lakes are also an important and generous food source, offering over 1,000 species of fish and some of the best freshwater fishing in the country. Our state's clear waters provide smallmouth and largemouth bass, northern pike, sunfish, perch, lake trout, and our pride and joy—buttery, flaky, walleye—the official state fish that makes everyone's heart race a little faster, widely regarded as a delicacy. In a class all its own is Lake Superior, the largest of the Great Lakes and the largest surface area of freshwater on Earth. Reaching 1,300 feet at its deepest point, its crystal clear waters are home to about eighty species of fish, including three kinds of salmon, Ciscoes, the prehistoric Lake Sturgeon, and many more. According to the Objibwe, the lake is protected by Nanabijou, Spirit of the Deep Sea Water.

Directly or indirectly, water affects all facets of life. Without water, there would be no vegetation and no wild rice—or *manoomin*—as it is called by the Ojibwe. A poised and graceful aquatic North American grass found mainly in the Great Lakes region, wild rice

grows in the shallow waters of small lakes, marshes, and slow-flowing streams. Minnesota's official state grain, wild rice is technically a seed boasting an earthy, nutty flavor. Chewy on the outside and tender on the inside, wild rice is prized throughout Minnesota. Several Native American cultures, including the Ojibwe, consider it a sacred gift. The harvest of true wild rice—not *cultivated* wild rice—is strictly regulated to ensure the reseeding and regrowth of this plant isn't interrupted and the health of this valuable resource remains intact.

Minnesotans take great pride in the diverse and natural beauty surrounding them. The state's topography is a treasure, from the remaining pockets of tallgrass prairie in the southwest corner of the state to the towering pine forests in the north, water is the thread weaving our landscape together. Lakes ranging from ten acres to tens of thousands of acres, trout streams, our protected Boundary Waters Canoe Area, Lake Superior, and the Mississippi River: ours is a state of water. These waters ebb and flow, inhale and exhale, breathing life and nourishment into everything they touch, bringing us waves of plenty.

Minnesota wouldn't be Minnesota without its first inhabitants: Minnesota Native Americans, almost exclusively Ojibwe and Dakota people, whose traditions and cultures have profoundly influenced the state's culture: our language and art scene; a widespread interest in hunting, fishing, and foraging; our taste for fish, game meats, bison, corn, wild rice (a critical ingredient in many a hot dish (casserole) Minnesotans are famous for), and maple syrup, which was first harvested and boiled down by the Ojibwe. Many of our cities, towns, lakes, and other significant landmarks are named from the Ojibwe or Dakotah languages. Moccasins, snowshoes, pride in local, indigenous foods, and quite likely our reverence for the natural world at large—the influences and contributions of Native Americans to Minnesota are truly immeasurable.

Wild Rice and Walleye Croquettes

2016: Chef Christian Pieper, Cafe Minnesota
in partnership with KC's Best Wild Rice

Walleye and wild rice—Minnesota's official state fish and official state grain—come together beautifully in these delicate croquettes, as if celebrating the riches of our state. Requiring some time and attention, these croquettes are not fast to assemble, but they are worth every bit of effort.

YIELD: 12–14
CROQUETTES

For croquettes:

3 cups hand-harvested wild rice

2 quarts vegetable stock

2 pints heavy cream

½ cup white wine

1 bunch fresh thyme (tied with butcher's twine)

2 teaspoons fresh cracked pepper

2 tablespoons ground cumin

2 pounds walleye, skinned and deboned

1 cup carrots, peeled and diced small

1½ cups celery, diced small

1 cup onion, diced small

1 tablespoon salt

To prepare the croquettes: Rinse wild rice thoroughly in a colander. Combine wild rice and vegetable stock in a sauce pot. Bring to a boil, then reduce to medium simmer for about 45 minutes, or until rice kernels split.

While rice is cooking, in a separate saucepan combine heavy cream with white wine, thyme, cracked pepper, and cumin. Bring to a boil, then reduce to medium simmer. Add cleaned walleye into reducing cream. Cook walleye 8–10 minutes in cream, or until cooked thoroughly—just before it starts to fall apart. Remove walleye with a slotted spoon; set aside to cool. When cooled, flake walleye by hand; set aside in the fridge.

After fish is removed, add carrots, celery, and onion to cream and reduce liquid by three-quarters of original amount. Be careful to not "break" the heavy cream (cook it so far that the fat separates), though you will reduce it to the point of almost breaking. Remove thyme; let cool for a moment.

In a large bowl mix rice with flaked walleye; slowly add cream and vegetable mixture (this is the binder). Add salt. Once mixed, taste for seasoning and adjust accordingly.

Form mixture into 4-ounce cakes (hockey puck shape) and let chill in fridge for 1 hour. If mixture is too loose to hold shape, add 1–3 tablespoons seasoned flour to the mixture to bind.

For dredge:

1 cup flour seasoned with 1 tablespoon seasoned salt (such as Lawry's)

4 eggs, beaten plus 2 tablespoons water

2 cups panko bread crumbs

3 cups canola oil (for pan-frying croquettes)

For aioli:

2 cucumbers, peeled, seeded, and sliced

2 tablespoons kosher salt

2 teaspoons fresh dill, chopped

juice of 1 lemon

1 teaspoon xanthan gum

1 cup extra-virgin olive oil

To dredge: Prepare 3 separate bowls for dredging: one with seasoned flour, one with egg mixture and panko bread-crumbs in the last. Coat chilled walleye cakes first in the flour, then thoroughly in egg, then finish in panko. Heat a sauté pan with canola oil to 350°F, using a thermometer to temp the oil; pan-fry cakes 2–3 minutes per side to a golden-brown sear. Serve walleye cakes hot.

To prepare the aioli: Place prepared cucumbers in a colander; cover with kosher salt to cure. Toss slightly so all cucumbers are salted. Let stand over a sink or another bowl for 1 hour to allow proper drainage. This extracts all bitter juices from cucumbers and gives them a salty cured flavor.

Drain cucumbers then add to a blender with dill, lemon juice, and xanthan gum. Puree until smooth. With blender running, slowly add extra-virgin olive oil through the small hole in lid. Taste for seasoning.

To serve: Top walleye cakes with aioli or serve on the side as a dip. Serve cakes as a main entrée or make smaller to serve as a starter.

Pan-Fried Trout with Lemon Beurre Blanc

2019: Chef Chris Young, Four Daughters Vineyard & Winery in partnership with Driftless Fish

Between the ultra-fresh trout and creamy, luxurious lemon beurre blanc, this dish is truly a melt-in-your-mouth experience. Serve with a glass of white wine and enjoy a fancy-tasting night dining in.

YIELD: 4–6 SERVINGS

For the trout:

1½ cups flour

2 eggs plus 1 egg yolk

½ cup milk

½ cup grated Parmesan

½ cup corn flakes, crushed finely

½ cup cornmeal

½ teaspoon garlic salt

¼ teaspoon white pepper

4 trout fillets

½ cup high heat oil for frying

salt, to taste

lemon wedges, for serving

For creamy beurre blanc:

1½ sticks cold unsalted butter, cut into tablespoon-size pieces, divided and kept chilled

1 tablespoon shallot, chopped fine

2 cloves garlic, peeled and mashed

3 sprigs fresh thyme

6 peppercorns

2 bay leaves

¼ cup dry white wine

3 tablespoons plus 1 teaspoon cream

2 tablespoons lemon juice

pinch kosher salt

pinch white pepper, or to taste

To prepare the trout: Place the flour in a long shallow dish. In a separate bowl whisk together eggs, yolk and milk. In a third shallow dish combine Parmesan, corn flakes, cornmeal, garlic salt, and white pepper; mix well.

Dredge each fillet first in flour, patting off any excess, then in egg mixture, and lastly in crumb mixture.

Heat oil in a large frying pan to medium-high. When oil is hot enough to react to a little flour dropped in, slide in the fillet, skin-side down and fry about 5 minutes until golden brown. Carefully flip the fillet and fry another 2–3 minutes until it is also crisp and golden.

Remove from pan and drain on paper towels. Keep warm while you repeat process with remaining fillets. Sprinkle the fried fillets with a little salt to taste.

To prepare the beurre blanc: Melt 1 tablespoon butter in a sauce pot over medium heat. Add shallots, garlic, thyme, peppercorns, and bay leaves to pot; sauté until aromatic, then add wine, cream, and lemon juice. Increase heat gently until just boiling, then reduce slightly to maintain a simmer. Remove bay leaves then add salt and pepper and whisk in remaining butter a little at a time until well incorporated. Strain, and season to taste. Add more lemon juice, if desired.

To serve: Top fillets with beurre blanc and garnish with lemon wedges.

Lake Superior Whitefish en Papillotte

2008–2009: Chef Judi Barsness, Chez Jude
in partnership with Dockside Fish Market

It sounds quite fanciful, but you don't have to be a chef to cook en papillotte. *En papillotte is a method for baking something in a folded packet of parchment paper or aluminum foil, which uses trapped steam to cook the food. Fish fillets are an ideal choice because the steam preserves precious moisture and flavor. Open papillotes carefully at the table, mindful of the escaping steam, so everyone can enjoy the aromas that erupt from inside.*

YIELD: 8 SERVINGS

8 sheets parchment paper

¼ cup unsalted butter, melted

2 tablespoons fresh squeezed Meyer lemon juice*

3 teaspoons Meyer lemon zest*

salt and freshly ground pepper, to taste

2 pounds potatoes, a mix of Yukon Gold, red, purple, and new potatoes, thinly sliced with skin on

2 pounds Lake Superior whitefish fillets, skinned, cut into 8-ounce portions**

½ pound asparagus, trimmed, cut into ½-inch sections

Preheat oven to 450°F. Fold sheets of parchment paper in half to form a 12 x 14-inch rectangle. Round corners with scissors.

In a small bowl mix together melted butter with Meyer lemon juice and zest, and season with salt and pepper. Dividing evenly, layer potato slices on right side of each parchment paper near middle fold, using some of each color. Season to taste with salt and pepper. Next, layer fish fillet, then vegetables, finishing with mushrooms. Top each with Meyer lemon butter, fresh chopped parsley, and a couple fresh chive stems.

Fold the left side of parchment over the filling and, beginning at the top, fold and crease the edges together securely to the end, so no juices escape and all steam remains in the pouch. You will finish with a small tail of parchment paper that you will fold under the pouch.

Place pouches in a single layer on baking sheet and bake until pouches are puffed quite a bit, 10–15 minutes.

recipe continues . . .

4 spring ramps or leeks, cut in half lengthwise

4 baby carrots, cut in half lengthwise

8 morel and/or shiitake mushrooms, sliced in half or quartered

1 teaspoon Italian flat-leaf parsley, chopped

16 fresh chive stems

extra fresh chive stems & chive flowers for garnish, if available

If Meyer lemons are not in season, use a combination of orange and lemon juice and zest

**Talk to your fishmonger about best substitutes for Lake Superior whitefish if you must. Cod, bass, grouper and haddock are all acceptable substitutes.*

To serve: Place each pouch on its own plate. Mindful of the hot steam trapped in the parchment, make a 3-inch cut in the middle of the parchment pouch using a sharp paring knife. Using two forks, carefully tear the parchment from the contents. Brush with remaining Meyer lemon butter, and garnish with fresh chive stems and chive flowers.

New Scenic Herring and Prosciutto Sandwich

Chef Scott Graden, New Scenic Cafe
in partnership with fisherman Stephen Dahl

The North Shore's iconic and cozy New Scenic Cafe has been serving guests local fare since opening in 1999, including fish from fisherman Stephen Dahl, who has delivered Lake Superior herring weekly since day one. Demand always outpaces his catch, especially as the fishing industry continues to steadily grow alongside the awareness of local foods in Minnesota. Blaming his crazy Nordic genes for his life as a fisherman, Stephen is a staunch supporter of the waters he fishes, always emphasizing the importance of protecting our natural resources.

YIELD: 4 SERVINGS

For fennel mustard vinaigrette:

1 tablespoon fennel seeds

½ cup rice wine vinegar

2 tablespoons lemon juice

2 tablespoons whole grain mustard

1 tablespoon garlic, minced

½ teaspoon kosher salt

½ teaspoon cracked black pepper

2 teaspoons honey

½ cup olive oil

1 cup canola oil

For lemon basil aioli:

2 tablespoons white wine

1 cup mayonnaise

To prepare the vinaigrette: In a small sauté pan, toast fennel seeds lightly until fragrant over medium heat. Cool and pulse in spice grinder.

Place all ingredients except oils in a blender. Blend on low speed to mix until mostly smooth.

While continuing to blend, slowly add oils to emulsify. After all oil has been added, adjust consistency by mixing in cold water until vinaigrette is just thin enough to pour. Store in refrigerator.

To prepare the aioli: Place all ingredients in a mixing bowl and whisk until evenly combined. Store in refrigerator.

To prepare the salad: Rinse frisée in cool water, and either spin it dry in a salad spinner or use a clean towel to gently blot it dry. Using a sharp knife, shave frisée into thin, wispy pieces and set aside.

Preheat oven to 400°F.

Place 2 tablespoons of butter in a large, oven-proof sauté pan, and heat gently over low heat, just long enough to melt the butter. Lay herring fillets in the pan, making sure they are not touching, and pour white wine over them.

1 tablespoon basil pesto*

1 teaspoon lemon zest

1 tablespoon lemon juice

½ teaspoon garlic, minced

½ teaspoon kosher salt

1 teaspoon honey

⅛ teaspoon white pepper

For the salad:

2 heads frisée

6 tablespoons unsalted butter, divided

4 fresh herring fillets (4–5 ounces each) or other whitefish

¼ cup white wine

cracked black pepper, to taste

4 slices prosciutto

8 slices sourdough ciabatta

2 tablespoons fennel mustard vinaigrette

½ cup lemon basil aioli

Season fillets with cracked black pepper, and then lay 1 slice of prosciutto across each, crumpling prosciutto slightly to give fish additional crispness when finished cooking.

Place pan in oven, and roast fillets for 7–10 minutes, until they are just cooked all the way through. While fillets are baking, spread butter on one side of all slices of sourdough ciabatta, and grill them on medium heat in a large sauté pan or on a griddle, until they are golden brown on buttered side. Remove bread slices from pan, and place them on serving plates.

In a small mixing bowl, toss the frisée with fennel mustard vinaigrette, until frisée is coated evenly. Divide dressed greens equally among four of the slices of bread, and then lay one herring filet on top of each bed of greens. Spread 1 or 2 tablespoons of lemon basil aioli on un-grilled side of other slices of bread, place them on top, and serve the sandwiches immediately, while the herring is nice and hot.

Store bought basil pesto can be replaced with a homemade variety from this book such as Sunny Seed Pesto page 59, Pepita Pesto page 140, or Garden Pesto page 57.

Gin-Cured Mackinaw

2016: Executive Chef T. J. Rawitzer, The Third Bird
in partnership with Far North Spirits

*"100 years ago, or so, the natives of Lake Superior referred
to lake trout as Mackinaw. I like the term Mackinaw; it has a
better sound to it and keeps a bit of history alive."*

—Chef T. J. Rawitzer

*For this gin-cured Mackinaw, Chef Rawitzer likes Far North Gustaf Navy Strength
Gin, which has layers of lavender, juniper, and honeysuckle with a trace of citrus. Far
North Spirits describes this gin as "a zesty, lingering expression of earth and sea."*

YIELD: 8 SMALL PLATES

For Mackinaw:

1 fillet Lake Superior
Mackinaw, roughly 1½
pounds

½ cup kosher salt

½ cup sugar

3 ounces gin

**For lightly pickled
vegetables:**

1 pound baby summer
vegetables, such as
carrots, cucumbers,
radishes

1 cup white vinegar

2 cups water

1 cup sugar

1 tablespoon salt

For garnish:

8 ounces crème fraîche

4 slices rye bread, diced
small and toasted

8 celery leaves

extra-virgin olive oil

lemon

To prepare the Mackinaw: Place fish on a clean work surface and remove any small pin bones with pliers or tweezers. Place fish on a sheet pan inserted with a wire rack. Mix salt and sugar together and evenly sprinkle mixture over fish. Lightly sprinkle gin over fish. Loosely cover with plastic wrap and place in the refrigerator for 3 days.

After 3 days, remove fish from the refrigerator and lightly rinse off any visible salt. Pat dry with a paper towel and slice as thinly as possible.

To prepare the vegetables: Trim and cut so they are all roughly the same size.

Bring vinegar, water, sugar, and salt to a boil in medium saucepot. Gently blanch each vegetable separately in liquid. For softer vegetables like cucumbers or squash, blanch for at least a minute. For harder vegetables like carrots, blanch at least 2 minutes. As each vegetable is done blanching, transfer to a bowl of ice water to stop the cooking process. Once cooled, place vegetables on a plate lined with a paper towel.

To plate: Place sliced fish on center of platter. Carefully arrange vegetables around fish. Dot crème fraîche around platter (about 1 ounce crème fraîche per serving). Garnish with toasted rye and celery leaves. Finish with a drizzle of olive oil and squeeze of lemon juice.

North Shore Bouillabaisse

2016: Chef Judi Barsness, Waves of Superior Cafe in partnership with Dockside Fish Market

"Being a chef is part craft and technique, part true culinary art. The plate is my canvas, and I paint it with food and sauces."
—Chef Judi Barsness

A second-generation chef, Judi Barsness adopted her mother's French-inspired philosophies and passion for fresh, seasonal foods early in life. Throughout her career, Judi perfected the art of combining ingredients from Minnesota's North Shore with other more exotic ingredients in classic French dishes, such as this bouillabaisse. Tip: Place a small bowl of the exquisite rouille on the table to add directly to the fish soup.

For rouille:

YIELD: ABOUT 1 CUP

2 large garlic cloves, peeled and crushed

1 red bell pepper, roasted, peeled, and seeded

1 egg yolk

1½-inch thick slice baguette, cut on the diagonal, crust removed (or 1 slice torn white bread, crust removed)

1 teaspoon Dijon mustard

juice of 1 fresh lemon

1 pinch saffron threads

¾–1 cup extra-virgin olive oil

salt and pepper, to taste

To make the rouille: In a food processor outfitted with a metal blade, combine all ingredients except olive oil, salt, and pepper.

Pulse until smooth. Slowly drizzle in olive oil and process continuously until mixture is thick and smooth. Season with salt and pepper to taste. Store, covered, in the refrigerator for up to one week.

To make the bouillabaisse: In a large pot, heat olive oil over medium-high heat. Add onions, leeks, and garlic. Cook until translucent, but not browned.

Add Pernod through parsley and a small amount of salt, crushed red pepper, and black pepper. Simmer 20 minutes. Add trout and walleye and bring back to a low simmer for 20 more minutes. Add mussels and clams and cook 5–10 minutes, or until shells open. Discard unopened shells. (If substituting shellfish, cook shrimp until just pink or scallops until opaque.)

For bouillabaisse:

YIELD: 8 SERVINGS

½ cup olive oil

1 cup onion, chopped

1 cup leeks, chopped

4 cloves garlic, peeled and minced

¼ cup Pernod

1 (28-ounce) can diced tomatoes, or equivalent of fresh peeled, seeded, and chopped tomatoes

2½ quarts clam juice or fish stock

1 (2-inch) piece orange peel

½ cup fennel, sliced thinly

2 pinches saffron threads

2 dried bay leaves

3 sprigs fresh thyme

2 tablespoons fresh flat-leaf parsley, chopped

sea salt, crushed red pepper, and fresh cracked black pepper, to taste

2 pounds total lake trout and walleye, cut into large chunks

2 pounds total mussels in shell (washed, debearded) and clams in shell (washed)*

If desired, substitute shrimp (peeled, deveined, tails on) and/or scallops (foot removed)

Taste broth and add more salt, pepper or crushed red pepper, if necessary.

Place fish and shellfish equally in bowls and cover with tomato saffron broth. Serve with crusty bread topped with rouille.

Summer Goddess Walleye

2012: Chef Paul Lynch, Firelake Grill House and Cocktail Bar in partnership with Red Lake Nation Fishery

Red Lake Nation Fishery strives to sustainably manage and harvest superior quality wild fish, ensuring the future health of fish populations on Red Lake. It is illegal to sell Minnesota-caught walleye unless it comes from Red Lake Nation, which is exempt from the rule because of its tribal status. Chef Paul's Summer Goddess Walleye is divine and will leave you in an altered state. Truly goddess-worthy!

YIELD: 4 SERVINGS

For green goddess dressing:

¼ cup plus 1 tablespoon mayonnaise

2 small cloves garlic, peeled and minced

1 anchovy fillet, mashed

¼ cup fresh minced flat-leaf parsley

1 tablespoon minced tarragon

1 tablespoon minced green onion

¼ cup sour cream

¼ cup buttermilk

½ lemon, juiced

1 tablespoon extra-virgin olive oil

salt and pepper, to taste

For garlic herb breadcrumbs:

2 cups bread crumbs

2 cloves garlic, peeled and minced

2 tablespoons finely chopped parsley

2 tablespoons finely minced chives

2 tablespoons finely minced tarragon

To prepare the dressing: Blend mayonnaise, garlic, anchovy, and herbs until fine and smooth. Add sour cream, buttermilk, and 2 teaspoons lemon juice. Drizzle in olive oil last. Season with salt and pepper. Taste and adjust seasonings and lemon, if necessary.

To prepare the breadcrumbs: Mix breadcrumbs, garlic, herbs and salt in a medium bowl. Drizzle with oil and combine with a fork until oil is incorporated.

To prepare the butter: Mix all ingredients together in a mixing bowl. Compound butter may be stored in a covered container in refrigerator for about 4 days.

To prepare the walleye: Preheat oven to 425°F.

Spread top of each walleye fillet with about 2 tablespoons green goddess dressing. Cover with herb breadcrumb mix. Place fish on a parchment-lined baking dish, breadcrumb side up, and bake until herb crumbs turn a light golden brown, about 8–10 minutes.

While walleye is cooking, heat a sauté pan over medium heat. When pan is hot, add olive oil and fennel, and sauté until fennel is crisp tender. Add green beans and radishes. Sauté until beans are heated through and radishes have started to soften. Finish with lemon garlic butter; toss to coat. Season with sea salt and black pepper.

To serve: Divide vegetables onto four plates, then arrange fish on vegetables. Serve with a ramekin of green goddess salad dressing and lemon wedge.

large pinch kosher salt

3 tablespoons olive oil

For lemon garlic butter:

1 stick unsalted butter, room temperature

1 teaspoon finely minced shallot

1 teaspoon peeled and finely minced garlic

½ teaspoon kosher salt

1 teaspoon Dijon mustard

1½ teaspoons Italian minced flat-leafed parsley

1 teaspoon finely minced chives

½ lemon, zested and juiced

½ teaspoon Tabasco sauce

1 scant tablespoon dry white wine

For walleye:

4 boneless walleye fillets

green goddess dressing

garlic herb bread crumb mix

1 tablespoon olive oil

1 small fennel bulb, cored and julienned, reserve a few fronds for garnish

8 ounces baby green beans, trimmed and blanched

4–5 radishes, cut in half and then quartered

1 tablespoon lemon garlic butter

sea salt and black pepper, to taste

1 lemon, cut into wedges

Angry Trout Cafe Trout Chowder

2006–2007: Angry Trout Cafe
in partnership with Dockside Fish Market

Easy, hearty, and oh-so-comforting, this versatile, well-rounded chowder could be made with any number of vegetables. If lake trout isn't available, use walleye or another favorite local fish instead.

YIELD: 6 SERVINGS

4 cups vegetable stock

2½ cups Yukon gold or red potatoes, diced

1 cup carrots, diced

4 tablespoons unsalted butter, divided

¼ cup red onion, chopped

1 clove garlic, peeled and minced

¼ cup celery, diced

1 bay leaf

1 teaspoon dried dill

salt and white pepper, to taste

8 ounces lake trout, cut into soup-sized chunks

3 tablespoons flour

¾ cup half-and-half

½ cup fresh Italian parsley, chopped, for garnish

In a large pot, boil potatoes and carrots in vegetable stock until tender.

In a fry pan sauté onion, garlic, and celery in 2 tablespoons butter until tender, then add to stock. Add bay leaf, dill, salt, and white pepper. Simmer for 5 minutes.

Add trout and simmer until trout is cooked through (about 5 minutes). Stir gently to avoid breaking up the fragile chunks of fish.

Make a roux by melting 2 tablespoons butter in a pan. Add flour and whisk over medium heat for about 3 minutes. Remove from heat, gradually add half-and-half while whisking until smooth. Do not cook any further. Add roux mixture to soup, stir gently, and heat until soup is just starting to boil, then remove from heat. Remove bay leaf and check seasonings. Garnish with freshly chopped Italian parsley.

Sunday Picnics

Farming is a community affair. Whether lending a hand with harvest, sharing equipment and resources, dishing about the latest research on rotation crops, or enlivening local markets, farmers know how to be good neighbors and build something bigger together. Farmers enrich communities. Whether in support or celebration, everyone brings something to the table to share.

Working Together on Prairie Drifter Farm

Theirs is a farm that is at its best when being shared with others. In fact, it's a farm specifically created to share with others. Their farm is a community farm.

It was a particularly powerful and unforgettable storm. Eighty-mile-per-hour winds whipped through the air, leaving a trail of damage and an indelible impression in its wake. On one farm alone the winds downed sixteen mature trees, mangled the greenhouse and hoop house, and punched a hole in the garage roof. Owned by Nick and Joan Olson, the landscape of Prairie Drifter Farm changed within minutes and imprinted the couple with a vivid, long-lasting reminder of why everyone needs a strong community to lean on.

The first day after the storm, Nick and Joan stood numb amidst the debris, unsure exactly how or where to begin restoring order. Then, because they're farmers and are constantly challenged to adapt to unforeseen circumstances, they sprung into action and put out a call for help to friends, family, and members of Prairie Drifter Farm, the community they've invested so much time and energy building throughout the years. In an outpouring of support, thirty people responded, ready to rally, including new farm members Nick and Joan had never met face-to-face before. Some brought meals or offered to watch their kids. Many others rolled up their sleeves and dug into some seriously physical work, cutting, moving, and hauling tree limbs. Nick will never forget the overwhelming sense of gratitude he and Joan felt that day, hauling brush alongside members for hours and being cushioned by their goodwill, kind words, and generosity. They weren't alone. People had their backs, reinforcing a belief Nick and Joan have always held: Farming isn't meant to be a solo endeavor.

Nestled in the transition zone between the prairie grasslands of western Minnesota and the deciduous forest of central Minnesota, Prairie Drifter Farm is a diverse Community Supported Agriculture (CSA) operation producing certified organic vegetables on six of thirty-three acres. After gaining knowledge and interest working and volunteering on CSA vegetable farms, Nick and Joan intentionally set up their own farm to be a CSA, motivated by their desire to grow a strong community in a rural space, a community rooted in meaningful social connections with others who also care about a healthy local food system. Though the CSA movement is gaining popularity, it is still considered a relatively alternative model to agriculture, especially when compared to large commodity farms. This is part of its beauty and appeal for farmers like Nick and Joan, whose success hinges on community support, not foreign trade or commodity prices. If Nick and Joan are willing to show up, and if their community is willing to show up for them, Prairie Drifter Farm can work.

Nick and Joan's community farm helps feed about 225 families over the course of a season and fosters deep connections between them and many of their "share members." Some members opt to work on the farm (work shares) in exchange for a seasonal membership, lightening the workload for Nick, Joan, and their employees and providing plenty of hours and opportunities to develop a close camaraderie. Many days there is a revolving door of people coming and going on the farm, a delight to Nick and Joan who want their kids to grow up with a broad definition of family. Festive farm celebrations or community work days at Prairie Drifter provide additional opportunities to galvanize folks around healthy food and cultivate social ties. Whether recceiving support during a time of crisis or celebrating one of life's milestones, Nick and Joan's relationship with many members extends far beyond simply providing them with vegetables. This element of connection is so central to their mission that if their business were structured so that vegetables were simply loaded onto a delivery truck and then disappeared—without the added value of knowing the people on the receiving end—they doubt they would be farming at all.

For members, belonging to a CSA can help cultivate an entirely new relationship with food and, often, the land from which it came. Members expand their palates and food moxie as they figure out how to handle mysterious new veggies like fennel, Chinese cabbage, or kohlrabi that may show up in their seasonal deliveries—foods they might bypass if left to their own routine buying habits. Families tend to eat healthier, consuming increased quantities and a greater diversity of hyper-fresh foods. People also express more enthusiasm about cooking and eating the beautiful produce because there is a connection with the place it was grown and the hands that grew it. Meals are savored, even revered. Nick and Joan hear about members gifting neighbors with extra produce from their overflowing boxes, then pausing in the doorway to chat and catch up about life. They witness members introducing themselves to each other at pre-arranged CSA pick-up sites, then exchanging ideas for how to prepare the vegetables in that week's delivery. And members routinely gush how taking a day to work outside on the farm is the highlight of their week, how meaningful it feels to help with the harvest and how digging in the dirt is akin to therapy. These are the reasons Nick and Joan do what they do; to feed their community, and to feed community itself.

Community Supported Agriculture farms have been on the rise since the early 2000's, in tandem with the local food movement. CSAs are an increasingly popular agriculture model in which consumers—or members—invest in a farm upfront by buying "shares" of that farmer's harvest for the season. Members then typically receive weekly or bi-weekly deliveries of ultra-fresh, seasonal produce throughout the summer and fall. While most CSA farms focus on delivering an abundance of vegetables, some offer seasonal fruits, eggs, or value-added products like honey, maple syrup, or jams. There are even meat and cheese CSAs.

For farmers, the CSA model is helpful because there's a clear picture of how many customers are committed for the season prior to planting, which streamlines the planning process and establishes some predictability and advance income. And while those nuts and bolts are critical in helping make small-scale farming more financially viable, equally important the CSA model helps make small-scale farming socially viable, connecting farmers with other like-minded people, usually in rural spaces where they can easily become physically and emotionally isolated.

As more people express concern over farming practices and want to know their farmer, CSAs help consumers get back in touch with the source of their food, and members feel good knowing their money is directly supporting a farmer's livelihood. Through this model, farmers and consumers essentially share the risks and rewards of farming, generating a feeling of togetherness, as was evident within the Prairie Drifter community after the 2017 storm. If, for instance, a wave of hail comes through in June and destroys a crop of tender lettuces, that loss doesn't fall solely on the farmer—it's absorbed by the entire membership, softening the blow for everyone. And while members most likely won't receive lettuce for a few weeks, chances are good they won't even miss it among the abundance of other vegetables they will receive.

Nick and Joan are human. From time to time hard days deflate their optimism and their minds wander to all the other things they could be doing with their lives that would provide a steadier paycheck—and most likely keep them dry and comfortable, too. Yet their work and their joy in bringing folks together around the three shared common values of community, environmental stewardship, and eating healthy always manages to tip the scale back in favor of farming. As they turn into bed at night, worn out, their need to feel connected and part of a broader mission is fulfilled.

On the back of the Olson's couch lies a colorful, handmade quilt gifted to them by a farm member, a token of gratitude for the abundance of healthy food she received as a result of Nick and Joan's careful planning, sweat, and labor. Over winter they'll bundle up in that quilt, probably as they're poring over seed catalogs and strategizing next year's growing season, physically enveloping themselves in her warmth and benevolence. It's a tangible reminder how their small-scale farm is making a difference and positively impacting peoples' lives around them—which is exactly what they set out to do.

Charred Broccoli with Hummus and Herbed Yogurt

2020: Chef Owners Mateo Mackbee & Erin Lucas, Model Citizen in partnership with Prairie Drifter Farm

Chefs Mateo and Erin wanted to create a dish that "tastes like the end of summer." They succeeded! This recipe simultaneously reflects Erin's love for hummus, vegetables, and Mediterranean cuisine while harnessing Mateo's obsession with wood and fire. Charring the broccoli adds a layer of rich caramelized flavor to the dish you don't want to skip.

YIELD: 1 PARTY PLATTER

For broccoli:

2 heads broccoli

2 tablespoons olive oil

salt and pepper, to taste

½ lemon

finishing salt, such as Maldon or fleur de sel, for final assembly

For hummus:

1 (15½-ounce) can garbanzo beans (chickpeas), drained and rinsed

2 cloves peeled garlic

⅓ cup tahini

¼ cup good olive oil

1 tablespoon lemon juice

¼ cup water

salt and pepper, to taste

To prepare the broccoli: Preheat grill to medium-high heat. Cut florets off broccoli stalks, leaving about an inch and a half of stem. Place on plate and drizzle with oil and salt. Char broccoli on grill until there is some good charring, or char in a hot cast iron pan over a medium flame. Take off heat and squeeze on lemon juice; season with pepper.

To prepare the hummus: Place chickpeas, garlic, and tahini in a food processor; blend on high while adding oil, lemon juice, and water. Blend for a few minutes, ensuring everything is blended smoothly. Remove from processor and set aside. Season to taste.

recipe continues . . .

For herbed yogurt:

1 cup plain Greek yogurt

½ teaspoon minced fresh flat-leaf parsley

½ teaspoon minced fresh dill

½ teaspoon minced fresh basil

juice of 1 lemon

salt and white pepper, to taste

For pickled red onions:

½ red onion, peeled and thinly sliced

½ cup champagne vinegar

½ cup water

½ cup sugar

pinch of salt

For toasted pepitas:

½ cup pepitas (pumpkin seeds)

1 teaspoon good olive oil

salt and pepper, to taste

To prepare the yogurt: Place yogurt in a bowl; add herbs and lemon juice, then mix together. Season to taste.

To prepare the red onions: Place red onions in non-reactive bowl or container. Bring champagne vinegar, water, sugar, and salt to a boil. Stir occasionally to dissolve sugar. When it just reaches a boil, pour over onions. Make sure there is enough liquid to cover onions.

To toast the pepitas: Preheat oven to 400°F. Mix pepitas, oil, salt and pepper in small bowl. Place on baking sheet and bake 12–15 minutes or until slightly golden brown. Set aside.

To assemble the dish: Spoon hummus on a platter. Sprinkle with a bit of finishing salt. Add charred broccoli. Drizzle on herbed yogurt and top with pickled red onions and toasted pepitas. Sprinkle a small pinch of finishing salt over everything. Serve warm or at room temperature.

Pesto Zucchini Noodles

2019: Manager Brian Nanoff, Truce Juice
in partnership with Big River Farms via Shared Ground Cooperative

Truce Juice began strictly as a juice bar but has steadily evolved to include new ways—always raw and vegan—to showcase the perfectly ripe bounty courtesy of their many farm partners, including Big River Farms. Big River Farms, a program of Minnesota Food Association (MFA), is an educational farm and food hub that supports beginning farmers from diverse backgrounds as they start organic farming businesses. MFA's farmer training programs primarily serve refugees and recent immigrants who learn skills around growing, marketing, and selling their food at fair prices.

YIELD: 5 SERVINGS

For pepita pesto:

¾ cup pepitas, toasted

6 cups loosely packed fresh spinach

1 cup loosely packed basil leaves

1½ tablespoons olive oil

1 tablespoon lemon juice

1 teaspoon garlic, minced

1 teaspoon black pepper

1 teaspoon salt

For zucchini noodles:

5 cups spiralized zucchini (or yellow summer squash)

1 cup red bell pepper, chopped

1½ cup pepita pesto

toasted pepitas, crushed (for garnish)

Place all ingredients for pesto in a food processor and pulse for 1–2 minutes, scraping the sides of bowl as needed.

Mix zucchini noodles well with pesto and bell pepper, garnish with crushed pepitas. Serve cold.

Basil Lemonade

2013: River Rock Coffee: Chef Christine "Montana" Rasmussen in partnership with Living Land Farm

This basil lemonade is the perfect, refreshing drink on a hot summer's day. Add some vodka or gin, and you have a winner of a cocktail.

YIELD: ½ GALLON

1 cup sugar

1 cup hot water

2¾ cups fresh basil, with stems

1 cup fresh squeezed lemon juice

5½ cups cold water

sprig of basil for garnish

Combine sugar and hot water. Stir until dissolved; set aside.

In a blender, combine basil, lemon juice, and cold water. Pulse until basil is pureed into fine pieces and the liquid has turned a bright green. Sieve out basil and discard. Combine lemon basil water with the cooled sugar water. Mix well. Pour over ice, garnish with a fresh sprig of basil, and enjoy.

Roasted Eggplant Salsa

2009: Spoonriver Cookbook by Brenda Langton
in partnership with Sandra Jean's Herbal Specialties

Brenda Langton, chef owner of two memorable Minneapolis restaurants, Cafe Brenda and Spoonriver, will forever be regarded as one of the pivotal pioneers of Minnesota's rich local food landscape. Farm fresh ingredients dominated her award-winning menus. Eggplants give this summer salsa a unique spin. This is a tasty dip with pita chips or try it as a quesadilla filling. It's also delicious atop broiled fish.

YIELD: 1 PARTY BOWL

For eggplants and peppers:

2 medium eggplants

1 red pepper

1 green pepper

olive oil for brushing

salt

For salsa:

1 large tomato, chopped

3 large garlic cloves, peeled and minced

½ cup olive oil

2 tablespoons cilantro, chopped

1 jalapeño, seeded and minced (optional)

1 medium lemon, juiced

1 small lime, juiced

4–6 green onions, sliced

1 teaspoon salt

To char eggplants—oven method: Cut off top and bottom of eggplant and discard. Slice eggplant in half lengthwise. Place on parchment-lined baking sheet, skin-side down. Brush halves on each side with olive oil and sprinkle with salt and pepper. Roast in 350°F oven for 25–30 minutes.

To char eggplants—grill method: Cut off top and bottom of eggplant and discard. Slice vertically into ¼-inch slices. Lightly brush both sides with olive oil and sprinkle with salt and pepper. Grill eggplant slices over medium heat about 10 minutes, turning once, or until deep golden brown on each side.

To char peppers: Place peppers over medium heat using an open flame on stove top or on grill, turning every so often with tongs, until skins blister. Place peppers in bowl and cover with a towel, about 10 minutes, to allow further steaming and easier peeling.

To assemble salsa: Once eggplants are charred, cool and remove skin, then chop remaining flesh of eggplant. Place in a bowl. Remove peppers from bowl, cool and peel, leaving a bit of the char for flavor. Remove the top and seeds, then dice and add to bowl with eggplant. Mix in all remaining ingredients. Taste and add additional salt and lemon juice if desired.

Charcuterie with Local Flavors

2008: Chef Mike Phillips, The Craftsman in partnership with Riverbend Farm

Considered a pioneering chef in Minnesota's widespread farm-to-plate mentality, Salumiere Mike Phillips has long-emphasized the importance of supporting small farms—both for superior quality and to preserve healthy rural communities. Mike's specialty is salumi, dry-cured pork products made from heritage breed hogs raised on sustainable farms. Whether sourcing pork for his Red Table Meat Co. salumi products or red onions for marmalade, Mike keeps it local by sourcing as much product from Minnesota as possible.

Salami on crostini with Red Onion Marmalade

YIELD: ABOUT 1 CUP

¼ cup olive oil

3 large red onions, thinly sliced

½ cup sugar

1 cup red wine vinegar

½ teaspoon mustard seeds

1 tablespoon grated orange zest

freshly ground black pepper

1 loaf crusty bread, sliced into ½-inch pieces

soppresata, thinly sliced (Red Table Meats Big Chet's salami recommended)

In a large sauté pan, warm olive oil over low heat. Add onions and cook, stirring often until softened, about 20 minutes. Add sugar, vinegar, mustard seeds, and orange zest and simmer until almost all liquid has evaporated and onions are syrupy, about 20 minutes longer. Remove from heat and season with lots of pepper. Let cool to room temperature. Marmalade will keep, tightly covered, in the refrigerator for up to two months. Bring to room temperature before serving.

Grill crusty bread and slather it with olive oil, then top with salami and red onion marmalade.

Dry-Cured Ham with Zelniki

YIELD: 2 DOZEN CRACKERS

2 cups all-purpose flour

2 cups sauerkraut, chopped fine

3–4 ounces unsalted butter, cut on a cheese grater

dry-cured ham or prosciutto

olive oil

freshly ground black pepper

Preheat oven to 425°F.

Combine flour and sauerkraut and grate butter into mix (mixture should have the consistency of a pie crust). Pinch off dough in pieces about a tablespoon in size and flatten with glass on prepared baking sheet.

Bake for 10 minutes. Reduce heat to 350°F and bake for about another 15 minutes. Watch crackers closely so they are crisp but not overbrowned. Cool completely on baking rack. Crackers should be crisp with a little chew in the center.

Thinly slice dry-cured prosciutto. Lay prosciutto on crackers, drizzle with olive oil, and top with freshly ground black pepper. These crackers will surprise you with their slightly sour flavor and toothiness. Great topped as directed or as an addictive snack on their own.

A Culture of Cooperation at HAFA

Most people do not get very far in life alone. More often than not, successes unfold when a community of peers, friends, and mentors lock arms, generously share resources and wisdom, and collectively align themselves toward a common mission. This is the essence and strength of the Hmong American Farmers Association (HAFA), where farmers have banded together and share everything from brain power to muscles, seeds to infrastructure, and land to dreams to create a thriving farming community.

The tradition of working in a community has always been an integral part of the Hmong culture and lifestyle. This interconnectedness extends to every branch and leaf of the Hmong, and it is especially felt in farming. Hmong people refer to working cooperatively as *pauv zog,* which essentially means "trading labor." Back in their homelands of Laos and Thailand, Hmong people customarily traded labor with others in their villages, ensuring everyone's land got planted, weeded, and harvested in turn. It didn't matter if people were related or not; they had a cooperative kinship. Even upon arriving in the US, a foreign, foreboding landscape for the Hmong, this spirit of cooperation didn't change; it strengthened. More than ever, farmers pooled their money together to help one another rent land and work that land *en masse* to secure a stable future for generations to come.

Pakou Hang, co-founder and first Executive Director of the Hmong American Farmers Association, was working for a social investment firm before embarking on a quest to help improve the livelihoods of Hmong American farmers in Minnesota. The farmers she knew were relying on their rich, agricultural roots to earn a living, but, like many beginning farmers, they faced significant obstacles accessing land and securing start-up capital—obstacles too big to easily overcome themselves. As a result, the majority were living in poverty.

Started in 2011, the Hmong American Farmers Association (HAFA) is a membership-based organization for Hmong farmers who depend on farming for their livelihoods. HAFA strives to advance the prosperity and intergenerational wealth of Hmong American farmers through cooperative endeavors, capacity building, and advocacy. The overarching belief is that the best people to support Hmong farmers are Hmong farmers themselves; therefore, education and training aimed at preserving generational knowledge and skills and empowering farmers are core to the organization. HAFA recognizes that many of the problems and obstacles in our present-day food system are simply too big to tackle solo; they require the power found in community—something that has never been forgotten in the soul of the Hmong people.

With every quest, there comes a plethora of challenges. First things first, HAFA needed accessible farmland, the single most important component to fulfill their mission. After many initial setbacks and struggles attempting to work with traditional lending sources, HAFA connected with an anonymous benefactor interested in supporting small farmers and immigrant farmers, successfully tackling this barrier. Once farmland was secured, their next step was to create a formal membership structure. Because farming is so intertwined with Hmong culture, HAFA established certain criteria to differentiate between the everyday, backyard gardener who grows food to sustain one's family and professional farmers who depend on farming for a financial livelihood. Members are required to have at least three years of experience farming, and they must farm at least three acres. Additionally, farmers are expected to have their own established markets, though HAFA does offer other various markets through their food hub, including workplace CSA's (community supported agriculture shares delivered to companies), Veggie Rx boxes (subsidized produce delivered to clinics for food insecure families), contracted sales with schools and food co-ops, and ad hoc sales generated from HAFA's weekly availability list.

From a farmer's perspective, these additional markets translate into increased financial security. Rather than sitting in the scorching, hot sun or gloomy, pouring rain all day at a farmers' market relying on unpredictable sales, farmers may know as early as February just how many hundreds or thousands of pounds of potatoes they will need to grow to help, for example, collectively fulfill a large contract for the St. Paul public school district.

Hmong people began coming to Minnesota in 1975 as political refugees after the Secret War of Laos. With them they brought rich, never-before-heard dialects, illustrious hand-stitched clothing, and an unyielding heritage of agriculture. Now, after almost four decades, there are more than 66,000 Hmong Americans in Minnesota, of which the Twin Cities of Minneapolis and St. Paul house the largest urban population of the Hmong people in the world.

Within just a few years of arriving in Minnesota, Hmong American farmers established a strong presence at the Minneapolis and St. Paul farmers' markets, reinvigorating the markets with stands of both familiar and exotic vegetables and row upon row of vibrant flowers. Hmong farmers helped evolve Minnesotans' stereotypical bland palates, introducing them to Japanese sweet potatoes, bok choy, bitter melon, lemongrass and much more, and reintroducing them to overlooked tastes like the delightful sweet burst of ground cherries, a Minnesota native once shunned as nothing more than a low-brow, ditch weed. Hmong farmers also helped Minnesotans reimagine what the face of a farmer looks like, showing that people of color and women could be farmers, too.

Because of this revitalization, the Minneapolis and St. Paul farmers' markets have not only become both an oasis and source of pride for residents but also a festive place to rendezvous with family or show off to out-of-town guests. Farmers' markets no longer just represent the fertility of farming; they also represent an inclusive, magnanimous, hopeful community.

The contributions of Hmong American farmers to Minnesota's economy and diverse tapestry run deep. They unquestionably stand out as leaders in the Twin Cities local food economy, having helped foster a renewed awareness and interest in local foods and small-scale farming in Minnesota. According to AgStar Financial Services, the local foods economy in Minnesota currently generates over $250 million in annual sales. Since Hmong American farmers now comprise more than 50 percent of all the farmers in the urban and suburban farmers markets in Minnesota, they undoubtedly make up a strong, integral core of this economy. Who would've imagined that a small ethnic group from the dense, humid jungles of Laos would become such a profound pillar in the epics of Minnesota history.

Large, valuable contracts like this—far too large for one member to handle—are shared among many members. Furthermore, farmers then share delivery costs, another significant expense.

HAFA sells large quantities of its produce to a non-profit food hub in St. Paul called The Good Acre, whose mission is to strengthen and connect farmers, food makers, and communities through good food. On its own, HAFA supplies produce to four school districts in Minnesota. Through The Good Acre's reach, HAFA produce helps feed 140,000 children in 24 school districts in Minnesota. Contributing nutritious, whole foods to schools, many of which their children and grandchildren attend, is deeply rewarding and a great source of pride for the farmers.

When developing HAFA and making decisions about its structure, immense thought was given to the logistical and technical aspects of farming. When creating the CSA boxes, the focus was squarely on the potential of growing another market for farmers. Yet, surprisingly, the real benefit to all of this has been something much deeper than anyone expected—meaningful connection. Two of HAFA's CSA members include a domestic violence shelter and a drop-in mental health center; every week both the shelter and the mental health center use the produce from their CSA boxes to create a beautiful, wholesome dinner to share with the people they serve. At the domestic violence shelter, every woman and child shows up to enjoy that meal of solidarity together, a rare occurrence. We know it in our hearts but sometimes forget: food is the universal language.

The HAFA farm buzzes with life and energy, and the sense of ownership, prosperity, and camaraderie among farmers radiates. The farmer-member responsible for tending the plot of land nearest HAFA's entrance beautifies her space with a brightly painted rain barrel and a cheerful planting of sunflowers, a warm and inviting welcome to both farmers and visitors. Grandkids run around the land, alternatively helping and playing. If one farmer doesn't have enough kale to fulfill an order or doesn't feel his product is fit to sell, he'll pass the order along to another farmer. At night, before leaving for the day, farmers check in with each other, asking if anyone needs or wants them to stay. Do they need help? Do they feel safe? Starting in the fall, as the days grow shorter and darkness falls earlier, dinner is served in the farmhouse so farmers can indulge in a hot meal, cider, or coffee with one another before heading home. Together they catch up about farming, family, and life.

It takes a village. Communities, by their very nature, bring together a multitude of ideas, opinions, and skills. Rich exchanges occur, fostering increased stability and deepened social ties, reminding everyone of their interconnectedness. For HAFA farmers, this cooperative exchange means the dream of earning a living from farming, preserving their cultural heritage, and owning farmland is alive and well.

Chicken Lettuce Wraps with Tiger Bite Sauce

2020: Chef Owner Yia Vang, Union Hmong Kitchen in partnership with Hmong American Farmers Association

Chef Owner Yia Vang cooks to carry on his parents' legacy and tell their story of escaping Laos and Thailand so Yia and his siblings could build better futures. Yia's dad taught him to grill over wood fire, and his mom cooked whatever was seasonally available to ensure her kids didn't go hungry. These experiences shape his Hmong cuisine today. Yia says, "Every dish has a narrative. If you follow a dish far enough, you get to the people behind the food. Our food is a reflection of my mom and dad's table. We're merely the vessel and hands that deliver it." You'll have plenty of leftover tiger bite sauce, which Chef Yia suggests serving on grilled fish, pork, or chicken.

YIELD: 6–8 WRAPS

For tiger bite sauce:

1 cup cherry tomatoes

1 tablespoon olive oil

salt and pepper

5–8 Thai chilies

4 cloves garlic, peeled

2 cups chopped cilantro

¼ cup fresh lime juice

2 tablespoons fish sauce

2 tablespoons oyster sauce

For dry rub:

2 teaspoons smoked paprika

1 teaspoon granulated garlic

1 teaspoon ground coriander

1 teaspoon ground cumin

1 teaspoon salt

To prepare the sauce: Toss whole tomatoes with olive oil, salt, and pepper. Spread out on a baking sheet and place under broiler for 15 minutes, or until soft and blistered. Alternatively, cherry tomatoes can be smoked in a smoker.

Place chilies and garlic in mortar and pestle; mash into a paste. Add cilantro and a pinch of salt; mash together with chilies and garlic. Add lime juice, fish sauce, oyster sauce, and roasted or smoked tomatoes. Stir until incorporated together. Taste and add salt, if desired

To prepare the dry rub: Combine all ingredients.

1 teaspoon pepper

1 teaspoon Korean chili
flakes

For lettuce wraps:

8 ounces boneless
chicken thighs

Little Gem or romaine
lettuce leaves

¼ cup loosely packed
mint, chopped

¼ cup loosely packed
cilantro, chopped

2–3 green onions, sliced

1 cucumber, sliced

2 radishes, thinly sliced

To prepare chicken: Rub chicken thighs with a little bit of oil, then coat with dry rub. Let sit overnight or for at least 3 hours, then grill over medium-high heat 10–12 minutes, turning, until cooked through.

To serve: Slice chicken and layer in lettuce wraps along with mint, cilantro, green onion, cucumber, radish, and tiger bite sauce.

Roasted Asparagus with Crispy Prosciutto and Gribiche

2018: Chef Owner Seth Lintelman & Co-Owner Elizabeth Lintelman, Cup N' Saucer in partnership with Elm Creek Veggies

Seth and Elizabeth Lintelman are the proud owners of Cup N' Saucer cafe in Sherburn because, unbelievably, they won it in an essay contest. With twenty years of restaurant and management experience between them, they'd always dreamed of owning their own restaurant. Then suddenly within two months of submitting their essay, the dream was theirs. An investor devised the contest in an attempt to keep the town's main street alive and chose the Lintelmans partly because they promised to procure as many ingredients locally as possible. Today they're one of the only restaurants in the surrounding five counties to do so, both for their everyday menu and their popular monthly tasting dinners, which are sold out well over a year in advance.

For asparagus:

1 pound asparagus,
   ends trimmed

extra-virgin olive oil

salt and freshly ground
   black pepper, to taste

2 slices crisped
   prosciutto, crumbled,
   for garnish

For gribiche:

pinch of salt

1 tablespoon Dijon
   mustard

1 tablespoon red wine
   vinegar

3 tablespoons extra-
   virgin olive oil

1 tablespoon capers,
   rinsed

2 hard-boiled eggs,
   finely chopped*

2 cornichons, finely
   chopped

1 tablespoon fresh flat-
   leaf parsley, chopped

pinch of red chili flakes

freshly ground pepper

For garlic scape pesto:

1 cup finely chopped
   garlic scapes (or ⅔
   cup finely chopped
   chives, plus ⅓ cup
   finely chopped garlic)

¾ cup extra-virgin olive
   oil

½ cup finely grated
   Parmesan

⅓ cup roasted, salted
   cashews

pepper

To prepare the asparagus: Liberally coat asparagus in olive oil and season with salt and freshly ground black pepper. Grill asparagus 5–8 minutes (depending on size of asparagus) over medium-high heat, turning once or twice. Asparagus should be lightly charred and tender, but not mushy.

To prepare the gribiche: In a bowl, mix all ingredients together. Taste and correct seasoning. The texture of this gribiche makes for a crumbly, savory topping. Mix the first four ingredients into a creamy paste before folding in the rest of the ingredients.

To prepare the pesto: Pulse garlic scapes, oil, Parmesan, and cashews in a food processor until finely chopped. Season with pepper.

To plate: Place warm grilled asparagus on bottom of platter. Top with sauce gribiche and garlic scape pesto. Garnish with prosciutto. Serve warm or at room temperature.

For a creamier gribiche, eggs should be soft-boiled.

Dolmades

**2020: Owner Anna Christoforides, Gardens of Salonica
in partnership with Prairie Hollow Farm**

*For twenty years, Anna Christoforides has relied on farmer Pam Benike of Prairie
Hollow Farm in Elgin for an extensive list of both expected and unexpected ingredients: seasonal mushrooms, fiddlehead ferns, ramps, garlic scapes, grape leaves,
cheese—and the list goes on. Anna follows both her creativity and the seasons when
making dolmades, sometimes incorporating fresh chive blossoms, ramps, or garlic
scapes for a springtime twist, or grating in carrots or zucchini during the height of
summer. Dolmades can also be made using Swiss chard or French sorrel leaves.*

For rice filling:

2 cups raw jasmine rice

1½ cups chopped green onions

2 cups grated onions

½ cup chopped fresh flat-leaf parsley

¼ cup extra-virgin olive oil

2 teaspoons sea salt

2 teaspoons white pepper

1 tablespoon dried mint

1 tablespoon chopped fresh dill

For dolmades:

1 pound prepared grape leaves, soaked/ sorted/stacked*

⅔ cup extra-virgin olive oil

6 cups boiling water

Any Greek import or Middle Eastern store should carry prepared grape leaves.

To make the rice filling: Mix all ingredients together and set aside.

To make dolmades: Preheat oven to 350°F.

Place underside of grape leaf up and snip off stem if longer than ¼-inch. Place approximately 1 tablespoon of filling close to stem edge. Starting from the stem end, fold bottom of leaf to cover filling. Proceed by folding one lobe side over the other, forming a 2-inch tube or round packet. Finish dolma by rolling the tube to the tip of leaf. Place folded side down in a 9 x 13 baking pan. Continue rolling and placing dolmades loosely, barely touching, as they will swell as the rice cooks. Cover bottom of pan with first layer. Make a second layer as needed.

When all the dolmades are rolled, drizzle top layer with the olive oil. Finish by slowing pouring boiling water over, which should not completely cover dolmades—allow ¼-inch to be above liquid. (Amount of water used will depend on size of pan and number of layers. It's possible to layer up to 4 rows, but the bottom row may become mushy as cooking will be more inconsistent.) Cover with parchment paper and foil wrap or with another pan upside down as a lid. Bake until rice is cooked, 40–50 minutes.

Anna's note: When using fresh vine leaves, pick only bright green leaves about the size of an open palm, then sort, rinse, and parboil in water. When cooked grape leaf dolmades are exposed to air, they may blacken—for this reason keep covered until ready to serve! When using Swiss chard leaves, cut off thick stalk and roll fresh (no parboiling); when using sorrel leaves, cut off heavy stems and roll up from stem end tucking the edges while rolling to tip.

Rural Renewal with Smude Enterprises

Farmers are integral to strong local economies. When farms thrive, small-town businesses and local economies tend to thrive alongside them. When farms struggle or disappear, rural communities become anemic and risk disappearing alongside them.

Tom and Jenni Smude's entrepreneurial odyssey is one laced with ingenuity and persistence. Tom Smude grew up farming, and he and Jenni began farming crops and cattle together in Pierz in 1998. Their unexpected journey building Smude Enterprises LLC, which makes premium, cold-pressed sunflower oil, was born out of a dire need on their farm around 2008. Several years of widespread drought had resulted in a diminished supply of corn and soybeans, forcing the Smudes to begin hauling in large amounts of additional protein and feed for their cattle. The astronomical trucking expenses from this were swallowing their profits, motivating them to explore alternative crops they could grow on their farm's sandy soil as feed for their four hundred steers.

They landed on gloriously vibrant, happy-faced sunflowers. When sunflowers are pressed and the oil is removed, a pellet—or flake—remains called sunflower meal. Sunflower meal is a nutritious, protein-rich feed for ruminants, so Tom and Jenni felt optimistic that adding sunflowers to their crop rotation could provide a solution to the protein deficit on their farm. Though the Smudes were focused on the potential of the sunflower meal to feed their cattle, sunflower oil is generally considered the more valuable product; therefore, it only made sense to sell that too. Their original plan was to sell the oil by the semiload for the biofuels industry, but shortly after they began operations the market became flooded with cheap oil and the economics of their plan went haywire. Prices plummeted, creating a scenario in which they would only earn half of what they had originally forecasted for their oil, leaving them stranded with a quality product and no obvious profitable home for it.

Desperation bred innovation. It was a fearful time, and they felt panicky. Their new plan would almost certainly fail if they couldn't demand a better price for their sunflower oil, so the Smudes got hustling. Within a few months they had garnered support from community resources and secured the necessary capital to build a small food-grade facility on their farm. With no prior experience producing food-grade products from start to finish, they turned to their supportive network of community members and experts to point them in the right direction. Scientists at the Agricultural Utilization Research Institute (AURI) in Minnesota developed a nutrition fact label for them, and a local friend designed their first product label. In 2010 they began bottling and selling their high-oleic, cold-pressed sunflower oil themselves, hoping to finally generate a return on their investment. They began with local farmers' markets. When Tom returned home one Saturday from a market with $300 in his pocket, he felt buoyed and wondered if they might actually be onto something.

By the end of that first season, word was spreading quickly about Smude's sunflower oil. Retailers were enthusiastic about stocking it, and farmers' market sales kept climbing, fueled by consumer interest in heart healthy, cold-pressed oils. By 2013 the Smudes had already outgrown their small on-farm bottling facility, a trend that has continued since. Two expansions later Smude Enterprises now occupies an impressive building in Pierz, which will allow them to process about six million pounds of sunflower oil a year, a significant increase from the eight hundred thousand pounds of oil they could process in their previous plant. Today Smude Sunflower Oil is now widely available throughout Minnesota and sales continue to increase.

None of this was easy, but through every stage of their expansion and growth, the Smudes were fortunate to have community resources such as Carol Anderson, Executive Director of a nonprofit economic development corporation in nearby Little Falls, on their side. Community developers understand how attracting and supporting family farmers and emerging entrepreneurs is a powerful strategy for revitalizing rural communities. Businesses create jobs and attract a workforce, providing a valuable tax base that supports the county, city, and school districts. From the beginning Carol advocated for the Smudes' idea, envisioning many potential benefits down the road, including the possibility that a successful sunflower plant could eventually provide opportunities for other local farmers to diversify their incomes if it resulted in a strong market for sunflowers.

Although their plan did not unfold perfectly and growth has been anything but linear, the Smudes embraced the necessary risks to get where they are and seem to have the winds of momentum behind them now. Robust community support tempered the risks, and now they are in a position to give back tenfold. Smude Enterprises currently employs twenty-three individuals from their community and plans to hire more in the coming years. Tom estimates their new plant could be processing *fifteen thousand* acres' worth of sunflowers in a few years—up from *fifteen hundred* acres in 2019. The Smudes only grow about one hundred acres of sunflowers themselves, which means they're going to need help. They would prefer to buy local sunflowers, which could indeed be a promising new market for surrounding farmers just as Carol Anderson predicted—a market not tied into trade agreements. Another side benefit is that farmers now have the option to buy local sunflower meal for cattle feed rather than paying an arm and a leg to haul feed in from elsewhere, which circles back to the initial impetus for Smude Enterprises. As Tom says, "It all works hand in hand."

The Smudes have also brought a boost to their local economy in more subtle ways. Truck drivers delivering sunflowers to the plant for pressing or drivers hauling oil out may stop at the gas station in town and fill their trucks. Then they might linger and enjoy a bite to eat at a restaurant before they hit the road. There's a palpable economic vibrancy in Pierz these days that gives the community a sense of hope and pride.

With a spirit of reciprocity, the Smudes are mindful to support their neighbors and encourage other community members to use their purchasing power with the local hardware, clothing, and grocery stores. Tom believes tight-knit communities are built when neighbors look out for one another and provide security for each other, especially during tough times. Even something simple, like buying a box of pencils at the local hardware store, can make a difference.

Farmers and producers like the Smudes are instrumental in establishing flourishing local and regional food systems. These local food systems not only nourish people, they also create a sturdy foundation for continued growth in small towns and rural communities. The Smudes have managed to strike a delicate balance between simultaneously thinking big and thinking locally in their continued expansion. Their story is one of many that speaks to the economic and social significance food and farming have on communities, yet it only scratches the surface of the total value they bring.

Roasted Harvest Vegetable Platter with Sunflower Aioli

2012: Chef Truman Olson, Chowgirls Killer Catering in partnership with Smude Enterprises

Every party needs a good vegetable platter, and every vegetable platter needs a really good sauce. If you can get your hands on Smude's unrefined, cold-pressed sunflower oil, treat yourself. The buttery tasting oil shines through in the mayonnaise and complements the earthy deliciousness of the roasted vegetables.

YIELD: 8-10 SERVINGS

For preserved lemon sunflower aioli:

2 egg yolks

1 tablespoon lemon juice

½ teaspoon dry mustard

salt and pepper, to taste

1 cup unrefined sunflower oil

½ cup canola oil

1 preserved lemon—rind, seeds, and membranes removed and minced

For the roasted vegetables:

6-8 small green-top carrots, halved lengthwise

1 head cauliflower, cut into medium florets

2-3 red, yellow, or orange bell peppers, cored, seeded and cut into wedges

1 small bunch asparagus

2 bunches scallions, peeled

½ cup sunflower oil

kosher salt and freshly ground pepper, to taste

To prepare the aioli: Beat yolks with lemon juice, mustard, salt and pepper. Continue beating rapidly while dropping oil into mixture, drop by drop. Do not speed up this part. After about ¼ cup of oil is incorporated and oil and egg yolk mixture are fully emulsified, oil can be incorporated in a steady stream while you continually beat the mixture. Fold in preserved lemon. Adjust seasonings. Serve alongside roasted vegetables.

To prepare the platter: Preheat oven to 400°F. Place all vegetables onto sheet pans, grouping according to cook times below. Drizzle vegetables with oil and season with salt and pepper.

Roast carrots and cauliflower about 20–25 minutes until tender. Roast bell peppers 12 minutes or until tender but still somewhat firm. Roast asparagus and scallions until asparagus is bright green and starting to brown, but still firm, about 8 minutes. Allow each vegetable to cool to room temperature as they come out of the oven. Arrange on a large platter.

Turkey Momos

2015: Chef Co-owner Rashmi Battachan and Chef Co-owner Sarala Kattel, Gorkha Palace in partnership with Ferndale Market

The words "local foods" have become synonymous with "fresh" and "high-quality," which is exactly what you'll find at Gorkha Palace in Northeast Minneapolis, where chefs and co-owners Rashmi and Sarala grind their own spices, make their own ghee, and source as much food locally as possible for their Nepali, Indian, and Tibetan cuisine. These turkey momos are spiked with layer upon layer of flavor, rightfully earning Gorkha Palace a cult following at the Mill City Farmers Market in Minneapolis. These will be a unique and pleasing addition to any potluck or gathering.

YIELD: ABOUT 6 DOZEN MOMOS

For filling:

1 pound ground turkey

2 cups cabbage, shredded

1 cup red or white onions, chopped

1 cup chives or green onions, chopped

½ cup tomatoes, diced

3 tablespoons ginger, minced

1 tablespoon garlic, minced

salt, to taste

½ cup vegetable oil

2 tablespoons ground cumin coriander mixed powder

2 teaspoons garam masala

1 tablespoon turmeric

chili powder, to taste

To prepare the filling: Mix all ingredients together at least 2 hours and up to overnight in advance. Cover with plastic wrap and keep refrigerated.

To prepare the momo chutney: Heat oil in a pan. Add garlic and sauté, then add tomatoes; stir for 5 minutes. Pour mixture into blender along with salt and cilantro or mint. Blend and serve with momos.

To prepare the momo wrappers: In a large bowl combine flour, oil, salt, and water. Mix well. Knead until dough becomes homogeneous in texture, 8–10 minutes. Cover and let stand for at least 30 minutes. Knead well again before making wrappers.

Shape small amounts of dough by rolling between palms into 1-inch dough balls. Dust working board with dry flour. Gently flatten dough balls on the board with your palm into 2-inch semi-flattened circles. Cover with a bowl or wet paper towels to prevent drying.

For well-executed momos, it is essential that the middle portion of each wrapper be slightly thicker than the edges to ensure steam will not tear the bottom. With this in mind, place one piece of semi-flattened dough on work surface, and using a rolling pin roll only the edges out until each wrapper is a 3-inch circle. Cover with bowl or wet paper towels again. Continue process with all wrappers.

For momo chutney:

2 tablespoons oil

2 cloves garlic, peeled and chopped

2 cups tomatoes, chopped

salt, to taste

½ cup fresh cilantro or mint leaves

For momo wrappers:

2 cups white flour

1 tablespoon oil

2 pinches salt

1 cup warm water

You can also use ready-made round potsticker wrappers found in grocery stores

To form momos: Hold wrapper on one palm. Add 1 tablespoon filling mixture in center. Use other hand to bring all edges together to the center, making pleats. Pinch and twist pleats to ensure absolute closure of stuffed dumplings. Continue with additional wrappers and filling.

To finish: Heat a steamer and oil steamer rack well so momos won't stick on the bottom. Arrange uncooked dumplings in the steamer, leaving even amounts of space among them. Plenty of space among momos is essential so steam can flow freely. Close lid and steam for 12–14 minutes. The momos will look really shiny when ready. Remove momos off steamer and serve immediately with chutney.

Beer Braised Pork Sliders

2012: Chef Craig Sharp, Terra Waconia
in partnership with Elmbrink Farm

*"Always cook with love and respect for ingredients, the
earth they come from, the people who grow them, and
most importantly, yourself and your intuition."*
                                        —*Chef Craig Sharp*

*This simple one-pot dish is easy to transport and reheats well. It's a basic recipe meant
to be adapted to different seasons and tastes. Chef Craig Sharp and owner Tracy
LeTourneau suggest pairing these sliders with a simple slaw made of julienned apples,
carrots, and cabbage mixed with a bit of rice vinegar and a touch of maple syrup.*

YIELD: 24 SANDWICHES

10 pounds Red Wattle
    Boston butt or other
    pork butt or shoulder

2 tablespoons salt

1–2 tablespoons
    cooking oil

1 large red onion, diced

3 bottles oatmeal stout

¼ cup brown sugar

1½ cups tomato paste

¼ cup maple syrup

1 tablespoon fresh
    black pepper

2 teaspoons red pepper
    flakes, to taste

24 slider buns

Remove bones from pork. When using Red Wattle pork, remove most of the outer layer of fat. Red Wattles have great marbling of intramuscular fat, so you don't have to worry about losing flavor. If not using Red Wattle, skip to next step.

Cut pork into pieces (about 3-inch cubes) and pat each piece with a paper towel, drying them on all sides. Salt pork well. Preheat a small amount of oil in a pot large enough to fit all the pork and enough cooking liquid to cover it. Add onions and pork and cook together, sweating the onion and searing the pork on all sides. The pork and onions will begin to release liquid; this is the beginning of your cooking liquid.

Stir in the beer, sugar, tomato paste, and maple syrup, as well as enough water to just cover the pork. Bring to a boil, then reduce heat to a simmer and cover. Simmer for 2–3 hours, stirring periodically. The pork is ready when you are able to easily pull it apart with a fork.

Remove pork from the pot to a plate. Heat cooking liquid to reduce. Pull pork apart with 2 forks and return it to the pot. Add black pepper and crushed red pepper. Adjust seasonings, if necessary. Reduce to desired consistency. Serve on slider buns.

Grilled Young Hen with Potatoes and Sweet Corn Relish

2004: Chef Owner Mike Phillips, Chet's Taverna

"If you work with local farmers, you have to learn to roll with the punches. Working with farmers isn't easy all the time, but if you're committed then you stay committed and figure it out. There's a learning curve on both sides."

—Chef Owner Mike Phillips

Open from 1997–2004, Chet's Taverna was a small, intimate neighborhood eatery, seating fewer than fifty people. On weekends the tiny establishment was consistently packed. Nothing compared to Chet's on a super cold winter's night. Warm and cozy inside, the windows would fog up and ice over, giving the interior of the restaurant a gorgeous glow, like a lit candle burning inside of an ice lantern.

YIELD: 6 SERVINGS

For young hens:

3 young hens (Cornish
   Game Hens or small
   chickens may be
   substituted)
4–5 tablespoons olive oil
2–3 teaspoons salt
1 teaspoon pepper

For potatoes:

1 pound fingerling
   potatoes
2–3 tablespoons olive oil
salt and pepper, to taste

For sweet corn relish:

6 ears of corn, kernels
   cut from the cobs
1 cipollini onion, diced
   small
1 clove garlic, peeled
   and minced
2 Hungarian hot wax
   peppers, diced fine*
½ red bell pepper, diced
   fine
1 large heirloom tomato
   such as Pruden's
   Purple or ½ pint
   of Sungold cherry
   tomatoes, diced
¼ cup chopped fennel
salami, such as Red
   Table Meat's Big
   Chet's Salami
¼ cup extra-virgin olive
   oil
2 teaspoons cider
   vinegar
4 teaspoons lime juice,
   freshly squeezed
1 teaspoon sea salt,
   more to taste
1 teaspoon fresh black
   pepper
a pinch sugar
fresh basil, chiffonade

To prepare the hens: Preheat grill to medium-hot.

Prep hens by cutting out backbones; this is called spatch-cocking, which results in even cooking throughout. To spatchcock, lie hens, backbone down, on a cutting board. Using a very sharp knife or sharp kitchen shears, cut along one side of the backbone then along the other. Remove backbone and discard. With palm of hand, press firmly to flatten the hen. Repeat with remaining hens.

Coat thoroughly with olive oil, salt, and pepper. Place hens on preheated grill, skin side down, with a foil-wrapped (room temperature) brick on top of each. Cover grill, and cook 25 minutes. Remove brick, flip chicken, and grill 10 more minutes or until meat thermometer reads 165°F.

Allow hens to rest 10 minutes on a cutting board.

To prepare the potatoes: Blanch fingerling potatoes in boiling salted water until al dente. Cool. Slice into ¼-inch sections and coat liberally with oil, salt and pepper.

Grill slices of fingerling potatoes 5–7 minutes alongside cooking hens until tender.

To prepare the relish: Mix corn, onions, garlic, peppers, tomatoes, fennel, and salami in a medium-sized bowl. Stir in olive oil, vinegar, lime juice, salt, pepper, and sugar. Taste and adjust as needed. Serve at room temperature.

To serve: Cut hens in half or pieces for plating. Place hen and fingerlings on a plate and top with ½ cup of relish on each. Garnish with chiffonade of basil.

Shishito peppers could be used in place of Hungarian peppers or Fresno or jalapeños, if you want more heat.

Note: Chef Mike uses a foil wrapped brick but any heat resistant heavy object, such as a cast iron pan, can be used.

Suppertime

Food has roots in family.
Family has roots in food.
Sharing meals with loved ones is one of life's great
pleasures and honors.

Returning Home to Pettit Pastures

It was probably the worst day of his life, the day he sold off his two hundred head of dairy cattle. Words alone can't do justice to the anguish Tim Pettit felt during that time, saying goodbye to the only livelihood he had ever known and wanted. Non-farmers can only imagine the weight it bears, but farmers get it—not only losing your animals but feeling as if you've lost part of yourself.

It was the 1980's farm crisis; interest rates were high, milk prices had bottomed out, and farmers like Tim Pettit were earning pennies—if anything—for their hard work. The USDA was telling farmers to *get big* if they wanted to survive, otherwise *get out* because there wasn't going to be a future for them in farming. Tim and his wife Alice had two young children at the time, and it seemed as if the writing was on the wall: raising a family on a dairy farm was going to be an ongoing struggle. After selling his milking cows, Tim raised dairy heifers for other farmers for a short time until he determined he needed to sell their land, too—land previously owned by his great-uncle. Jake, their son, was only nine years old at the time, but he remembers it being a dark time for his family, how the auction was a terribly sad day.

Tim moved on to a long career in construction, and when Jake became an adult he joined his dad, working together as pipe fitters in the ammonia industry. Since ammonia is used in refrigeration, their work brought them inside food plants and slaughter houses across the country, giving them an intimate and disconcerting view into how mass quantities of cheeses and meats are handled in the US. During this time it became clear the father-son duo worked well together, shared a strong work ethic, and enjoyed each other's company even during long stints on the road. They also realized neither of them liked what they saw inside the industrial world of food processing; both felt drawn toward a healthier, more transparent food system.

Ever since Jake was a little boy, his mom Alice has lightheartedly referred to him as "Tim's clone." Besides getting along swimmingly, Tim and Jake think eerily alike, frequently saying out loud what the other was thinking at that exact moment. It happens often enough that it doesn't surprise anyone anymore. As the decades passed and Tim neared retirement, Jake planted a seed, asking his dad whether he had ever considered farming again, knowing full-well how much he still missed it. The truth was Tim always thought about it; despite the misfortune he'd endured in the '80s, he had never lost his desire to return to farming. He admitted this to Jake but followed quickly with an objection—he didn't want to be tied down three hundred and sixty-five days a year like he had been with dairy cattle. It turns out Jake had another idea; he'd been reading about raising grass-fed beef cattle and thought it sounded like a worthwhile endeavor they could pursue as a team. Tim could resume a life of farming he loved but Jake would share the responsibility and risk. Together, Jake proposed, they could create a quality product on their own terms while subverting the conventional food system.

It was a genesis, and the wheels began turning.

Given his experience running a conventional dairy operation, Tim initially felt skeptical about raising cattle on grass, but his long hiatus from farming had also broken any strong attachment or preconceived ideas he had held about right or wrong farming practices. He welcomed the new science Jake presented with curiosity and an open mind. Jake, knee-deep in research, was learning how grass-fed beef could not only produce a healthy product for consumers but also restore the health of soil through the addition of organic matter. The research also suggested how increased organic matter then enables soil to store carbon, creating a situation in which raising cattle on pastures fosters a neutral or positive environmental impact. It seemed like a win-win opportunity, and so they began.

In 2012 Tim and Jake, along with their spouses, bought a farm in Milaca and launched Pettit Pastures just as grass-fed beef was gaining a strong foothold in the market. But the farm they bought was in rough shape; half the land had been over-farmed and was nutrient-poor, and the other half consisted of severely overgrown and neglected pasture-land that had not been grazed in thirty years. Starting at ground zero but undeterred, they proceeded one step at a time, installing water lines, erecting fences, introducing heritage pigs to feast on the invasive buckthorn crowding their pastures, and seeding their land with a diverse mix of grasses, forbs, and legumes—the key to healthy pastures and cattle. Then they began rotationally grazing their cattle every one to three days—a balancing act that teeters on knowing exactly how to keep plants in a strong, nutritious stage for the cattle while also giving the soil what it needs. Just as the research promised, it wasn't long before improvements in their soil biology and overall land were visible to the naked eye.

Encouraging signs of life and health appeared everywhere on their parcel of earth, assuring their efforts were not in vain. Angleworms returned to the soil, as well as beneficial insects and spiders. Pastures began growing in lusher and greener than before, and plants recovered more quickly after a grazing. Soil tests now confirm improved nutrient density and increased organic matter, which skillfully sponges up rainfall and prevents their land from flooding as often as it did. And every year the quality of their meat gets better. Tim never dreamed how strong of a connection exists between cattle and rebuilding soil health, but he's a believer now. The results feel like a miracle. Tim and Jake are still a ways from where they want to be, but they're also a long way from where they were.

Farming together has reminded the father-son partners how anytime you work with others —family or not—it's not always going to be easy (even for clones). Sometimes their perspectives clash, but mostly Tim and Jake complement each other. Because Jake main-tains an off-farm job, Tim runs the majority of the farm's day-to-day operations, though Jake helps often after work and on weekends. As a direct market farm that sells all of its own meat, they also have a business to run, which Jake generally steers, taking the lead on marketing, sales, deliveries, and anything related to the Internet. They've found a rhythm that works.

After a thirty-year break from farming, Tim Pettit has found his way home again, work-ing alongside Jake. There's no other way to explain it; farming runs through his blood. And though the economics of the 1980s may have pushed him out, nothing could keep him away. The farm is where he's comfortable, where he feels he belongs. As Tim watches their cattle move from pasture to pasture, belly-high in grass, grazing tranquilly, the love he feels for the land and their cattle rises to the surface and he feels whole. Pettit Pastures is both an ecological restoration and a restoration of the farmer who has always lived inside Tim Pettit. The past and the present are reconciled.

Sloppy Joe with Crispy Fried Onions

2018: Main Street Farmer Eatery in partnership with Pettit Pastures

You can't go wrong with a good sloppy joe, and trust us—this is a tip-top sloppy joe. Using a combination of beef and smoked pork topped with crispy fried onions, the team at Main Street Farmer Eatery has taken an everyday family classic from something ordinary to something pretty special. This recipe builds in flavor so plan to start with a simply seasoned shredded smoked pork, which can be purchased from the butcher or made at home in the oven or crockpot using Liquid Smoke. (Here's a secret: sometimes chefs use liquid smoke.)

YIELD: 8 SERVINGS

For sloppy joe sauce:

¼ white onion, diced small

½ red pepper, diced small

1 tablespoon steak seasoning

2 cloves garlic, peeled and minced

¼ cup Memphis-style (vinegar-forward) barbecue sauce

¼ cup Worcestershire sauce

½ cup ketchup

2 teaspoons tomato paste

2 dashes Tabasco

For crispy fried onions:

1 white onion, sliced ¼-inch thick

¾ cup buttermilk

1 egg, beaten

salt and pepper, to taste

1 cup corn flour

2 teaspoons steak seasoning

To prepare the sauce: Sweat onion and red pepper in oil over medium-high heat until onion is translucent. Add steak seasoning and cook to incorporate. Add all remaining ingredients and simmer on low for several minutes. Sauce can be used immediately or chilled and stored in the refrigerator.

To prepare the crispy onions: Combine buttermilk, egg, salt, and pepper in a medium bowl. In a separate bowl, mix together corn flour, steak seasoning, and barbecue seasoning.

Heat oil in pan to 365°F.

Toss onion in corn flour mixture until coated, then dip in buttermilk. Shake off excess liquid, then add again to the corn flour mixture and turn until coated.

Lower onion rings into hot frying oil, leaving plenty of room between slices. Fry on one side for 60 to 90 seconds and flip, repeating until golden brown. Remove and drain on towels. Repeat with remaining onion slices.

2 teaspoons barbecue seasoning, store bought or from the North Shore Cider Braised Pulled Pork

canola or olive oil, for frying, at least 1-inch deep in your pan

For sloppy joe:

1 pound ground beef

1 pound pulled smoked pork*

sloppy joe sauce

buns, buttered and toasted on a grill

crispy fried onions

pickles, optional

*For simple smokey pulled pork (or use your favorite recipe):

3 pounds pork shoulder

salt and pepper

¼ cup broth or water

1 tablespoon liquid smoke

To prepare the sloppy joe: Brown beef in a skillet. Drain fat, then mix in smoked pork. Add sloppy joe sauce to skillet and heat through.

Build sandwiches with a generous portion of sloppy joe mixture, topped with crunchy onions and pickles, as desired.

*To prepare simple smokey pulled pork: Season pork generously with salt and pepper and place in a dutch oven or crockpot. Pour broth or water around pork and add liquid smoke. Cover with lid and cook at 300°F for 1 hour per pound of pork or, if using a crockpot, on low for 8 hours or on high for 4 hours. Meat should shred easily with 2 forks when done. You'll have plenty of leftover pulled pork which would make a great addition to serve with the Red Flannel Hash, page 36.

Herb Roasted Chicken with Farro Risotto

2015: Chef Mike Rakun, Mill Valley Kitchen in partnership with Kadejan, Inc.

The health-conscious cuisine at Mill Valley Kitchen is thoughtfully crafted to enhance the healthy lifestyle of its patrons. From listing the nutritional content of each dish on the menu to knowing their farmers personally, the team at Mill Valley Kitchen strives for total transparency. Farro, the ancient whole grain used in Chef Mike's risotto, is a type of high-protein, high-fiber wheat with a lovely, chewy texture.

YIELD: 4 SERVINGS

For chicken:

4 (6-ounce) skin-on, boneless chicken breasts

1 teaspoon salt

8 cracks freshly ground black pepper

4 tablespoons olive oil

6 sprigs fresh thyme

½ cup dry white wine

2 cups chicken stock

For garnish:

watercress or fresh thyme

To prepare the chicken: Preheat oven to 450°F.

Season chicken breasts with salt and pepper. Heat olive oil in large sauté pan over medium-high heat. Add chicken breasts skin side up and cook 3 minutes. Add thyme and flip chicken skin side down. Place pan in oven and roast for 10 minutes, or until chicken reaches an internal temperature of 165°F. Set chicken aside to rest; pour off excess cooking oil. Discard thyme sprigs.

Add wine to skillet and bring to a boil over medium-high heat. Reduce wine by half then add stock and reduce to 1 cup. Add salt to taste. Garnish with watercress or fresh thyme.

recipe continues . . .

For farro:

2 cups farro

4 cups water

2 tablespoons olive oil

2 teaspoons garlic, minced

1 tablespoon shallot, minced

½ cup mushrooms, diced small (shiitake, button, portabella)

2 cups chicken stock

¼ cup heavy cream

1 teaspoon salt

½ teaspoon pepper

¼ cup Parmesan or other hard local cheese, grated

To prepare the farro: Rinse farro under cold running water in a fine mesh strainer. Place in a pot with water and bring to a low simmer over medium heat. Cover and simmer until all water is absorbed, 15–30 minutes.

Heat olive oil in a heavy-bottom pan over medium heat. Sweat garlic and shallots until translucent. Add mushrooms and sauté until lightly browned. Add cooked farro, stock, cream, salt, and pepper. Stirring constantly, continue to cook farro until most of the liquid has been absorbed. Fold in cheese.

To serve: Place farro risotto in the center of shallow bowls. Slice chicken and place on top of risotto. Warm white wine reduction then drizzle over chicken. Garnish plates with watercress or thyme sprigs.

Barley Risotto with Lamb and Icelandic Skyr

2012: Chef Ian Pierce, 128 Cafe
in partnership with Star Thrower Farm

"Food is an art that touches all the senses. That's why I'm drawn to cook."

—Chef Ian Pierce

This hearty risotto feels like a big hug. The addition of Skyr, a tangy Icelandic yogurt sheep cheese, holds all the flavors of this dish together. Grab a big bowl and snuggle in.

YIELD: 6 SERVINGS

For barley:

1½ cups water

½ teaspoon salt

1 cup barley (pearl or hulled)

For spice blend:

1 teaspoon dry juniper berries

1 teaspoon coriander seeds

½ teaspoon caraway seeds

¼ teaspoon cumin seeds

3 cloves (whole)

For risotto:

2 teaspoons vegetable or olive oil

2 teaspoons butter

½ cup carrots, diced medium

½ cup red onions, diced small

To prepare the barley: Bring water and salt to a boil, add barley, and cover with a tight-fitting lid. Reduce heat to a simmer, and cook about 30 minutes. Barley should soak up all the water and still have a light chew to it. Spread on a tray to cool. Once cool, place barley in a bowl and cover. Refrigerate 1 hour to overnight.

To prepare the spice blend: In a dry saucepan over low-medium heat, toast spices until fragrant. Shake pan often as spices are toasting to prevent burning. Cool thoroughly, then grind finely.

To prepare the risotto: Heat a medium-large sauté pan over medium heat. Once hot, add oil and butter for a minute until hot, but not smoking. Add carrots, onions, and kale. Cook until fragrant and a little golden. Add garlic and ginger, and sauté until fragrant and golden, but not browned. Immediately add stock. Add cooked and cooled barley, spice blend, salt and pepper, and stir well. Simmer and stir until stock is reduced by half. Add lamb and herbs, taking care not to overcook them. Taste occasionally and tweak seasoning, if desired.

½ cup kale, chopped small

1½ tablespoons garlic, peeled and minced

2 teaspoons ginger root, minced

2 cups chicken stock

2 cups cooked barley

2 teaspoons spice blend

2 teaspoons kosher or sea salt

½ teaspoon black pepper

1 cup braised lamb meat, pulled or cut into 1-inch pieces (such as braised lamb, see page 222)

2 tablespoons fresh flat-leaf parsley, chopped (plus additional for garnish)

2 teaspoons fresh thyme leaves, chopped

⅓ – ½ cup Icelandic Skyr (plus additional for garnish)

When liquid is almost absorbed, stir in Skyr over low-medium heat. Check final seasonings. Risotto is done when most of the liquid is absorbed, although there should be a little "gravy" at the bottom of the pan.

Garnish risotto with a few spoonfuls of Skyr and some parsley leaves.

Pad Prik Khing: Long Bean and Pork Stir Fry

2011: Chef Owner Joe Hatch-Surisook, Sen Yai Sen Lek in partnership with Fischer Family Farms Pork

Chef Owner Joe Hatch-Surisook of Sen Yai Sen Lek presents Thai food as he remembers it growing up. Undoubtedly Thai, this simple stir-fry packs a flavor punch.

YIELD: 4 SERVINGS

- 2 tablespoons vegetable oil
- 1 pound pork loin, thinly sliced, marinated in 1 tablespoon fish sauce for 5 minutes
- 1 garlic clove, peeled and chopped
- 2 cups yard-long beans or green beans, cut into 1-inch pieces
- 2 tablespoons prik khing or red curry paste
- 1½ tablespoons fish sauce
- 4 kaffir lime leaves*, chiffonade
- 2 tablespoons water or stock
- red bell pepper (mild) or red Serrano pepper (hot), seeded and julienned, for garnish
- steamed rice, for serving

Heat vegetable oil in a wok or large fry pan (14-inch diameter or larger) over high heat. When pan and oil are hot, add garlic and pork and stir-fry approximately 1 minute. Add long beans and continue to stir-fry until pork is done and long beans are still crisp. Remove pork and long beans to a plate.

Return the wok or pan to medium heat, add curry paste and stir-fry until fragrant. Return the pork and long beans to the wok and continue to stir-fry, tossing/coating the pork and long beans with curry paste. Add fish sauce and half of the kaffir lime leaves. Deglaze with water or stock and stir-fry until thoroughly mixed. Remove to a plate and garnish with the other half of the shredded lime leaves and julienned red peppers. Serve with steamed rice.

Note: the entire cooking process should take no more than 4–5 minutes at most. Long beans should maintain their crispness.

*Kaffir lime leaves are available at Asian markets and some supermarkets.

Orange Butter-Roasted Carrots with Buttermilk Ranch Dressing

2020: Chef Owner Erick Harcey, Willard's
in partnership with Iron Shoe Farm

The classic carrot and ranch dressing combo gets dressed up and made over with some bright orange butter and a homemade savory buttermilk ranch dressing, elevating a simple kid favorite from ho-hum to tantalizing.

YIELD: 6-8 SERVINGS

For carrots:

2 pounds whole, washed and peeled carrots

salt and pepper, to taste

scant ½ cup orange juice

3 tablespoons unsalted butter, melted

2 small sprigs rosemary, cut into small pieces keeping leaves on the stem.

For ranch dressing:

YIELD: ABOUT 1 CUP

¼ cup mayonnaise

¼ cup sour cream

1 tablespoon buttermilk

1 tablespoon white miso

2 tablespoons fresh chives, chopped

1 tablespoon fresh flat-leaf parsley, chopped

1 tablespoon plus ¾ teaspoon onion powder

¼ teaspoon garlic powder

dash of fish sauce

dash of tamari

dash of hot sauce

2-3 teaspoons fresh lemon juice

To serve:

fresh dill, torn into pieces

hazelnuts, toasted and rough chopped

To prepare the carrots: Preheat oven to 400°F.

Place carrots on a baking sheet and season with salt and pepper. In a bowl combine orange juice and butter. Pour butter mixture over the carrots and, using a pastry brush, spread the butter mixture all over the carrots so that they are well coated. Add rosemary sprig pieces on top of carrots.

Place carrots in the oven to roast. While carrots are roasting, shake the pan a few times to turn the carrots and redistribute butter mixture. Roasting time should be 20–25 minutes until carrots are tender but not browned. If your carrots are thin, reduce to 15–20 minutes.

To prepare the dressing: Combine all ingredients except lemon juice; mix well. Add a teaspoon of lemon juice. Taste, and add more, if desired.

To serve: Remove carrots with tongs and place them on a platter. Drizzle with desired amount of ranch and top with a small handful of dill. Sprinkle hazelnuts over the dish and serve.

Hasselback Sweet Potato

2019: Owner Kari Grittner and Chef Tom Grittner,
Tillie's Farmhouse in partnership with Countryside Apple Farms

Hasselback potatoes are thinly sliced but not quite sliced through, leaving the potato intact as it bakes. Basting the potato with oil before it goes in the oven results in a crispy outside and a soft, creamy inside—a lovely textural dance. The sweet, heady, apple-y sauce is wildly delicious and also perfectly suited for pork tenderloin or chops.

4 medium-size sweet potatoes, peeled

3 tablespoons plus 2 teaspoons oil, divided

1 cup natural apple juice

¼ red onion, julienned

1 tart, red apple like SweeTango, Haralson, or Regent, julienned

2 fresh sage leaves, julienned

1 tablespoon freshly squeezed lemon juice

2 tablespoons unsalted butter

salt and pepper, to taste

Preheat oven to 425°F.

Make a series of ⅛-inch slices along each potato, slicing ⅔ of the way through. If you like, place chopsticks or wooden spoons on long sides of sweet potato before slicing. This can be helpful so you don't cut all the way through.

Place potatoes on a baking sheet and, using a silicone pastry brush, brush the outside of each potato and in between the hasselback slits with about 3 tablespoons oil. Roast until center of potatoes are tender and the outside is crisp, 50 minutes–1 hour. Halfway through roasting time, remove potatoes from oven and run a fork or spoon gently across the tops of the potatoes, using light pressure to fan the slices and separate from one another.

While potatoes roast, prepare sauce.

Boil apple juice until reduced by half.

In a wide fry pan, over medium-high heat, sauté onions, apples, and sage in 2 teaspoons oil until starting to brown. Add reduced apple juice and bring to a boil. Take pan off heat, add the lemon and then slowly stir in butter until melted and emulsified. Season with salt and pepper. Pour sauce over baked sweet potatoes.

Fall Greens Salad with Curry-Roasted Squash

2018: Chef Craig Sharp, Terra Waconia
in partnership with The Horticultural Research Center

Chef Craig loves the intensity of hardy fall greens like spinach, arugula, mustard greens, and kale for this salad, with a personal preference for leaning heavily on arugula and mustard greens. The addition of toasted walnuts and apples provides a satisfying crunch and sweetness, but the star is definitely the squash.

YIELD: 4 LARGE SALADS

For apple cider vinaigrette:

¼ cup avocado oil

2 tablespoons apple cider vinegar

1 tablespoon honey

1 tablespoon grainy mustard

salt and pepper, to taste

For the salad:

3 tablespoons sunflower oil

1 teaspoon curry powder

1 red kuri or buttercup squash, peeled and diced into ½-inch cubes

salt, to taste

1 pound hardy fall greens, cut or torn into pieces—if using arugula or mustard greens, leave whole

1 Honeycrisp apple, sliced

4 ounces blue cheese, crumbled

½ cup walnuts, toasted

To prepare the vinaigrette: Combine ingredients and shake well.

To prepare the salad: Preheat oven to 350°F.

In a warmed skillet heat sunflower oil and curry powder together. When curry powder becomes aromatic and starts to toast—but before it begins to smoke—add diced squash and salt. Sauté squash until it begins to caramelize, then transfer to a lined baking sheet and roast for roughly 20 minutes. Squash should be lightly browned on the outside and soft with a little bite. Squash may be served warm or cold.

Toss greens with apple slices and apple cider vinaigrette. Add squash and top with blue cheese and toasted walnuts.

Handmade Spaetzle with Sweet Corn, Bacon, and Fresh Sage

2005–2006: Chef Alex Roberts, Restaurant Alma
in partnership with Otter Creek Growers

Restaurant Alma, named after the Spanish phrase "alma del tierra" or "soul of the earth," has highlighted sustainable Minnesota food producers on its fresh-daily menu since opening in 1999. Chef Alex's spaetzle is deeply satisfying—and it makes the house smell amazing! If you don't have a spaetzle maker, use a colander with large holes. Once the dough has rested, the dish will come together in a slick 20 minutes.

YIELD: 4 SERVINGS

For spaetzle:

2 cups all-purpose flour

1½ teaspoons salt

⅛ teaspoon freshly ground nutmeg

½ teaspoon freshly ground pepper

¾ cup milk

4 eggs, beaten

salt for cooking water

olive oil

For sauce:

⅓ cup bacon, minced

2 tablespoons coarsely chopped fresh sage

freshly ground black pepper, to taste

2½ cups sweet corn kernels

¼ cup dry white wine

¼ cup water

1¼ tablespoons unsalted butter, plus more for sautéing

¼ cup Parmesan or other local hard cheese

salt to taste

To prepare the spaetzle: Add flour, salt, nutmeg, and pepper to a large bowl and stir. Add milk and eggs. Mix well. Allow batter to rest 15 minutes.

Bring a large saucepot of water to a boil, add salt, then reduce to a simmer. Place a colander or spaetzle maker over saucepot of simmering water and push batter through using spaetzle or other flat blade, allowing dumplings to drop into simmering water below. Cook 3–4 minutes; spaetzle will rise to the surface when cooked through. Pour spaetzle into colander and rinse with cool water. When cool, toss with a little olive oil to prevent sticking. Set aside.

To prepare the sauce: In a large skillet, cook bacon with a bit of butter over medium heat, stirring frequently until slightly browned. Remove 2 tablespoons cooked bacon and reserve for finishing dish. Add sage and a few grinds of black pepper, followed by corn and wine. Once wine has evaporated, add water, butter, and Parmesan. Stir constantly until water, butter, and cheese form a creamy sauce.

Add reserved spaetzle and stir until warmed through. Taste and adjust salt and pepper as desired. Serve with additional Parmesan and reserved bacon, if desired.

Living a Legacy at Ferndale Market

Visiting Ferndale Market turkey farm is like attending a big, boisterous family get-together—except with turkeys. The pasture party begins with a single turkey sensing a guest's arrival. A head pops up among the sea of white birds in the distance and excitedly alerts the flock—somebody new has arrived! Chatter ripples throughout the group, and the turkeys crane their bright blue and red heads to get a better view. Then, wings spread wide, they hastily propel themselves toward the newcomer, looking as though they could topple over at any moment in their frenzied rush to say hello. Enveloping the guest as if he is the last to show at a family reunion, the turkeys form a clumsy welcoming committee. Then a wave of uproarious enthusiasm erupts, spreading from one big, beautiful bird to the next, culminating in a collective mix of gobbles and cackles, which is surely saying, *"Welcome to Ferndale! Aren't you a sight for sore eyes? So glad you're here!"*

The interest these turkeys have in people, however, pales in comparison to how interested the farmers here are in the lifestyle of their birds. The generational thread of thoughtfully raising turkeys stretches back eighty years for the Peterson family. Walking the same fields his grandfather walked for five decades, John Peterson, third generation farmer at Ferndale Market, remembers his grandfather Dale often and feels tremendous gratitude for the life trajectory Dale created for their family back in 1939 when he launched the widely revered and distinctive turkey farm, Ferndale.

Ferndale Market is an independently owned, family farm raising 150,000 Broad Breasted White turkeys annually, and though it's the most common breed to raise domestically, Ferndale turkeys aren't like other turkeys. These turkeys are as unique as the Petersons and their devoted staff, who do everything within reach to support a good life for their birds, ultimately in exchange for the animals' lives. Ferndale turkeys are raised primarily outdoors where they enjoy sunshine, space to roam, fresh air, and exceptionally robust health as a result of their perfectly suited living conditions. None of which is an accident.

Founder Dale Peterson was a man with a plan and part of the first wave of turkey farmers in Minnesota. Both daring and practical, Dale was a product of the Great Depression and made it his goal to provide an affordable, low-cost protein for people. After studying poultry science at North Dakota State University and then getting his feet wet farming in North Dakota for a couple years, he embarked on a search for the ideal piece of property to raise his free-range birds. Turkeys don't do well in damp conditions, so Dale needed land with sandy soil that would drain thoroughly and provide a dry environment, which he ultimately found in Cannon Falls. Shortly after putting down roots and starting to raise turkeys he met his future bride, Fern. Fern and Dale became Ferndale, and so their story began.

Today the second and third generations of the Peterson family follow the exact blueprint laid out by Dale in 1939. John and his wife Erica moved back home to the family farm in 2008 post college, after realizing just how intense their interest and passion for local food systems had become. They joined John's parents, Dick and Jane, who never strayed from or lost faith in Dale's plan. During years of staggering consolidation and growth in the world of poultry, Dick and Jane had quietly bucked the agricultural trend of moving turkeys indoors, all in the name of practicality. If their system wasn't broken, they reasoned there was no need to fix it. The Petersons have never wavered in their beliefs:

Bigger doesn't always mean better, newer and shinier can't always compete with tried and true. This sets Ferndale apart among modern-day turkey farmers. Despite the fact that Minnesota farmers raise more turkeys than any other state in the nation—forty-five million annually—John estimates the number of free-range turkey growers left could be counted on two hands.

Ferndale turkeys are comedic show offs, proudly strutting their stuff to whoever is paying attention. Visitors to the farm can't help but smile at their curiosity and silliness, their cackles and murmurs. Even though John grew up with turkeys his whole life, he still delights in watching them, often finding himself getting lost in their animated antics on evening strolls out to the fields. Though it may sound exaggerated and anthropomorphic, the turkeys display playfulness and humor, no doubt encouraged by a natural habitat that allows them space to express innate behaviors. Baby chicks called poults are nurtured in a heated brooder barn, where they are hand-fed and hand-watered until old enough to be moved outdoors full-time. Once outside, turkeys are rotated to fresh grassy pasture each week where they can forage all summer long and seek shade under wood shelters when needed. By receiving what they need to thrive naturally, the birds enjoy remarkably good health and are raised entirely without antibiotics.

Building on Dale's sturdy foundation, John and Erica brought their own spin to the farm when they moved back, wanting to be involved not only with Ferndale but also with other farmers and the process by which food makes its way onto consumers' plates. They became instrumental in transitioning the farm to direct marketing and transforming Ferndale's former hatchery into a bustling, on-farm local foods grocery store, which connects shoppers with products from over seventy other farmers and community members. Now Ferndale Market exemplifies a true farm-to-table business where the Ferndale family knows the faces of their consumers, and consumers know the faces of their farmers. Everybody is braided together in a system built on integrity, quality, and relationships.

Dale passed away in 1989, but three generations later and eighty years after Fern and Dale began the journey, his legacy is alive and well. John feels incredibly proud to carry on his grandfather's legacy and share it with his own young son. He cracks a grin as he considers how amusing his grandfather would find the fuss frequently made over their farming practices today, how fascinated the public is by the *innovative* and *unusual* practice of raising turkeys outside. John imagines his grandfather scratching his head and asking, "What's the big deal?" After all, Dale wasn't trying to create a niche market at the time; he was simply raising his birds the way everybody did—seasonally and outdoors, geared toward both the Minnesota production season and, of course, Thanksgiving. It's a recipe for success that everyone in the family feels lucky to have inherited and honored to preserve. Perhaps even the turkeys.

Harry's Homemade Turkey Quinoa Burger

2020: Owner Harry Brand, Harry's Scratch Kitchen in partnership with Ferndale Market

A self-described "Italian boy from New York," Harry Brand grew up helping his grand-mother in the kitchen, a rare privilege not typically shared with boys in his family. Though she mostly gave him mundane tasks—shelling peas, grinding sausage, stirring sauces—those experiences sparked Harry's interest in crafting flavorsome food and feeding others well. In this not-so-average turkey burger, quinoa lends a pleasing texture and keeps the burger moist. The chipotle mayo leftovers are versatile and can be used in a variety of ways: as a sandwich spread or topping for fish tacos, or mixed with hard- boiled egg yolks for spicy deviled eggs or with goat cheese for a zippy dip.

YIELD: 4 BURGERS

For chipotle mayonnaise:

YIELD: ABOUT 1 CUP

2 chipotle chilis (from canned chipotles in adobo)

½ cup mayonnaise

¼ cup sour cream

1 tablespoon adobo sauce

1 tablespoon lime juice, about half a lime

For burgers:

1 cup chicken stock or water

4 tablespoons dry red quinoa

1 pound turkey breast with skin, or 1 pound ground turkey

4 tablespoons celery, diced fine

To prepare the mayonnaise: Chop or puree chipotles, then combine all ingredients in a small bowl. Whisk or fold together until thoroughly combined. Cover and chill until needed.

To prepare the burgers: Bring stock or water to a boil; add quinoa. Return to a boil. Turn off heat and let quinoa sit, covered, for 5 minutes. Drain well and cool.

If using turkey breast, run turkey through medium coarse grinder assembly. Alternatively, using a very sharp knife, cut turkey breast with skin into 1-inch cubes and pulse in a food processor until meat is ground. Hand dice any skin that didn't process.

In a large bowl combine turkey, quinoa, celery, salt, pepper, and garlic; mix together well. The mixture should hold together in a firm and slightly sticky ball. Place in refrigerator for 1 hour, then portion into 4-ounce patties. Keep cold until ready to use.

Season patties with kosher salt and cracked pepper. On a grill or in a non-stick frying pan that has been heated to medium-high, cook patties until lightly browned. Flip, then turn heat to low and cook about 4 minutes until starting to

¼ teaspoon salt

¼ teaspoon freshly
ground black pepper

¼ teaspoon granulated
garlic

For serving:

4 brioche buns,
buttered and toasted

1 avocado, sliced into
quarters

chipotle mayo

firm. Turn heat back up to medium-high to lightly brown the patty. Remove from heat. The turkey burgers should be cooked to 165°F.

To serve: Place each patty on a butter toasted brioche bun topped with avocado and a side of chipotle mayo to finish.

Grilled Lavender and Rosemary Crusted Pork Tenderloin with Heirloom Tomato Relish

2004: Chef Owner Lenny Russo, Heartland Contemporary Midwestern Restaurant

Chef Owner Lenny Russo, along with wife and partner Meg Hoehn, opened the beloved Heartland Contemporary Midwestern Restaurant in October of 2002, winning many awards for the elevated, seasonal dishes served at the quaint Mac-Groveland neighborhood restaurant. Heartland grew into a much larger space in Lowertown, St. Paul before eventually closing in 2016, but its stamp will forever remain in the Twin Cities dining scene and Russo will long be recognized as one of the first prominent chefs to insist farm fresh food from Minnesota could be as good as food anywhere else in the world. Chef Russo was raised in an Italian immigrant family that bought virtually all its food from neighboring farmers and artisans. In fact, he was ten years old before he stepped inside a supermarket, instilling in him an unwavering commitment to the importance of connecting with and supporting farmers.

This recipe is an impressive centerpiece but a quick prep for either a weeknight family meal or entertaining guests. The high-impact flavors are sure to be a hit.

YIELD: 4 SERVINGS

For pork:

5 tablespoons fresh rosemary, chopped

2 tablespoons dried lavender

2½ teaspoons fine sea salt

½ teaspoon black pepper, freshly ground

2 tablespoons sunflower oil

2½ pounds pork tenderloin

To prepare the pork: In a small bowl, mix together rosemary, lavender, salt and black pepper. Brush meat on both sides with sunflower oil and generously coat meat in herb mixture.

Grill pork over moderate heat for approximately 4 minutes on each side. Allow to rest before slicing. Spoon relish onto four serving plates and place pork slices on top.

recipe continues . . .

For relish:

2 teaspoons fine sea
  salt

2 tablespoons apple
  cider vinegar

2 tablespoons sunflower
  oil

1 tablespoon walnut oil

4 heirloom tomatoes,
  peeled, seeded, and
  diced

¼ cup green onions,
  thinly sliced

1 teaspoon garlic,
  peeled and minced

2 tablespoons fresh
  mint, chopped

½ teaspoon black
  pepper, freshly
  ground

To prepare the relish: Dissolve salt in vinegar in a mixing bowl. Whisk in oils. Add the rest of the ingredients. Mix well and set aside.

When pork is ready for slicing, spoon relish onto 4 serving plates and place pork slices on top.

Flank Steak with Orange Gremolata

2007: Chef Scott Pampuch, Corner Table
in partnership with Earth-Be-Glad Farm

Chef Scott Pampuch's career is a continually evolving story. From restaurant owner to consultant, executive chef to speaker and trainer, Scott's notable career tells the tale of a steadfast passion for flavorful, responsible food. No matter the role he's in, one thing has never changed: a commitment to food that reflects local, seasonal agriculture as closely as possible.

Though this is a fairly simple dish to prepare, it's chock full of flavor with the gremolata balancing the richness of the beef and the sweetness of the onions beautifully. Consider playing with the herby condiment by using lemons or other fresh herbs like mint.

YIELD: 4 SERVINGS

For gremolata:

1 tablespoon garlic, peeled and minced (about 1 medium clove)

¼ cup fresh flat-leaf parsley leaves, minced

1 tablespoon freshly grated orange zest (about ½ a navel orange)

For the steak:

1½ teaspoons balsamic vinegar

¼ cup olive oil

salt and pepper, to taste

1 pound flank steak

4 slices red onion, cut ⅓-inch thick, secured with wooden toothpicks

To prepare the gremolata: In a bowl toss together garlic, parsley, and zest.

To prepare the steak: In a shallow baking dish, large enough to hold steak and onion slices in one layer, whisk together vinegar, oil, and salt and pepper to taste. Add steak and onions and turn to coat with marinade. Marinate steak and onions, covered, for 15 minutes, flipping halfway through.

Preheat grill to medium-high heat.

Drain steak and onions and grill on an oiled rack set 5–6 inches over glowing coals. For steak, grill 5 minutes on each side for medium-rare. Grill onions until tender and starting to brown. Transfer to a cutting board and let stand 10 minutes.

To serve: Slice steak thin across grain. Serve steak and onions sprinkled with gremolata.

Roasted Beet and Ricotta Toast

2013: Chef Paul Berglund, The Bachelor Farmer
in partnership with Laughing Loon Farm

Eloquent and simple, these toasts are beautiful and impressive without a ton of effort. The beets can be roasted ahead of time and then brought to room temperature along with the cheese. The shallot vinaigrette can also be made ahead of time, but add the herbs just before assembly. Sometimes simple, straightforward food is the best.

4 medium-size beets, different colors, if possible; red, orange, and yellow show their color well when roasted

¼ cup rendered duck fat, room temperature (check with your butcher or specialty food store; or use the rendered duck fat from the duck breast recipe on page 202; it freezes well)

3 teaspoons kosher salt, divided

¼ cup almonds, raw

1 teaspoon plus 1 tablespoon grape-seed oil

1 small shallot, peeled and finely diced

½ teaspoon cider vinegar

1 pinch sugar

4 sprigs fresh flat-leaf parsley, finely chopped

1 sprig tarragon, finely chopped

1 cup ricotta, fresh, hand dipped is best

8 slices Scandinavian rye or any rye bread, toasted

Preheat oven to 350°F.

Peel beets and thinly slice to ⅛-inch thick with a mandolin. If you do not have a mandolin, cut beets in half lengthwise, then slice into ⅛-inch-thick slices. Place beets on a sheet pan with parchment paper. Brush with duck fat and sprinkle with 1 teaspoon kosher salt. Flip the beets over, brush other side with duck fat, and sprinkle with another 1 teaspoon salt.

Roast beets in the oven for approximately 20 minutes, flipping them over halfway through, until beets are fork tender but not crispy. Remove beets from oven and cool.

Place almonds on a baking sheet and roast in oven for about 10 minutes until fragrant and browned. Place in a bowl; toss with 1 teaspoon of grape-seed oil and ½ teaspoon salt. Transfer back to baking sheet and allow to cool. When cooled, rough chop them and set aside.

Place shallot in a small bowl and add cider vinegar, ½ teaspoon salt, and sugar. Let rest 15 minutes. Resting helps to take the bite out of the raw shallot. Then add the herbs and remaining tablespoon of grape-seed oil to the shallot mixture and combine. Taste and correct seasonings, if necessary.

To assemble: spread 2 tablespoons ricotta on each piece of toast and place on a platter. Add beets on top of cheese, varying the colors. Sprinkle shallot-herb mixture over beets then scatter almonds on beets and serve.

Cauliflower Fritters

2016: Chef Stewart Woodman, Culinary Director
at Kaskaid Hospitality
in partnership with Redhead Creamery

Chef Stewart Woodman first gained an appreciation for farmers at age nineteen during a brief stint picking strawberries. The grueling, back-breaking work opened his eyes to the intensity of the physical labor some farmers endure, and he never saw them the same. Over the years his appreciation has deepened through the rich day-to-day exchanges he shares with farmers dropping off goods. He sees farmers as his partners in helping to create memorable dining experiences for guests and has come to feel personally invested in their aspirations and successes.

For batter:

1 egg, separated

⅛ teaspoon salt

1 teaspoon unsalted butter, softened

½ cup plus 2 tablespoons all-purpose flour

½ cup water

2 teaspoons brandy

For cheddar sauce:

2 tablespoons unsalted butter

2 tablespoons flour

1 cup skim milk

¾ teaspoon salt

1 cup sharp, white cheddar, finely shredded

For cauliflower:

1 head cauliflower

1 tablespoon salt

6 quarts water

For fritters:

3 cups canola oil

kosher salt to taste

nutmeg, whole

To prepare the batter: In a medium bowl, whisk egg white to soft peaks; set aside.

In a clean medium bowl, whisk egg yolk, salt, and butter until thick. Add about a third of the flour to yolk mixture and whisk. Add about a third of the water to mixture and whisk. Add brandy. Continue whisking batter and adding water and flour, alternating between them, until all ingredients are fully incorporated. Fold in whipped egg whites. Refrigerate until needed.

To prepare the cheddar sauce: Melt butter over medium heat in medium pot. Add flour. Cook 5 minutes over medium-low heat. Stir constantly using a wooden spoon.

Add milk and salt. Turn heat to medium-high and stir constantly while bringing to a boil, then reduce heat to low. Simmer 8–12 minutes, stirring occasionally to prevent burning on the bottom of pan.

Stir in cheese over low heat for 30 seconds. Cover sauce and keep warm.

To prepare the cauliflower: Remove core from cauliflower and break remaining head into 2-inch florets. Bring salt and water to a boil in a large pot. Cook cauliflower until tender, about 5 minutes. Drain cauliflower into strainer, rinse under cold water until cool. Once cool hold in the refrigerator until ready to fry.

To make the fritters: Heat oil to 375°F in 1½-quart pot. Pour batter into medium bowl; add blanched cauliflower. Mix well.

Using a spoon, drop 6–8 coated florets into hot oil. Cook until golden brown—about 2 minutes. Using a slotted spoon, remove crisped florets to a paper towel. Immediately sprinkle with a pinch of salt. Work in batches until all florets have been cooked.

Spoon cheddar sauce onto a plate, then place florets on top of sauce. Grate nutmeg over cauliflower. Serve immediately.

Glazed Duck Breast with Stone Fruit Salsa

2004: Chef Russell Klein, W. A. Frost and Company
in partnership with Wild Acres

Chef Russell's duck recipe is utter perfection. The sweet glaze and accompanying stone fruit salsa strips away any hint of gaminess non-duck fans fear, leaving a perfectly balanced and composed dish. Both pretty and tasty, leftover salsa is outstanding served on pork or salmon or on top of a block of soft goat cheese with crackers.

For glaze:

1 teaspoon allspice
   berries

1 cinnamon stick

2 tablespoons coriander
   seed

½ teaspoon black
   peppercorns

½ cup wildflower honey

For stone fruit salsa:

YIELD: ABOUT 3 CUPS

½ pound assorted stone
   fruit, such as apricots,
   cherries, plums, etc.,
   diced ¼-inch

1 small shallot, minced

2 Fresno chilies, diced

4 dashes Tabasco

1 tablespoon
   champagne vinegar

1 jalapeño pepper,
   seeded and diced

½ bunch cilantro,
   chopped

3 dashes Worcestershire
   sauce

1 tablespoon extra-
   virgin olive oil

salt and pepper, to taste

For duck:

2 duck breasts

kosher salt and freshly
   ground black pepper,
   to taste

To prepare the glaze: Lightly toast spices in a skillet until fragrant over medium heat. Remove to a plate and cool. In a spice grinder or blender, grind cooled spices to a fine powder.

Mix spices and honey together in a saucepan and simmer gently until reduced by half. Reserve in a warm place.

To prepare the salsa: Mix ingredients together; allow to stand for 1 hour to let flavors come together.

To prepare the duck: Preheat oven to 350°F.

Score the fat on skin side of the duck, about ½-inch deep. Season both sides of duck with salt and pepper. Place breasts, fat side down in a warm sauté pan on medium heat. Slowly render the duck of excess fat, draining the pan as you go, reserving fat for another use, if desired. You may need to press down on the edges of the breast so that all the fat is rendered.

Once fat is rendered place pan in oven and cook for about 6 minutes, or until medium-rare. Remove duck from pan and let rest on a cutting board. Brush skin side with glaze and allow the duck to rest for 5–10 minutes before slicing. Arrange duck on plates and garnish with salsa.

Grilled Hanger Steaks with Swiss Chard and Tomato

2019: Chef JD Fratzke, Bar Brigade
in partnership with Thousand Hills Cattle Company

A suppertime meal this easy that tastes this good deserves a round of applause. Chef JD Fratzke has perfected the art of preparing steaks, in part because he believes in sourcing the best quality meat possible. Throughout the years JD has partnered with Thousand Hills Cattle Company to help him deliver the unforgettable, widely lauded entrées he's known for. The farmers at Thousand Hills Cattle Company all follow a specific grazing plan to produce their delicious, 100 percent grass-fed beef. The trick to successfully preparing grass fed beef—don't overcook it.

For swiss chard and tomato:

1 cup heirloom tomato, diced

salt and pepper

juice of 1 lemon, divided

4 tablespoons olive oil, divided

2 scallions, rinsed and chopped

1 teaspoon fresh thyme, chopped

2 cloves garlic, peeled, thinly sliced

1 bunch Swiss chard, rinsed, stemmed, chopped

2 ounces white wine

For steaks:

2 (10-ounce) hanger steaks, trimmed

kosher salt, to taste

black pepper, ground fresh, to taste

olive oil

optional: blue cheese for serving

To prepare the swiss chard and tomato: Place diced tomato in a non-reactive bowl. Add a few generous pinches of salt, 1 tablespoon of lemon juice, 2 tablespoons of olive oil, scallions, and thyme. Stir to coat evenly and leave at room temperature.

Heat a cast iron pan or heavy skillet to medium heat. Add 2 tablespoons olive oil; when warm, add sliced garlic. When garlic starts to soften and cook around the edges, add chard and wine. Stir vigorously to wilt chard, then reduce heat to low and cook until wine has reduced by about half. Add half of the remaining lemon juice, season with salt and pepper, taste and add more seasoning and lemon juice to taste.

To prepare the steaks: Heat grill to high heat. Season hanger steaks generously with salt and pepper. Lightly drizzle with olive oil. Set aside at room temperature.

Grill steaks over high heat for 3–4 minutes on each side for medium rare. Remove steaks and let rest for 10 minutes.

To plate: Slice steaks against the grain. Add any juices from the steaks to the tomato mixture. Divide swiss chard among 4 plates. If using blue cheese, add pieces of it to the hot chard on the plate. Add the tomatoes with juices and top with the hanger steak slices.

Cozy

Financial pressures, vulnerable business partnerships, bullying weather, physical aches and pains; there is no end to the challenges farmers endure. Farmers' ambitions and aspirations lie shrouded in uncertainties. Each day, each year, optimism and fortitude wrestle with powerful forces, many of which feel opposing and entirely outside of one's control. To be human is to seek comfort during trying times.

Forging Ahead at Yker Acres

Since becoming pig farmers in 2014, Matt and Sara Weik have alternated between feeling as if they're on top of the world, riding the winds of fortune, and periods of feeling down-trodden and powerless. They are not alone in their struggles. This is the story of every farmer. To pursue a life of farming is to know—with absolute certainty—it's going to be a wild ride on a treacherous and bumpy road. But deciding to be a farmer means putting your head down, anticipating and bracing for those inevitable bumps and bruises, and deciding to persist anyway.

Farming is a mental, emotional, and physical workout. There is never enough money on a farm to begin with, and unexpected costs pop up around every corner. The unpredictable nature of farming forces people to be adaptable. Catastrophic weather events can wipe out crops overnight, dramatically raise the cost of feed, destroy valuable property, and cause a cascade of consequences lasting years. Farmers know there are simply too many moving parts and opportunities for things to go wrong on a farm to expect otherwise. Something always seems to be breaking or falling through, including business relationships, which hinge on strong cash flow and stability from both parties and can change on a dime. Even as beginning farmers, Matt and Sara of Yker Acres in Carlton have already surfed through enough challenges to develop an ironclad trust in their abilities, but that doesn't mean the uphill battles haven't felt defeating at times.

The Weiks have never been ones to chase money, and they certainly didn't get into farming expecting to earn a lot. Actually, they never intended to become farmers at all. Their tale of becoming full-time pig farmers originates from a fortuitous three-way collision involving a deep reverence for nature and animals, a dedication to raising their own food, and their son Josey's talent and passion for cycling.

Their tale began with Josey's dream to race cyclo-cross professionally in Europe. He needed money and decided to raise pigs to fund his trip. This seemingly innocent decision dramatically shifted the course of his family's life when a pioneering chef in Minnesota's local food movement (and fellow cyclist) caught wind of Josey's entrepreneurial efforts and wanted to support him. The chef bought some pork, liked what he tasted, and wanted more. And then much more. Even after Josey left to race competitively in Europe, his temporary fundraiser continued to grow and quickly took on a life of its own. Matt and Sara, inspired by the opportunity unfolding and the idea of raising animals together, ambitiously picked up where Josey left off and officially launched Yker Acres in January of 2014. Today the family raises heritage breed pigs on pasture year round, and their Mangalitsa, Large Black, and Tamworth hogs frolic, play, and socialize—not unlike big, friendly dogs—in the lowest stress environment possible.

Like most modern-day beginning farmers, the Weiks didn't inherit a farmstead and had to build their operation from scratch—an expensive endeavor, especially as their business grew. Within just a few years of starting Yker Acres, the Weiks had reached capacity on their small sixteen-acre farm, and demand for their pork wholly supported expansion. Needing more land, equipment, and infrastructure to keep up, they made the bold decision to secure financing and take on more risk. Unfortunately, finding a lender brave enough to take a chance on a farmer is no small feat, even for picture-perfect borrowers like the Weiks. Their credit was impeccable—solid enough to buy a new truck or tractor without any fuss—they owned their small farm and vehicles outright, had no debt, and had three years of steady, continuous business growth behind them. Yet, despite a stellar track record, banks repeatedly denied them because they were farmers. Even banks federally subsidized to loan money to farmers denied them, concluding Matt and Sara's model of selling direct-to-consumer rather than to the commodity market was "too far outside the box and too risky." After six agonizing months of being told 'no,' Matt finally made a viable connection with a farmland finance company providing mortgages to small organic farmers. Yker Acres grew from sixteen acres to one hundred sixty acres, and the future looked bright.

But their streak of adversity continued. Just after scaling up, winds shifted and demand temporarily declined; the Weiks unexpectedly lost one of their largest buyers and a driving force behind their rapid growth. It happens in business. Customers come and go—and then sometimes come back. It wasn't personal, nor was it about quality or availability. The decision was rooted in numbers, and it was a devastating blow that left them scrambling underneath their new mortgage. With no choice than to rebound as quickly as possible, they added multiple new restaurant partners and learned an important lesson about diversifying their customer portfolio. While this was the first time they lost a partner, they soon learned it wouldn't be the last. Figuring out how to be financially sustainable is an ongoing challenge. Unlike many other entrepreneurial pursuits, if Yker Acres doesn't survive, not only will Matt and Sara lose their business, they'll also lose their home. This pressure and stress feels suffocating at times.

Just as business setbacks and the pervasive undercurrent of uncertainty build mental strength and resiliency, farm chores themselves build physical strength. Farming is physically strenuous even for relatively young, fit people like the Weiks. Though only in his late forties, Matt's body is starting to feel pretty beat up. The rigorous and repetitive activities of daily chores rival those demanded of athletes: hoisting themselves over gates innumerable times a day, repeatedly climbing in and out of the skid loader or tractor, lifting five-gallon buckets of water and twenty-three pound buckets of feed, forcing an ice chipper through frozen water or a pitchfork into rock-solid bedding in the dead of winter. The farm is an exhausting jungle gym, and their recovery time is minimal. Even Josey, *an elite, competitive cyclist*, added twenty pounds of muscle his first summer back working full-time on the farm. Sometimes when Matt wakes up in the morning, he can't move his wrists. The pain and damage of farming is taking a toll.

Despite the intense physical exertion, there are nights when Matt and Sara struggle to sleep, their minds busy with worry. At times it seems they're star-crossed farmers, unable to catch a break, fighting a system that makes it far too difficult to earn a living. Farming pushes their limits. But the deep, personal satisfaction they derive from positively contributing to the welfare of their animals and community urges them to persevere. Brief moments of self-pity are quickly soothed by the balm of appreciative customers, uplifting reminders that their work matters. Strong self-discipline pushes them out the door when it's thirty-five degrees, rainy and windy, and they don't have a choice to skip work that day. After all, the farm never closes for bad weather. Even on those blustery days, knowing they're going to get wet and feel unimaginably cold, the Weik family considers it a sincere privilege to provide families with responsibly raised food. They do not take this responsibility lightly, and so they remain on the wild ride they started, resolved and ready for the next round of challenges inevitably lurking around the bend.

OMC Smokehouse Pork and Grits

2018: Chef Owners Louis Hanson, Tom Hanson,
and Jaima Hanson, OMC Smokehouse
in partnership with Mirror Lakes Beeworks and Yker Acres

There's something in this dish for everyone. For the adventurous home cook with a smoker on hand, this smoked pork recipe straight from the pros at OMC (Oink, Moo, Cluck) Smokehouse is right up your alley. Prepare to be the hit of the neighborhood. For those not interested in smoking meat, cook the pork as desired but make sure to use the dry rub and barbecue sauce. No matter what, treat yourself to the cheddar jalapeño grits. Trust us.

For pork dry rub:

1¾ cups organic cane sugar

3 tablespoons sea salt

2 tablespoons paprika

1½ tablespoons chili powder

1½ tablespoons black pepper

2 teaspoons granulated garlic

1 teaspoon ground cumin

½ teaspoon dried sage

pinch of cinnamon

For the pork:

1 (3- to 4-pound) pork butt

1 cup pork rub, divided

3 gallons water, plus more for braising

8 cups water

1 cup cider vinegar, divided

For cheddar jalapeño grits:

3 cups cold water

1 cup 2 percent milk

2 teaspoons salt

½ teaspoon black pepper

1 cup coarse yellow cornmeal

1 small jalapeño, seeded and minced, or less for less heat

1 tablespoon unsalted butter

⅓ cup shredded cheddar

To prepare the rub: Combine all ingredients in a mixing bowl. Store any leftover rub in airtight container for later use.

To prepare the pork: Rub pork butt liberally with ¾ cup pork dry rub. Place pork butt on a sheet pan and cover with plastic wrap. Place in a refrigerator to sit for 2–3 days.

Load the smoker with wood, sugar maple and oak are suggested for the best taste. Place pork butt on rack in smoker. Add about 3 gallons water to pan in smoker. Smoke pork butt, according to smoker instructions, for 6–8 hours or until the pork reaches 170°F. Check every 2 hours to ensure constant temperature.

¼ cup shredded gouda

2 tablespoons sour cream

For chipotle cilantro barbecue sauce:

2 cups tomato sauce

1 cup apple cider vinegar

½ cup brown sugar

½ cup rhubarb cranberry jelly (recipe follows)

¼ cup local honey

2 tablespoons molasses

1 tablespoon fresh lemon juice

1 tablespoon Worcestershire

1½ teaspoons freshly ground black pepper

1½ teaspoons onion powder

1½ teaspoons prepared mustard

dash liquid smoke

1 tablespoon chipotle in adobo sauce

½ cup plus 2 tablespoons fresh cilantro, chopped

For cranberry rhubarb jelly:

½ cup cranberries

½ cup fresh rhubarb, chopped

½ cup organic cane sugar

¼ cup organic apple juice

Preheat oven to 250°F. Remove pork from smoker and place into a deep pot such as a dutch oven. Add water so it is covering just over half of the pork butt. Add ½ cup cider vinegar. Heat in oven until the internal temperature reaches 203°F, about another hour. Pork should be fork tender all the way through.

Remove pork butt from dutch oven and place into a large dish. Discard fat on top of liquid, reserving pork juice. Scrape off top fat cap on pork and pull meat into large chunks. Mix in additional ¼ cup dry rub, remaining cider vinegar, and reserved pork juices gently as you pull the meat. Shred pork, discarding any large pieces of fat. Do not overmix pork.

To prepare the grits: Combine water, milk, salt and pepper in a small stock pot and bring to a gentle boil. Slowly add cornmeal while whisking to avoid lumps.

Turn heat to low and let simmer. Add jalapeños, stirring frequently until cornmeal texture is no longer gritty, about an hour. Turn off heat and fold in butter, cheeses, and sour cream. Season to taste.

To prepare the barbecue sauce: In a large stockpot, combine all ingredients except chipotle and cilantro. Bring sauce to a boil, then reduce to a simmer. Simmer for 45 minutes. Stir frequently.

Remove from heat and add chopped cilantro and chipotle. Using a stick blender, puree until smooth or put everything into a blender and puree.

To prepare the jelly: Place all ingredients into a large stockpot and bring to a boil, stirring frequently. Turn down heat and simmer for 30–45 minutes. Blend finished product with a stick blender and allow to cool; or cool, then blend in a standing blender.

To serve: Spoon grits onto plate and top with a generous helping of pork. Serve Chipotle Cilantro Barbecue Sauce and Cranberry Rhubarb Jelly on the side.

Lucia's Braised Pot Roast with Roasted Root Vegetables

2008–2009: Chef Lucia Watson, Lucia's
in partnership with Hidden Stream Farm

Minnesota chefs have long relied on Lisa and Eric Klein of Hidden Stream Farm to supply them with everything from animal protein to vegetables. Lisa and Eric raise grass-fed beef, pork, and pastured chickens and also run a "food hub," which Lisa started to help farmer friends move their surpluses. Today it has grown into a vibrant network of farmers working together to supply grocery stores, restaurants, and farmers markets. This simple pot roast is packed with flavor. Leftovers are delicious served as a sandwich.

For the roast:

3-4 pounds beef chuck roast

kosher salt, to taste

freshly ground pepper, to taste

¼ cup olive oil

1 cup carrots, diced

1 cup celery, diced

1 cup yellow onion, diced

½ cup red wine

3 tablespoons tomato paste

1 teaspoon fresh thyme, chopped

1 teaspoon fresh flat-leaf parsley, chopped

1 teaspoon fresh rosemary, chopped

1 head garlic, ½-inch from top removed to expose cloves

6-8 cups beef or chicken stock, or combination

For roasted root vegetables:

6 cups assorted root vegetables, cut as desired, but into similar size pieces (carrots, parsnips potatoes, rutabaga, celery root)

½ cup olive oil

kosher salt

freshly ground pepper

Preheat oven to 425°F.

To prepare the roast: Season both sides of meat generously with kosher salt and pepper. Heat olive oil over high heat in a heavy pot until almost smoking. Add roast and brown on all sides. Remove from pan and set aside. Lower the temperature to medium-high. Add carrots, celery, and onion and cook for about 5 minutes. Add red wine and cook about 5 more minutes. Stir in tomato paste, thyme, parsley and rosemary. Add garlic and enough stock to just about cover roast. Bring to simmer then reduce heat and cook on stovetop, covered, for 3-4 hours. Alternatively, place into an oven set at 300°F for the same amount of time. Meat should fall apart when done.

Remove meat from pot and strain liquid. Discard vegetables. Return liquid to heat and cook over moderate heat until it thickens. Return meat to pot to rewarm. Gently pull apart and serve with root vegetables.

To prepare the vegetables: Toss vegetables in olive oil, salt and pepper on a sheet pan. Roast about 25 minutes until tender and caramelized.

Wild Mushroom Fricassee with Jalapeño and Honey Glazed Onions

2007–2008: Chef Matt Schoeller, Signatures
in partnership with Whitewater Gardens

The word fricassee *usually refers to a dish made from sautéed and stewed meat, often chicken, served in a creamy white sauce. In this recipe mushrooms take center stage rather than meat, creating a thoroughly satisfying vegetarian fricassee. Serve with creamy polenta.*

YIELD: 4–6 SERVINGS

For fricassee:

4 tablespoons unsalted butter

2 pounds wild mushrooms, best available mix

1 medium yellow onion, diced

2 large cloves garlic, peeled and minced

1 cup red wine

¼ cup heavy cream

2 teaspoons fresh marjoram

creamy polenta, page 223

For onions:

8 small onions (cipollini or smaller type onion), peeled and left whole

¼ cup honey

1 jalapeño pepper, seeded and diced fine

To prepare the fricassee: Melt butter in a large saucepan on medium-high heat, then sweat mushrooms, onions, and garlic in butter. Add wine, reduce heat, and simmer until reduced by half. Add cream and reduce to thicken. Stir in marjoram.

To prepare the onions: Preheat oven to 350°F. Place peeled onions in a shallow baking pan with fitted lid. Blend honey and jalapeño in a blender or food processor and drizzle over onions. Cover, place in oven, and roast until soft, 30–40 minutes.

To serve: Place warm, prepared polenta into a shallow bowl. Top with wild mushroom fricassee. Add 2–3 roasted onions to each bowl. Drizzle onions with warm jalapeño honey sauce from onion pan. Finish each dish with a drizzle of mushroom juices.

Braised Pork Shank with Smoked Bacon Risotto and Crabapples

2006–2007: Chef Owner Jim Kyndberg, Bayport Cookery
in partnership with Fischer Family Farms Pork

"Life is a journey, so take along plenty of good food and drink."
—Chef Jim Kyndberg

Though Bayport Cookery is no longer, its legacy lives on through beautiful dishes like this one. Bayport Cookery was all about highlighting local flavors in a warm and inviting atmosphere. Though the local food movement was still centered in the Twin Cities, Chef Kyndberg was brave enough to take his philosophy of supporting farmers outside this epicenter to a new audience. Perfect for a chilly day when you need some inner warmth, this "low and slow" dish will reward you richly for the time you invest.

YIELD: 6 SERVINGS

For pork shanks and sauce:

4 tablespoons extra-virgin olive oil

3–4 pork shanks (3–5 pounds)

4 teaspoons salt

3 teaspoons pepper

1 cup yellow onions, chopped

1 cup carrots, chopped

1 cup celery, chopped

2 sprigs fresh thyme

1 bay leaf

3 whole peppercorns

3 whole allspice

2–3 cups chicken stock

2–3 cups water

1 tablespoon unsalted butter

salt and pepper, to taste

To prepare the pork: Preheat oven to 200°F.

Heat olive oil in a skillet over medium high. Season pork shanks with salt and pepper, then brown all sides in skillet. Transfer shanks to a roasting pan or dutch oven and add onions, carrots, celery, thyme, bay leaf, peppercorns and allspice. Add chicken stock and water in equal amounts to halfway cover the shanks. Cover with a lid or foil and slowly braise shanks for 3-4 hours, flipping shanks halfway through the cooking process. Meat will fall off the bone when done.

Remove meat from roasting pan; set aside. Strain liquid through a fine mesh sieve and skim any fat from top of liquid. Heat liquid in a saucepot until reduced by half. Stir in butter and season to taste.

To prepare the risotto: In a heavy saucepan, cook bacon over medium heat until lightly browned. Add onions and garlic and sauté until translucent. Stir in rice and sauté until lightly golden brown. Add wine and 1 cup stock. Stir until liquid is absorbed. Continue adding stock or water 1 cup at a time, stirring continuously and allowing each cup to get absorbed before adding the next, to slowly cook

For risotto:

8 slices smoked bacon, chopped

1 medium onion, diced

1 clove garlic, peeled and minced

2⅓ cups Italian Arborio rice

½ cup white wine

9 cups stock or water (hot)

1 cup grated Parmesan

salt and pepper, to taste

½ cup cream (optional)

For crabapple garnish:

8 chestnut crabapples, or firm-flesh tart apple, skins left on

1 tablespoon unsalted butter

¼ cup apple juice or white/rose wine

3 cups arugula, loosely packed

rice. Stir in cheese and season to taste. Rice is done when creamy; grains should be al dente. Add cream to desired consistency.

To prepare the garnish: Remove crabapple cores and slice into thin wedges. Heat skillet over medium heat and melt butter. Sauté apples in butter until lightly browned. Add apple juice and simmer until most of the liquid has been absorbed. Remove from heat and add arugula. Stir greens until wilted.

To plate: Spoon risotto on center of plates; remove pieces of pork from shanks and shred lightly Place pork on top of risotto, spoon crabapples and arugula on top of pork and drizzle on braising sauce.

Lamb Ragout with Creamy Polenta and Camembert

2009–2010: Chef Mike Phillips, The Craftsman in partnership with Star Thrower Farm

For those lucky enough to have dined at The Craftsman, chances are good you savored one of Chef Mike Phillips's legendary ragouts. Mike insists the secret to a really good ragout or bolognese begins with sweating guanciale and vegetables together. Guanciale is cured pork made from the cheeks of a pig and is full of collagen, which gives sauces a velvety mouth feeling you don't get if left out. The chicken liver is important too, adding a subtle layer of sweetness. Always committed to using whole animals, every cut and part found delicious homes in his ragouts. This recipe yields quite a bit of leftover braising liquid with good quality gelatin. Consider freezing the liquid in small portions to reuse later, stirring it into simmered cream and tossing with pasta or adding to soup bases for a richer flavor.

YIELD: 8-10 SERVINGS

For braised lamb:

lamb shoulder plus 2 lamb shanks (5 pounds lamb)

kosher salt and freshly ground black pepper, to taste

2 tablespoons olive oil

½ yellow onion, chopped

½ cup carrot, chopped

½ cup celery, chopped

7 garlic cloves, peeled and smashed

⅓ cup tomato paste

2 cups red wine

8 cups beef or chicken stock

2 bay leaves

To prepare the lamb: Preheat oven to 400°F.

Season lamb with salt and pepper. Heat oil in a heavy-bottom braising pan or large dutch oven. Brown lamb on all sides and remove from pan. Drain fat.

Add vegetables and garlic to pan. Season with 1 tablespoon salt and 1/2 teaspoon pepper and sauté until browned, scraping bits from bottom of pan. Add tomato paste, stirring to coat vegetables. Add wine and return lamb to pan. Add stock and bay leaves. Cover pan and braise in oven until meat falls apart, about 3 hours. Remove lamb from pot and chill braising liquid. When lamb is cool enough to handle, pull meat off the bones and set aside. Remove fat from chilled braising liquid. Strain and discard vegetables. Reserve stock.

To prepare the ragout: In a heavy bottom saucepot, sweat guanciale or pancetta, vegetables, garlic, and bay leaf covered on low heat. When onions and pancetta are translucent, add lamb meat and a few cups of braising liquid until lamb is fully saturated. Heat lamb at a low simmer until hot,

For ragout:

½ cup guanciale or pancetta, diced

½ cup yellow onion, diced

⅓ cup carrot, diced

⅓ cup celery, diced

1 clove garlic, peeled and chopped

1 small bay leaf

½ cup lamb or chicken liver, chopped

reserved meat and braising liquid

For creamy polenta:

8 cups boiling salted water

2 cups polenta

½ stick butter

salt and pepper, to taste

To serve:

1 cup Camembert

fresh Parmesan

adding more braising liquid as necessary. Taste and adjust seasonings.

To prepare the polenta: Boil water in a heavy bottom pot. Add polenta slowly, stirring with a whisk. Reduce heat to low and cook for about an hour, stirring frequently with a whisk. When polenta is soft and grains are tender, remove from heat. Add butter and adjust seasonings.

To serve: Ladle polenta into a wide bowl. Scoop a tablespoon of Camembert cheese out of the rind and dot on top of polenta. Repeat with a few more tablespoons, to taste. Ladle ragout on top. Grate Parmesan over the top.

Roasted Garlic Cream Soup with Parsley Oil

2005–2006: Chef Owner Lenny Russo, Heartland Contemporary Midwestern Restaurant
in partnership with Cedar Summit Farm

Creamy and rich yet simple to prepare, this soup embodies comfort and is the perfect antidote to a cold wintery day.

YIELD: ABOUT 8 CUPS

For soup:

5 large whole garlic bulbs

4 tablespoons unsalted butter, room temperature (divided)

1 cup whole milk

½ teaspoon fine sea salt, plus more for finishing

¼ teaspoon finely ground white pepper, plus more for finishing

1 quart heavy cream

2 cups vegetable broth or homemade court-bouillon

2 tablespoons cream sherry

1 bouquet garni of 1 fresh bay leaf and 2 sprigs fresh thyme

For parsley oil:

1 bunch fresh Italian parsley

1 cup sunflower oil

Preheat oven to 400°F.

Cut tops off garlic bulbs to expose cloves and place root side down in a baking dish; dot with 2 tablespoons butter. Cover dish tightly with lid or foil and bake for 40–45 minutes. Remove and cool. Press garlic pulp out of skins and place in a blender with milk, ½ teaspoon sea salt, and ¼ teaspoon white pepper. Puree, then add to a small saucepan. Heat to a simmer and allow flavors to meld, about 10 minutes.

While roasted garlic milk mixture is heating, heat cream and broth in a medium saucepan over low- to medium-heat. Add sherry and bouquet garni, season, and simmer 20 minutes, whisking occasionally to prevent scalding. Remove bouquet garni. Add roasted garlic milk to cream mixture, whisking until thoroughly combined. Allow soup to simmer for 5 more minutes then remove from heat and whisk in remaining 2 tablespoons butter.

Puree parsley with sunflower oil using a blender or food processor. Pour oil through a fine strainer and discard pulp. Ladle soup into bowls and drizzle parsley oil into soup.

Swede Hollow Meatballs

2009: Chef JD Fratzke, The Strip Club Meat & Fish
in partnership with Thousand Hills Cattle Co.

*Black truffle powder, sherry, brandy—these aren't your typical Swedish meatballs;
these are flavor bomb meatballs. Though the black truffle powder is a specialty
ingredient, it helps develop a bold and enticing depth of flavor in the gravy. Don't
skip it. These meatballs are delicious served over mashed potatoes and topped with a
small dollop of lingonberry sauce from Daybreak, if possible. Some sliced and salted
cucumbers or your favorite cucumber salad make a pleasant side.*

For meatballs:

1 cup yellow onion, chopped

½ cup garlic, peeled and minced

1 egg

¼ cup balsamic vinegar

1 pound ground grass-fed beef

1 pound ground pastured pork

2 tablespoons ground allspice

2 tablespoons sea salt

1½ tablespoons smoked paprika

1 tablespoon fresh cracked black pepper

¼ cup breadcrumbs

For simmering liquid:

2 quarts chicken stock

⅔ cup madeira or cream sherry

⅓ cup brandy

2 cinnamon sticks

3 large sprigs fresh rosemary

For gravy:

½ cup unsalted butter

½ cup flour

1 tablespoon ground black truffle powder

2 quarts meatball simmering liquid, hot

pinch of sea salt

pinch of black pepper

To prepare the meatballs: Place onions, garlic, egg, and balsamic vinegar in bowl of food processor and puree into a loose paste. Transfer to a large mixing bowl and add remaining meatball ingredients. Mix well by hand until all ingredients are well incorporated. Cover with plastic wrap and transfer to the refrigerator to set, about an hour.

To prepare simmering liquid: While the meatball mixture rests, make the simmering liquid. Heat a large saucepan or dutch oven on the stove top over medium and add chicken stock, madeira or sherry, brandy, cinnamon stick, and fresh rosemary. When stock begins to boil, reduce heat to low and simmer.

Remove meatball mixture from refrigerator. Roll into meatballs slightly smaller than a golf ball and place onto a plate or baking sheet.

When meatballs are all rolled, lower half into the simmering liquid and cook for 10 minutes. Remove with a slotted spoon and place on a rimmed baking sheet and repeat with the second half of the meatballs.

To prepare the gravy: Place a large sauté pan over medium-low heat and melt butter. Whisk in flour and black truffle powder until a light paste forms. Whisk in hot meatball liquid and keep whisking until thick. Taste the gravy and adjust with salt and pepper to taste.

Add meatballs to gravy and simmer for a few minutes until very hot and serve.

Porter Braised Bison Roast

2016: Executive Chef Paul Lynch, FireLake Grill House & Cocktail Bar in partnership with Eichten's Bison

Nearly 30 years ago Ed Eichten and sister Eileen were looking for a meat alternative to complement the award-winning cheese business started by their parents. They took a chance on bison, beginning with one animal. When the meat sold out in ten days, they purchased thirteen additional animals. Today they maintain a herd of roughly one hundred fifty majestic bison, which graze on roomy pastures on their farm in Center City.

YIELD: 6–8 SERVINGS

- 8 slices bacon, cut into ½-inch pieces
- 3 pounds bison chuck roast
- kosher salt, to taste
- freshly ground black pepper, to taste
- 2 small yellow onions, peeled, sliced 1-inch thick
- 6 tablespoons Dijon mustard
- 3 tablespoons tomato paste
- 2 cups dark porter beer
- 3 cups au jus or very rich beef stock*
- ⅔ cup red wine vinegar
- 9 green peppercorns, crushed
- 1 large bay leaf
- 1 large sprig fresh sage
- 2 sprigs fresh thyme

braising juice from Lucia's pot roast on page 214 is perfect

Preheat oven to 350°F.

Heat a dutch oven or heavy bottom braiser to medium and add bacon. Cook until the fat is just rendered. Remove with a slotted spoon and set aside.

Cut bison across the grain into 2 large slabs, season with salt and pepper, and then brown in bacon fat. After all bison is browned, remove meat from the pan and pour off fat. Add onions to pot and cook until browned, about 5 minutes. Add mustard and tomato paste; cook 2 minutes. Add beer, au jus, red wine vinegar, and green peppercorns. Bring to a boil. Add bay leaf and return bison and bacon to pan. Cover and cook in oven until tender, approximately 2 hours 45 minutes or until meat separates easily using 2 forks.

Cool meat in braising liquid, then skim excess fat from top. Remove meat and slice into pieces, then place into a baking dish and pour some of the braising liquid over the top. Cover and reheat in the oven. While bison is reheating, strain remaining braising liquid into a pan and add sage and thyme. Bring to a simmer, then reduce to coating consistency, about 15 minutes. Serve bison with sauce.

Bison roast can be prepared 48 hours in advance. When ready to serve, simply reheat roast with reduced sauce in a covered dish at 350°F.

The Resiliency of Shepherd's Way Farms

There are a couple prerequisites to becoming a farmer. One is the love of a good challenge. The other is resiliency. If either is missing, chances are the story isn't going to end well.

Farmsteads are naturally idyllic, which might explain why pictures and stories depicting farm life too often conjure up overly romanticized visions of a much harsher reality. Images of tidy, groomed fields, perfectly painted red barns, baby animals, and vivid sunsets offer idealized glimpses of life on a farm but fail to show its inherent messiness and cracks. In truth a life of farming, however bucolic and purposeful, is also synonymous with hardship, just as life itself cannot escape hardship. These hardships come in all shapes and sizes and, too frequently, are sneaky reminders of how many things lie outside one's control. Sometimes it is hard to tell which challenges are big and which are small.

Luckily, challenges don't scare Jodi Ohlsen Read of Shepherd's Way Farms in Nerstrand. She and husband Steven Read both possess the sincere love of a challenge and seem as though they were born to overcome obstacles. *"Challenges are opportunities,"* is a phrase Steven repeats often, no doubt gleaned from decades weathering a hardscrabble life on their farmstead sheep dairy and creamery, where he and Jodi raised four sons and built a trailblazing business together. Though having problems can be frustrating and draining, for people like the Reads it also keeps them engaged and fuels them with a sense of purpose. They actually see challenges as part of the draw of being a farmer. Throughout the years the Reads have learned how adversity can ignite surprisingly creative solutions and forge connections, how being pushed to expand forces positive growth. They've learned what they're made of.

College sweethearts who married young, Jodi and Steven knew early on in their relationship they wanted to pursue meaningful work together that involved creativity, respect, and caring for land, animals, and the environment. Perhaps most importantly, they wanted to construct a life where family and work weren't divided. While in graduate school for agricultural education, Steven was introduced to the concept of raising sheep, an idea that stubbornly embedded itself in the couple's minds and wouldn't let go. In 1994, trusting an inkling that farming might provide the lifestyle they sought, Jodi and Steven bought forty sheep and began their family-based, family-run farm, Shepherd's Way Farms.

In the beginning they sold milk from their East Friesian crosses through a dairy cooperative. But when a main buyer abruptly pulled out and left the Reads with excess milk, they were pushed to evolve. Jodi and Steven dove into the challenge head first, researching and seeking expertise at the University of Minnesota where they quickly made their first batch of cheese with the lead cheesemaker. Jodi soon began immersing herself in learning the art and science of artisan sheep milk cheesemaking and became one of the first producers of sheep milk cheese in the nation. It was 1998 and sheep milk cheeses, still extremely rare in the US, were frequently met with suspicion, hesitation, and the need for basic education. Some folks had no idea sheep could even be milked;

others were convinced the Reads were actually making goat cheese. Yet despite consumer hesitation, Jodi's cheeses were immediately well-received and quickly winning awards. *Challenges are opportunities.*

The demands of farming are ongoing, often unforgiving, and most always untimely. Decades of running both a farm and production facility have turned Jodi and Steven into professional problem solvers. With so many moving parts raising livestock and making cheese, repairs on their farm happen weekly and are never surprising—they're expected. To make matters more intense, amidst all the chaos, the farm doesn't pause when something breaks—even if it's the farmer herself. Like the time Jodi accidentally stepped in a hole her dog dug and broke her ankle. The very next day she and Steven made cheese together. What else could they do? The vats were already full of milk and she couldn't very well tell the sheep to hold their milk for five days while she elevated her foot. Long hours, staffing challenges, the inability to take an extended vacation together: Jodi classifies all these examples—even her broken ankle—as small nuisances. Yet each illustrates a more realistic picture of farmers' lives: The farm's needs come first. Simply shutting the door on unfinished work and going home is never an option.

Without a doubt the Reads' biggest hardship hit in January of 2005, an unimaginably tragic event that would test their mettle for years. Two arson fires, just days apart, ripped through their property and changed everything—their family, farm, and future—in a matter of hours. First, someone set their round bales on fire in the middle of the night. A neighbor, awake early for work, saw the flames and quickly alerted both the fire department and the Reads. While terrible and pointless, it paled in comparison to the utterly horrific site the same neighbor woke to several nights later: the Reads' lambing barn engulfed in flames. Moving as quickly as possible, Jodi and Steven did everything they could to rescue sheep while fire departments from several communities worked to stop the devastating blaze, but ultimately they lost their lamb nursery and all of their lambs, many of their adult sheep, and their large free stall barn.

This cruel, catastrophic act brought vast repercussions. The Reads ultimately lost over four hundred sheep and were unable to breed or lamb their own animals for many years. Prior to the tragedy they had one of the largest dairy sheep herds in the country; sixteen years later they're left raising half the number of animals they did then. Jodi and Steven had to let all of their staff go, and then they took a hard look at whether or not they still wanted to farm. Unbelievably, despite everything—the trauma, uncertainty, the difficult financial reality ahead—they determined they did and began slowly and intentionally rebuilding Shepherd's Way Farms.

While the fire was devastating beyond belief, the outpouring of emotional and financial kindness and generosity that followed somehow managed to dwarf the tragedy, humbling the Reads. The hardship forced Jodi, Steven, and their sons to dig deep and draw on inner resources they hadn't known existed, resiliency they had no idea they could muster. In this most vulnerable time power and strength emerged, emanating from both their immediate family and also their extended food and farming family, which felt equally stunned and attacked by the fire. Minnesota's tight-knit local foods community quickly enveloped them in a protective warmth, and the Reads discovered just how threaded together they are with others. Though life felt frighteningly fragile, the Reads also realized they were not alone in their pain and found fortitude in connection. Even now people throughout Minnesota still remember and reference the fire as if it were their own, because in many ways it was. Everybody is connected to farming somehow.

Jodi and Steven live in an old farmhouse built in the late 1800s. There is a window facing the west pasture where the sheep often roam, and the view from that window in winter is bleak, a monochromatic gray and white snowscape. As Jodi looks out and watches the wind whip across the snowy fields, she sometimes wonders how many other farm families have stood in that exact same spot over the decades and simply resolved to endure whatever came their way, just as they have done time and time again.

The Reads are one of the most well-known farmstead sheep cheesemaking families in the nation. But this never was their goal—their goal was to raise their sons on a farm and create a lifestyle with purpose. Each day, as they tenderly care for their herd and produce artisan cheese, everything they do, everything they make, is in pursuit of this goal. They believe the small family-based farm holds an important place in society, and so they endure. Their history of hardships, big and small, have certainly played a big role in their story, but they do not allow them to become their story's ending.

Croque Monsieur

2012: Chef Jeffrey Lundmark, Domacin Restaurant and Wine Bar in partnership with Shepherd's Way Farms

Chef Jeffrey elevates the already perfectly pleasing Croque Monsieur into a gooey, velvety, mind-altering experience. Settle in with a thick cloth napkin (you'll need it) and do your best to savor each bite. If you can't get your hands on Shepherd's Hope cheese by Shepherd's Way Farms, substitute a local burrata or mozzarella instead.

For the Croque Monsieur:

8 (½-inch) slices brioche bread, or a good cottage loaf

4–6 tablespoons unsalted butter, room temperature

5–6 ounces Shepherd's Hope cheese, cut into 8 slices

12 slices prosciutto, thinly sliced and crisped over medium heat in cast-iron skillet

For Mornay sauce:

1½ cups whole milk

1 cup heavy cream

4 tablespoons unsalted butter

½ cup yellow onion, finely diced

4 tablespoons flour

2 bay leaves

½ teaspoon whole black peppercorns

2 tablespoons Dijon mustard

1 cup Shepherd's Way Friesago cheese, grated (or a good-quality Asiago-like cheese)

salt and white pepper, to taste

½ teaspoon freshly grated nutmeg, or to taste

finely sliced chives, for garnish

To prepare the Croque Monsieur: Preheat oven to 350°F.

Heat 2 large skillets over medium-low heat. Spread butter evenly over one side of each brioche slice. Place 4 slices of bread buttered side down on a clean work surface. Place a slice of cheese on each slice of bread, followed by 3 crisped slices of prosciutto. Top each sandwich with remaining cheese slices, and finish with the last 4 pieces of bread, buttered side up.

Using a large spatula, transfer sandwiches to preheated skillets. Fry until golden brown on one side, 3–4 minutes. Flip sandwiches and transfer skillets to oven for 5–6 minutes, or until bottoms are golden and cheese is melted.

To prepare the sauce: Combine whole milk and cream. Melt butter in a saucepan over medium heat. Add onions and sauté until translucent. Whisk in flour and cook 3–4 minutes, stirring occasionally. Turn heat to high and whisk in ⅓ of milk and cream mixture. When sauce comes to a boil, add another third and repeat until all the milk and cream mixture is absorbed. Add bay leaves, peppercorns, and mustard. Reduce heat to low and simmer 30–45 minutes. Strain sauce through a mesh sieve into a small sauce pot and add cheese, whisking until melted. Season with salt, pepper, and nutmeg to taste.

Return sauce to stove top and warm gently over low heat. Keep a close eye on it, using a whisk to ensure it does not scorch or congeal.

To serve: Cut each sandwich on the diagonal. Place on plates, then ladle ½ cup of warm Mornay sauce on each sandwich. Garnish with chives.

Tomato and Bread Soup

2006–2007: Chef Owner Alex Roberts, Restaurant Alma in partnership with Otter Creek Growers

Restaurant Alma's cozy and elegant atmosphere matches the cozy and elegant food it consistently presents. Chef Alex's spin on tomato soup, dressed up with rustic bread, makes for a lovely grown-up version of the childhood classic.

12 small to medium whole tomatoes (if summer tomatoes are not available, use fresh vine-ripened tomatoes or Romas)

¾ cup extra-virgin olive oil

¼ cup fresh garlic, peeled and thinly sliced

¼ cup fresh basil, chopped

4 cups homemade (or good quality) chicken or vegetable stock

1 tablespoon tomato paste

2-inch sprig fresh rosemary

⅛ cup Parmesan or other favorite hard cheese

1 bay leaf

sea salt and freshly ground pepper, to taste

2 cups dried rustic bread (ciabatta-type), diced

Preheat oven to 350°F.

Roast whole tomatoes on a parchment-lined rimmed baking sheet until they split and release their juices, 30–45 minutes. Allow to cool, then remove and discard tomato skins, reserving juices. Lightly pulse remaining tomato in a food processor until chunky but uniform, and mix with reserved juices.

Heat olive oil in a soup pot over medium-high heat until hot, then add garlic and stir vigorously until lightly browned and fragrant. Add basil, roasted tomatoes, stock, tomato paste, rosemary, Parmesan, bay leaf, and salt and pepper, to taste. Simmer on medium heat for 20 minutes. Remove from heat. Remove rosemary sprig and bay leaf. Whisk in bread just before serving. Garnish soup with Parmesan, fresh basil, or toasted croutons, if desired.

Beef Short Rib "Bourguignon"

2009–2010: Chef Jon Radle, Grand Cafe
in partnership with Thousand Hills Cattle Co.

Though not a traditional bourguignon, this beef short rib stew produces the same melt-in-your-mouth results we expect from a classic bourguignon. To make the most of the rich sauce, serve with mashed potatoes, polenta, or egg noodles.

YIELD: 4 SERVINGS

- 6 beef short ribs, cut 2-inches wide
- salt and pepper, to taste
- flour for dusting
- 4 slices bacon, diced
- 8 ounces mushrooms, cleaned and chopped
- 6 cloves garlic, peeled and smashed
- 2 sprigs fresh thyme
- 1 bay leaf
- 2 cups red wine
- 1 quart beef stock

Preheat oven to 325°F.

Generously season ribs with salt and pepper and dust all surfaces with flour. Heat a dutch oven over medium heat. Add bacon and cook until crisp. Remove bacon and drain on a paper towel-lined plate. Set aside. Using rendered bacon fat, sear ribs until all sides are well-browned. You may need to do this in batches to avoid overcrowding the pan. Remove ribs to a rimmed plate or pan.

To dutch oven, add mushrooms, garlic, thyme, and bay leaf. Once mushrooms are softened and tender, deglaze pan with red wine. Reduce liquid by half and add ribs back into the pan. Add beef stock and cover with a lid or foil, then place in preheated oven. Braise until tender, 2½–3 hours. Remove ribs and keep warm. Place pan back on the stove over medium heat. Remove thyme and bay leaf and add bacon back into the braising liquid. Reduce until liquid is slightly thickened. Taste and adjust seasonings, if necessary.

Plate ribs and spoon bacon and braising liquid over meat to serve.

Cornbread with Slow-Cooked Red Beans

2008–2009: Chef Owner Alex Roberts, Restaurant Alma & Brasa in partnership with Cedar Summit Farm

Chef Alex's buttery cornbread alongside perfectly salty, slow-cooked red beans is the definition of Southern comfort. The addition of bacon, onion, lots of seasonings, and a ham hock builds a robust, satisfying flavor profile. Cornbread and red beans are the best of friends. You'll enjoy and look forward to these leftovers for days.

YIELD: 8-10 SERVINGS

For slow-cooked red beans:

2 cups red beans or pinto beans, soaked overnight at room temperature

¼ cup bacon, chopped

1 tablespoon olive oil

½ medium yellow onion, roughly chopped

½ medium green pepper, roughly chopped

3 cloves garlic, peeled

1 tablespoon tomato paste

½ teaspoon ground cumin

1 teaspoon fresh thyme, chopped

1 teaspoon dried oregano

½ teaspoon kosher salt, plus more to taste

1 teaspoon black pepper

1 smoked ham hock

To prepare the beans: Rinse soaked beans. Sauté bacon in olive oil in a dutch oven at medium heat to render fat. Puree onion, green pepper and garlic in a food processor and add to pan. Gently sauté for about 5 minutes. Add tomato paste, cumin, thyme, oregano, ½ teaspoon salt, pepper, and 2 tablespoons water. Simmer gently for 5 minutes until tomato paste begins to fry. Add beans, ham hock, 4 cups water, and vinegar to pot. Bring to a boil then reduce to a simmer and cook until very tender, 4–5 hours covered on the stovetop or in a 300°F oven. You can also do this in a slow cooker on low for 8 hours or on high for 4 hours.

When beans are tender, remove from heat and remove ham hock from pot. Pull meat off hock and add desired amount back to beans. Simmer another 10 minutes or so. Taste and adjust salt after ham is cooked and beans are tender.

recipe continues...

6 cups cold water plus 2 tablespoons

2 tablespoons white wine vinegar

For cornbread:

YIELD: 18 MUFFINS OR A 9 X 12-INCH PAN OF CORNBREAD

1⅛ cups all-purpose flour

1 cup cornmeal

1¼ teaspoons baking powder

1 teaspoon salt

¼ cup sugar

2 eggs, beaten

1½ cups buttermilk

½ cup unsalted butter, melted

½ cup creamed corn (½ cup sweet corn simmered in ¼ cup cream for 10 minutes, then pureed)

To prepare the cornbread: Preheat oven to 400°F.

Combine dry ingredients in a large mixing bowl. Add eggs, buttermilk, and melted butter. Mix thoroughly, and fold in creamed corn. Bake in buttered pan about 25 minutes or until a toothpick comes out clean when inserted and removed.

Braised Lamb with Garbanzo Beans

2020: Chef Owner Erik Kleven, Bleu Duck Kitchen
in partnership with The Berryhill Farm

Briny kalamata olives, salty anchovies, and toothy garbanzo beans all come together with local lamb and vegetables to create a flavor and texture wonderland. Roasting the lamb on the bone results in a deeply flavorful leg of lamb. Delicious served with polenta, jasmine rice, or mashed potatoes.

YIELD: 6–8 SERVINGS

1 (4-pound) lamb leg, bone-in

1 cup flour, seasoned with salt and pepper

¼ cup olive oil

1 cup yellow onion, diced

½ cup carrots, diced

½ cup celery, diced

8–10 whole garlic cloves, peeled

2 cups red wine

3 (14-ounce) cans diced tomatoes or 4 cups fresh tomatoes, chopped

2 bay leaves

1 lemon, sliced

8 anchovy fillets, optional

3 (15½-ounce) cans garbanzo beans

1 cup kalamata olives, chopped

3 stems fresh rosemary

1 quart beef stock

Preheat oven to 300°F.

Place seasoned flour in a large bowl. Place lamb leg in bowl and turn until covered with flour mixture.

In a heavy bottomed, deep-sided pot, heat olive oil over medium-high heat. Add lamb and sear well on all sides. Remove meat from pan and set aside on a plate. Add onion, carrots, celery, and garlic to pot; sauté 1 minute.

Add red wine and deglaze pot, scraping up any bits as the wine heats. Place lamb back into pot on top of vegetables; add remaining ingredients around lamb leg.

Cover pot and slow cook in oven for 3½–4 hours, or until lamb can be easily pulled apart with a fork. Remove lamb and pull apart into large chunks, saving vegetables and braising juices to serve along with the lamb.

Braised Chicken with Tomatoes and Heirloom Beans

2012: Chef Lucia Watson, Lucia's Restaurant, Wine Bar and To Go in partnership with Encore Farm

Lucia Watson, award-winning chef, author, and agricultural advocate has always loved to cook, a love inspired by her grandmother. For Lucia, food is about nurturing others, from the farmers who grow and raise food to the people who ultimately eat it. Always willing to take a chance on a farmer, Lucia became Paula Foreman of Encore Farm's first customer. Paula grows heirloom varieties of edible dry beans, heirloom corn for cornmeal, and other small grains. Paula chose dry heirloom beans as her first crop after learning about the decline of food diversity brought on by increasingly standardized industrial farming.

For heirloom beans:

1 cup dried heirloom beans (may substitute with dried Great Northern or navy white beans)

3 tablespoons olive oil, divided

1 bay leaf

1 whole tomato, chunked

3–4 garlic cloves, unpeeled

pinch of salt

For chicken:

1½ pounds chicken thighs and legs (about 4 pieces)

salt and pepper, to taste

4 tablespoons olive oil, divided

1 medium yellow onion, diced

2 cloves garlic, peeled and smashed

1 red pepper, diced

1 yellow pepper, diced

big splash red wine

2–3 cups tomatoes, diced (fresh is best)

2 cups low-sodium chicken stock

1 sprig each of fresh rosemary, thyme, and flat-leaf parsley

1 bay leaf

2 cups cooked heirloom beans

To prepare the beans: Generously cover beans with water and soak overnight in the refrigerator. Drain beans and lightly rinse with cold water, then place in a heavy kettle and cover with plenty of cold water (at least 3 inches above the beans). Add 1 tablespoon olive oil, bay leaf, tomato, garlic, and a pinch of salt. Bring beans to a boil, then reduce heat. Cook until tender to the bite, partially covered, 1–3 hours, depending on how dry and delicate beans are. Drain, discarding bay leaf, garlic and tomato pieces. Cool to room temperature and stir in 1–2 tablespoons olive oil to coat beans.

To prepare the chicken: Season chicken well with salt and pepper. In a deep, heavy skillet, heat 2 tablespoons oil until just smoking. Add chicken and brown all over. Remove and

For garnish:

citrus zest, lemon or orange

fresh herbs (such as basil and mint), chopped or torn

optional, crusty bread, for serving

optional, your favorite hard cheese for topping

set aside. In same skillet, add 2 more tablespoons olive oil, then onion, garlic, and peppers. Cook over medium-high heat, stirring frequently, for about 3 minutes. Add wine, stir, and cook down for a few minutes. Add tomatoes, stock, rosemary, thyme, parsley, bay leaf, and salt and pepper to taste. Nestle chicken into pot and cook covered over medium-low heat, about 40 minutes. Test for doneness, inserting a meat thermometer into thickest part of meat (it should read 165°F). Remove any big pieces of herbs and stir in cooked beans.

Mix fresh herbs with citrus zest. To serve, dish chicken, vegetables, beans, and broth into bowls. Sprinkle with garnish. Serve with crusty bread and freshly grated hard cheese, if desired.

Stewed Winter Squash and Black-Eyed Peas with Sage Polenta Triangles

2009–2010: Owner Danny Schwartzman, Common Roots Cafe in partnership with Riverbend Farm

Danny Schwartzman has been sourcing products from Greg Reynolds of Riverbend Farm since Common Roots opened; Greg even helped Common Roots establish its restaurant garden. Danny especially loves the handmade polenta Greg makes with his hand-shucked corn. When the three components of this recipe come together, it's magical, but feel free to use the components separately. The tomato sauce is crazy delicious and could be used in a shakshuka or served with pasta. If you have kids, puree the sauce first and they'll have no idea it is full of veggies.

YIELD: 8 SERVINGS

For polenta triangles:

4 cups water

3 tablespoons unsalted butter

2 cups polenta

½ cup Parmesan or local hard cheese of your choice, shredded

3 tablespoons fresh sage, chopped

salt and pepper, to taste

For squash and black-eyed peas:

1 cup butternut or any winter squash, peeled and diced medium

2 tablespoons olive oil, divided

salt and pepper, to taste

1 cup dry black-eyed peas, soaked overnight

To prepare the polenta: Bring water to a boil in a medium sauté pan. Add butter and reduce heat to medium. Slowly whisk in polenta until it thickens. Add shredded cheese and sage, and stir until smooth. Season to taste with salt and pepper, and remove from heat. Spread polenta ½-inch thick on a cookie sheet to cool and harden. Then cut into triangles. Preparing the polenta to this point ahead, at least a couple hours, will ensure it has time to completely cool and harden.

To prepare the squash and black-eyed peas: Preheat oven to 350°F.

Toss squash in 1 tablespoon olive oil and season with salt and pepper. Place on a sheet pan and roast 15–20 minutes, until tender.

Meanwhile rinse soaked black-eyed peas and drain well.

Heat 1 tablespoon oil in a large pot. Add onion and garlic. When fragrant and beginning to soften add spices. Stir well then add carrots, bay leaf, and black-eyed peas. Add enough vegetable stock to barely cover mixture, 2–3 cups. Bring to a slow boil. Cover and cook beans until tender, about 1 hour. After 30 minutes, check to see that the mixture is still

¼ yellow onion, chopped

1 clove garlic, peeled and minced

2 teaspoons paprika

1 teaspoon ground cumin

1 medium carrot, diced

1 bay leaf

1 quart vegetable stock

For tomato sauce:

3 tablespoons olive oil

1 cup celery, chopped

1 yellow onion, chopped

2 garlic cloves, peeled and chopped

½ cup roasted red pepper, chopped

1 bay leaf

1 teaspoon dried thyme

1 (14½-ounce) can whole peeled tomatoes, pureed

1 teaspoon cayenne pepper

1 teaspoon hot sauce

kosher salt and freshly ground black pepper, to taste

¼ cup fresh flat-leaf parsley, chopped

covered with stock; if not, add more. Continue checking every 15 minutes. If you run out of stock, use water. When peas are tender, add roasted squash and season with salt and pepper to taste.

To prepare the sauce: In a medium saucepan, heat oil then add celery, onion and garlic. Lightly sauté vegetables then add red pepper, bay leaf, thyme and tomatoes. Stir well and bring to a simmer. Simmer for about an hour until thick and deeply savory. Add cayenne, hot sauce and season to taste with salt and pepper. Remove from heat, let cool, then add chopped parsley.

To serve: Rewarm polenta triangles in oven at 350°F or on stovetop. For stovetop method, add 1 tablespoon olive oil to a nonstick skillet and heat to medium. Add polenta triangles to pan and reheat on both sides.

Spread tomato sauce around edge of plate. Place polenta triangles on plate. Spoon squash and black-eyed peas over polenta.

Sweets

A life spent doing what you've dreamed of doing, no matter how hard the work has been, is a sweet life. Effort, grit, and purpose foster a sense of contentment, the feeling that life has been well lived. Sit down, relax, and enjoy a treat. You've worked hard, and the day is over now.

Riverbend Farm: A Farming Love Story

Farmer Greg Reynolds's standard joke is that if he had grown up on a farm, he'd have known better than to become a farmer. No matter how deadpan he tries to deliver this joke, Greg's broad smile and twinkling eyes instantly give him away. He's not fooling anybody—certainly not anyone who knows him. Greg is doing the work he was born to do despite not actually being born a farmer. Greg chose to become a farmer, his life bending and winding along the way, just as the river running alongside his farm bends and winds, following the path it carves.

While it is true that Greg didn't grow up on a farm, both his parents did, and his childhood was filled with a *lifetime* of unfiltered stories from the gritty farm life quilting his family's past. Yet something inside him felt drawn to farm anyway, perhaps a magnetic generational connection to the soil. His mother's family lost their farm in North Dakota during the 1930's after a five-year drought, and his dad's family farm was passed on to his uncle. Since Greg didn't inherit land, he knew if he really wanted to farm someday he would have to pursue an education first and earn enough money to buy a farm later.

And so he did, all the while safeguarding his long-term goal of farming in his back pocket. Before anyone in Minnesota's food community knew him, and before he knew anyone, Greg got a degree in physics and went on to work for a Minnesota-based company, which, by today's definitions, would qualify as a high-tech start-up. The company measured rocket exhaust, split laser beams, and determined the speed of particles in airstreams by calculating the shift in the frequency of light. Greg, with an aptitude for science and problem solving, was a natural at translating the company's technology for customers. But after twenty years, despite feeling thoroughly engaged with his career, he decided it was time to bring his long-held vision to life, a change of focus also influenced by the post-Vietnam war back-to-the-land movement. Greg and his wife Mary, a licensed psychologist, sold their home in Connecticut where the company had relocated them and returned to Minnesota just in time for the great Halloween blizzard of 1991, perhaps an omen of life ahead.

Knowing they wanted a farmstead proximate to a large potential market, Greg and Mary found eighty acres of land just thirty miles outside of Minneapolis and embarked on the next phase of their lives. Having no map outlining the road to success, Greg leaned on his experience in science, sales, and problem solving, as well as a strong internal compass, to build both their farm and a network for their food. Focused on growing organic vegetables, Greg initially hoped to sell his produce within Minnesota's expanding system of natural foods co-ops, but he quickly learned that market was largely spoken for and hard to penetrate. Undeterred, his next thought was, *Restaurants use a lot of food, too,* prompting him to begin cold calling local restaurants, introducing himself as the owner of a new farm—Riverbend Farm—and asking whether they would be interested in buying any local, organic food. He endured plenty of rejection, but when the response was positive, his first follow-up question was, "Is there something we can grow for you?"

Through good old-fashioned cold calling, door-knocking, dropping off food samples for chefs, and—on at least one occasion—simply strolling back into a restaurant kitchen and saying, "I'm a farmer, I just had breakfast here, and I should be selling to your restaurant," Greg steadily built a foundation of committed chef partners. Drawn to his impeccable and clean produce, reliability, and good-natured personality, one chef led to another, then another, and another until eventually he was working with dozens of restaurants. Greg's reputation for excellence now precedes him within both Minnesota's restaurant and farm communities. And while it's impossible to credit a single farmer or chef with sparking Minnesota's interconnected, robust local foods community, Greg Reynolds has certainly been a linchpin.

Riverbend Farm is now twenty-five years old, and there have been plenty of occasions when Greg seriously thought about throwing in the towel, especially as the effects of climate change throw the most unkind curveballs, sometimes thwarting an entire season's worth of work. July and August of 2017 were unusually cool and wet, creating the perfect conditions for a nasty late blight, which swept through Riverbend and wiped out all the tomatoes just as they were starting to ripen, along with the potatoes. Searing heat in July of 2018 killed the blossoms on all their peppers and stressed everything in the fields, only to be followed by an exceedingly wet and uncharacteristically cool 2019, which messed with the corn and warm season crops. Uncontrollable weather events like these make farmers want to surrender. Riverbend, like every other farm, can't afford major crop losses.

Yet, according to Greg, farming is an addictive pursuit, and once it gets its hooks in you it's tough to give up. There is a persistent voice whispering that next time—next year—will surely be better, if you just hang in there a little longer. The sense that success is lurking around the corner is alluring. Greg jokes that this way of thinking is pathological; more likely it is pure and simple optimism and determination.

A standout within Minnesota's farming community, Greg Reynolds has been an important spokesperson for local producers, opening doors many others have now passed through over the years. He's been instrumental in creating relationship marketing with restaurants, groundbreaking in selecting and saving seeds, and incredibly productive in terms of providing large volumes of healthy, organic food; yet that which feels most rewarding to him is the Riverbend community formed over the years, the fulfillment he finds working with customers and the "crop mob regulars" who show up, rain or shine, to help at community work days on the farm.

Everything he's accomplished has been done with a straightforward, matter-of-fact, authentic, down-to-earth humility and the unwavering support of Mary, who maintained her psychology practice while helping on the farm more than most people know. If it weren't for Mary, Greg says he would likely have starved years ago, working in the fields and not stopping to eat. But beyond keeping him fed during long workdays, Mary herself has invested her own time, energy, labor, and love into Riverbend. Nobody runs a farm alone.

Has it all been worth it? Financially speaking, probably not. Greg is the first to admit he and Mary would probably have a lot more money if he had stuck with his other career path. But in virtually every other definition of success, yes—it has been worth it. In exchange for money, Greg has had the privilege of spending the last twenty-five years doing something he really wanted to do. There are problems to solve and a real sense of doing something meaningful, having something to show for a day's work. He got to write his own life's script, spend a lot of time outdoors, live in a beautiful spot, and be involved in making a little piece of the world a better place. He and Mary have built lasting friendships within a supportive community of people all connected around land and the food produced on their land. And, while the financial rewards haven't always been stellar, they still made a living. Despite requiring incredibly long and physical hours, farming feeds the souls of farmers in a way nothing else can. It's impossible to put a price on that picture of success.

Strawberry Rhubarb Cobbler

2007–2008: Owner Tracy Singleton, Birchwood Cafe in partnership with Riverbend Farm

Birchwood Cafe, located in the Seward neighborhood of Minneapolis, is a true community gathering place. For owner Tracy Singleton, supporting small, local farmers, who she believes are a vital component of a healthy food system, is central to Birchwood's mission to serve "Real Good Food." The Birchwood team takes their cues from farmer friends, who guide and inspire their creativity in the kitchen, including Greg Reynolds of Riverbend Farm. Greg has supplied Birchwood with fresh food for over twenty years. Wonderful served warm with vanilla ice cream or whipped cream, this cobbler is easy and flavorful, with the perfect balance of sweetness.

YIELD: 12 SERVINGS

For filling:

3 pints strawberries, quartered

2 pounds fresh rhubarb, sliced ½-inch thick

1½ cups sugar

3 tablespoons cornstarch

½ teaspoon cinnamon

1 big pinch nutmeg

For topping:

1½ cups flour

½ cup yellow ground cornmeal

½ cup sugar

1 tablespoon baking powder

¼ teaspoon salt

6 tablespoons cold unsalted butter, cut into pieces

¾ cup heavy cream, plus more if needed

¼ cup coarse sugar

To prepare the filling: Preheat oven to 350°F

Mix all ingredients together in a bowl. Pour into a buttered 9 x 13-inch pan. Bake 30–40 minutes. Stir occasionally until fruit is bubbly around the edges and juices are glossy.

To prepare the topping: Combine all dry ingredients except coarse sugar. Cut butter into dry mixture using 2 forks or a pastry blender until it has the consistency of coarse sand. Add ½ cup heavy cream and start to mix. Gradually add the remaining ¼ cup cream until a soft dough forms. If dough doesn't form, add a tablespoon more cream; repeat if necessary. Take care not to over mix. Break off ¼-cup size pieces of dough, flatten slightly with your fingers, and place evenly over baked fruit. Sprinkle dough topping with coarse sugar. Return to oven and bake 25–30 minutes until golden brown. Cool and serve.

Viennese Apple Strudel

2015: Chef Owner Robert Ulrich, Mendoberri Cafe & Wine Bar in partnership with Westcott Orchard and Hidden Stream Farm

For the experienced baker in the house—or someone interested in a challenge—Chef Robert's classic and celebrated Viennese Apple Strudel is the dessert for you. This fancy strudel is a true work of art. For those wishing for the sweet rewards without the challenge, store-bought puff pastry in place of the homemade strudel dough will also yield deliciousness. A native of Austria, Chef Robert has fond memories growing up in a home filled with the aromas of scratch-cooked meals, desserts, and even home-made wine. Using ingredients with integrity to create food with integrity, even in our fast-paced world, is of primary importance to him.

YIELD: ABOUT
12 PORTIONS

For strudel dough:

1¾ cups all-purpose flour

1 tablespoon vegetable oil

1 whole egg

pinch of salt

juice from 1 lemon

½ cup warm water

For apple filling:

2 pounds tart apples like Red Free, Paula Red, or Granny Smith

½ cup sugar

½ cup chopped walnuts

¼ cup raisins

2 tablespoons rum

1 teaspoon cinnamon

1 teaspoon lemon zest

1 teaspoon lemon juice

½ cup unseasoned breadcrumbs

To prepare the dough: Sift flour into a small hill onto a working surface. Create a well in the center.

In a mixing bowl blend together oil, egg, salt, lemon juice, and water. Using your left hand, slowly add liquid mixture in small amounts into the flour well. Combine slowly with your right hand to incorporate all ingredients.

Knead dough until it has an elastic feel to it and becomes shiny, about 5 minutes. Set aside onto a floured board. Cover with a warm bowl and let rest for at least 30 minutes while you prepare the filling.

To prepare the filling: Preheat oven to 350°F.

Peel, core, and slice apples. If working slowly, store sliced apples in a large bowl of water and lemon juice while work-ing to prevent oxidation. Remove excess water before pro-ceeding. (Skip this step if working quickly.) Mix apples with sugar, walnuts, raisins, rum, cinnamon, lemon zest, and lemon juice. Blend together well.

Toast breadcrumbs in a sauté pan over medium heat until light golden brown. Add 4 tablespoons melted butter. Com-bine with apple mixture.

Cover a table with a clean, old tablecloth. Dust well with flour. Knead dough thoroughly once more for a couple

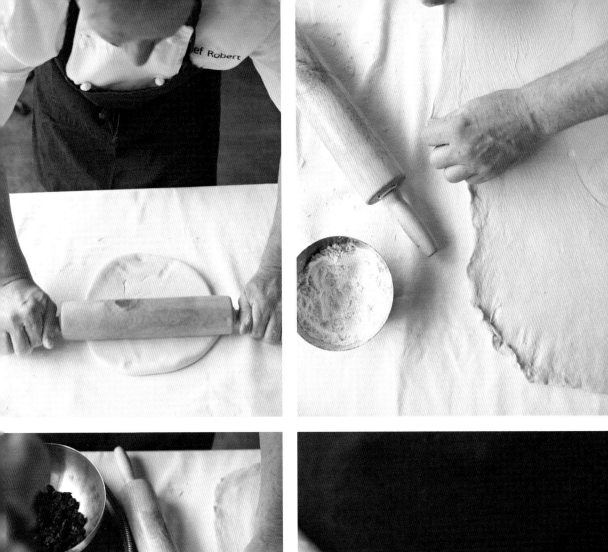

¾ cup melted unsalted butter, divided

To serve:

powdered sugar

vanilla ice cream

minutes, then roll dough into a rectangle. Using a rolling pin or the back of your hands, carefully stretch dough until about 36 x 18 inches and almost see-through. Cut off excess thick edges.

Carefully spread apple filling onto lower ⅔ of the dough lengthwise, then carefully fold in the left and right ends of dough 3–4 inches over the apple mixture. With the help of the tablecloth carefully roll the strudel, beginning at the bottom, into one long log. When you reach the end of the filling, fold over the last ⅓ of the dough to close the strudel.

Place onto a buttered parchment-lined baking sheet and brush top with remaining melted butter. Bake for 30–45 minutes.

To serve: Dust warm strudel with powdered sugar. Slice and serve with vanilla ice cream.

Hazelnut Shortbread Sandwich Cookies

2009–2010: Owner Lisa Lindberg, Amboy Cottage Cafe in partnership with Hope Creamery

Jam, frosting, and hazelnuts make these delicate, pretty sandwich cookies feel lovely and special. Lisa says, "This is an old Swedish recipe used by our family every Christmas for our Swedish Smorgasbord. Best made a day ahead of your tea party. They freeze very well."

Lisa relies on butter from Hope Creamery, one of the only independently owned creameries in the state, for her baked delights. Hope butter is considered the freshest around thanks to the old-fashioned, hands-on, small-batch operation used to make it. Their premium, luxurious butter is made fresh every week and never stored.

YIELD: ABOUT 3 DOZEN SANDWICH COOKIES

- 1 cup unsalted butter, room temperature
- ½ cup granulated sugar
- ½ cup hazelnuts, ground
- 2 cups organic white flour, divided
- 1 cup powdered sugar
- 2 tablespoons water
- 1 cup currant jelly
- ½ cup hazelnuts, toasted and roughly chopped, for topping

Preheat oven to 325°F.

Cream butter with sugar. Mix in hazelnuts and 1½ cups flour. Mix and add more flour until your dough starts to shape. It should hold together when shaped but still be slightly fragile. Shape the dough into a 1½-inch thick log and wrap in plastic wrap. Chill thoroughly in refrigerator, rotating the dough to keep round shape as it chills. Unwrap dough and, using a very sharp knife, slice into ⅛-inch rounds. Bake on an ungreased baking sheet until browned, 16–18 minutes. Cool slightly and remove to rack.

While cookies cool, stir together powdered sugar and water to make a glaze. Once cool, spread half of the cookies with currant jelly and sandwich them together with the plain cookie halves. Drizzle glaze over tops of cookies. Sprinkle with toasted chopped hazelnuts.

Citrus Pound Cake with Blueberry Compote

2007–2008: Chef Owner Jim Kyndberg, Bayport Cookery
in partnership with PastureLand Dairy Co-op

Fresh and bright, this pound cake is all kinds of wonderful. If you don't have Port on hand for the blueberry compote, you can use water, but the addition of Port is noticeable and brings a beautiful depth forward that makes buying a bottle worth every penny. Though straightforward to bake, this dessert tastes fancy.

YIELD: 1 9 X 5-INCH
POUND CAKE

For pound cake:

1 cup unsalted butter, softened

1⅓ cups sugar

3 large eggs plus 3 yolks, lightly beaten

1 teaspoon vanilla extract

2 teaspoons freshly squeezed orange juice

1½ cups cake flour

½ teaspoon salt

zest of 1 lemon

crème fraîche

lemon thyme or mint, for garnish

For blueberry compote:

1 pint blueberries

⅓ cup sugar

3 tablespoons lemon juice

1 teaspoon cornstarch mixed with 1 tablespoon Port wine (or water)

To prepare the pound cake: Preheat oven to 325°F.

Beat butter with a mixer on medium until smooth and shiny, approximately 30 seconds. Turn mixer to medium-low and add sugar. Mix until fluffy, approximately 5 minutes. Add eggs, vanilla, and orange juice. Once incorporated, beat on medium-high until fluffy again. Sift flour in a separate bowl and stir in salt and citrus zest. With mixer on low, add flour mixture to batter half a cup at a time, stopping occasionally to scrape sides of bowl. Do not over mix. Stop as soon as flour mixture is incorporated.

Pour batter into a buttered 9 x 5-inch loaf pan. Bake for 60–70 minutes or until you can insert a toothpick in the center and have it come out clean. Cool on wire rack until room temperature. Remove from pan and continue to cool on a wire rack.

To prepare the compote: Mix all ingredients together in a small saucepan. Bring to a boil while stirring constantly over medium-high heat, 2–3 minutes. Taste to make sure cornstarch has cooked out. Let cool before serving.

Slice pound cake, top with blueberry compote and crème fraîche. Garnish with lemon thyme or fresh mint.

Cherry Madeleines with Cherry Glaze

2018: Owner Anne Andrus, Honey & Rye Bakehouse in partnership with York Farm

Anne Andrus, owner of Honey & Rye Bakehouse in St. Louis Park, has manifested her dream of owning a little, stand-alone shop where she can spend her days knuckle-deep in dough, baking to her heart's delight. Given Minnesota's short summers, Anne savors every bit of ripe summertime goodness she can get her hands on, including Minnesota-hardy fruit like the cherries she uses in these dainty, delectable madeleines, which are as delightful to the eye as to one's palate.

YIELD: 24 COOKIES

For cookies:

1 cup unsalted butter

2 cups pastry flour

2 teaspoons baking powder

pinch of salt

1 cup granulated sugar

2 tablespoons brown sugar

2 tablespoons honey

5 eggs

1 cup chopped cherries, patted dry*

For cherry glaze:

2 cups powdered (confectioners) sugar

¼ cup fresh cherries*

juice of ½ lemon

2–4 tablespoons hot water

If fresh cherries are out of season, substitute high-quality frozen cherries.

To prepare the cookies: Preheat oven to 375°F.

Melt butter in a small bowl and reserve. Sift flour, baking powder and salt into a separate bowl. Whisk sugars, honey, and eggs in a separate bowl, just to incorporate.

Fold dry ingredients into wet ingredients in 2–3 batches, until just incorporated. Add melted, slightly cooled butter. Fold in gently, just to incorporate. Gently fold in chopped cherries, just to incorporate. Chill before baking (30 minutes or overnight).

Spoon or scoop batter into buttered madeleine pan, filling each cup about ¾ full.

Bake 10–12 minutes, rotating pan halfway through. Cookies are done when there is browning around the edges and a signature "bump" in the center. They should spring back when gently pressed. Remove from pan onto wire rack.

To prepare the cherry glaze: Sift powdered sugar. Mash cherries in sifted sugar and allow juices to release. Add water as needed to achieve pourable consistency—if too thin, add more sugar; if too thick, add more water. While cookies are still warm but cool enough to handle, dip one end in cherry glaze. Allow to cool to set the glaze before serving.

Roasted Butternut Squash Crème Brûlée

2008–2009: Chef JP Samuelson, JP American Bistro
in partnership with Deer Creek Farm

YIELD: 6 SERVINGS

1 cup butternut squash, peeled and cubed

olive oil

kosher salt

2 cups heavy cream

1 cup whole milk

¾ cup granulated sugar, divided

1 teaspoon Chinese five-spice powder

6 large egg yolks

pinch of salt

Toss squash with a light drizzle of olive oil and a little bit of salt. Place on a sheet pan and roast for about 25 minutes, until fork tender. Allow to cool slightly then puree in a food processor.

In a heavy saucepan over medium heat, bring heavy cream, milk, ¼ cup of sugar, roasted squash puree, and Chinese 5 spice powder to a simmer. Meanwhile, whisk together the egg yolks and another ¼ cup of sugar in a bowl. Remove cream mixture from heat and add a little to the egg yolk mixture to warm it, whisking constantly to ensure the yolks don't curdle. Slowly pour egg yolk mixture into hot cream mixture, whisking the cream as you pour. Taste cream mixture and add more Chinese 5 spice powder if preferred. Allow to cool. Strain through a fine sieve and stir in the salt. Chill for at least 2 hours and up to 2 days.

Preheat oven to 350°F. When ready to bake, pour cream mixture into six 4-ounce ramekins. Arrange ramekins in a deep baking pan with sides at least 3 inches high. Pour enough very hot water into the baking pan to reach ⅔ of the way up the sides of the ramekins. Cover tightly with foil. Carefully place pan in middle rack of oven. Bake custards for 30 minutes, then let out a little steam and bake for another 15–20 minutes longer, until they are set around the edges but still slightly jiggly in the center. Cool and refrigerate if serving later.

Just before serving, divide remaining ¼ cup sugar evenly among ramekins and spread along the surface of each custard. Use a kitchen torch to brown the sugar, or place under a broiler set to high heat, watching carefully to prevent burning. Tops should be deeply browned and caramel in color.

Thunder Cookies

2015: Positively Third Street Bakery
in partnership with Locally Laid Egg Company

Once Jason Amundson got it in his head to become a farmer, no amount of reasoning could derail him from pursuing his calling. Now he and his wife Lucie, owners of Locally Laid Egg Company, raise happy hens who lay eggs with sturdy, glowing orange yolks prized by bakers and cooks around the state, including those at Positively Third Street Bakery. Through farming Jason and Lucie hope to help shore up rural communities by nudging more people toward real, local food.

YIELD: ABOUT 5 DOZEN COOKIES

1 pound unsalted butter, room temperature

2 cups brown sugar

1½ cups white sugar

2 eggs

1¼ cups salted, natural peanut butter

1½ teaspoons baking soda

1½ teaspoons salt

2 cups thick rolled oats

4 cups whole wheat pastry flour

1¾ cups chocolate chips

Preheat oven to 375°F.

Combine butter, brown sugar, and white sugar; mix well until creamed together and no visible butter lumps remain.

Add eggs and mix until incorporated, then add peanut butter and mix until well combined. Add baking soda, salt, and oats. Stir well. Next, mix in whole wheat pastry flour. Finally, stir in chocolate chips. If you used a mixer for the batter, switch to hand mixing for this step.

Place heaping spoonfuls of cookie dough onto baking sheets, allowing plenty of space to spread. Bake cookies in preheated oven for 10–11 minutes. Let cool on sheet for a couple minutes then transfer to cooling rack.

Note: If you prefer a very soft and moist cookie, use slightly less flour—closer to 3½ cups. For a firmer cookie, add a bit more flour. After you make a few batches, you will learn what you prefer.

Church Basement Apple Crisp

2009–2010: Chef Owner Nathalie Johnson, Signature Cafe and Catering in partnership with Whistling Well Farm

Chef Nathalie Johnson and husband Tony Parsons, former owners of Signature Cafe and Catering in the Prospect Park neighborhood of Minneapolis, were known for creating down-home, approachable dishes made from the freshest seasonal ingredients they could get their hands on. This simple and familiar crisp is a perfect example—easy, trustworthy, and scrumptious.

YIELD: 12 SERVINGS

- 1 cup unsalted butter, room temperature
- 1-2 cups granulated sugar, divided
- 2 cups brown sugar
- 2 cups white flour
- 1 teaspoon salt
- 8-10 tart Minnesota apples (such as Haralson or Cortland), peeled, cored, and sliced

Preheat oven to 375°F.

Cream butter with 1 cup granulated sugar and 2 cups brown sugar with mixer until light in color, 3–4 minutes on medium-high speed. Slowly add flour. Add salt. When all is well-incorporated, place in refrigerator and prepare apples. In a well-buttered 9 x 13-inch pan, layer bottom of pan with apples. Sprinkle with granulated sugar—start with ½ cup, amount depends on tartness of apples. Cover with brown sugar topping. Bake 30–45 minutes, until apples are tender and top is crumbly and browned.

Acknowledgments

There are many people to thank for their role in bringing *The Farmer and The Chef* to life. First and foremost, every page of this book is inspired by farmers. For those who dedicate their lives to growing and raising food and nurturing the land, yours is a difficult and often thankless job; we simply cannot express enough gratitude for the work you do. Thank you especially to those farmers who set time aside to talk with us at length, treat us to farm tours, and patiently answer our questions. We appreciate your vulnerability, thoughtfulness, and honesty. For the restaurant owners, chefs, and cooks who commit to partnering with farmers and using your talents and platforms to support a healthy local food system, we also owe you a debt of gratitude. Minnesota is an agricultural leader and world-class food community because of all of you.

To the key folks who got Minnesota Cooks rolling in the beginning: former MFU President Doug Peterson, Chef Andrew Zimmern, Jim Ennis—special thanks to each of you for your vision, creative spark, and for laying Minnesota Cooks' sturdy foundation. To all of our farmer and chef participants, sponsors, volunteers, event panelists, dignitaries, and emcees who have braved the Minnesota State Fair during the searing heat of August to celebrate local foods with us, thank you for showing up. Mary Lahammer, thank you for your unwavering and enthusiastic support of the program and for believing in its potential beyond its original conception. We are so grateful to have you on our team. Thank you also to the Minnesota State Fair for giving us a prominent stage at the "Great Minnesota Get-Together" to shine the spotlight on local foods.

This book would not be what it is without the forward-thinking culture and innovative spirit of Minnesota Farmers Union. Minnesota Farmers Union President Gary Wertish and MFU's Executive Committee, thank you for being bold leaders who leapt at the chance to harness a unique, exciting opportunity—and for believing in us to carry it through on behalf of the organization. We are incredibly grateful to work with visionary leaders and dedicated colleagues who care about making a difference and amplifying the voice of farmers.

Funding and support for this project was provided by Minnesota Farmers Union Foundation and Farmers Union Industries Foundation. Additional significant funding was provided by the Minnesota Department of Agriculture's Minnesota Grown Program, for which we are deeply grateful. Paul Hugunin, Karen Lanthier, Carrie Tollefson, and the entire team at Minnesota Grown have been invaluable, long-term partners in our shared mission to support farmers and promote local foods. It is a joy to work hand-in-hand with you.

Becca Camacho and Caroline Glawe, our talented and patient recipe testers, spent a huge chunk of 2019 stowed away in their kitchens, recreating each restaurant recipe to make sure it would fly with the home cook. Thank you for your attention to detail, diligence, and endurance. It felt comforting to know these recipes were in such capable hands.

To our friends and families who have listened to us ramble endlessly about the smallest, grittiest details of this book and who have patiently waited for us to join the land of the living again—thank you for proofreading, caring, and encouraging us to keep going. Thank you for understanding when we had to cancel plans.

To all the consumers who shop at farmers markets, belong to a CSA, dine at farm-to-table restaurants, or otherwise buy directly from a farmer—your thoughtful choices are meaningful, important, and make a profound difference. Thanks for being part of a grassroots tribe creating thoughtful change!

Lastly, a special thank you to Bruce Miller, our third team member and co-conspirator for the last decade, who helped bring *The Farmer and The Chef* to life. Bruce, thank you for trusting us to carry out this project on behalf of the team. You have been with us every step of the way, influencing our decisions, even when we could no longer see or talk to you. Thank you for all the savory waffles, fried shishito peppers, and stories we got to share throughout the years. You are missed.

Claudine and Katie

Recipe Index

About the Authors

Minnesota Farmers Union (MFU) works to protect and enhance the economic interests and quality of life for family farmers, ranchers, and rural communities of Minnesota. The Minnesota Cooks™ program and *The Farmer and The Chef* are created with support from MFU President Gary Wertish and the MFU Executive Committee and in partnership with the Minnesota Department of Agriculture's Minnesota Grown Program.

Claudine Arndt is the manager of Minnesota Cooks™, a local foods program of MFU that served as the inspiration for *The Farmer and The Chef*. She is the primary author of the book's stories, drawing from her dedication to local foods, a healthy lifestyle, and her unique ability to connect with others' experiences. Also a nutrition counselor and owner of Wellness with Claudine, she encourages others to choose quality, local foods.

Katie Cannon is the photographer for the Minnesota Cooks™ program; the public television program, *Farm Fresh Road Trip*; and *The Farmer and The Chef*. Beyond photography, Katie's creativity helped shape and finesse each recipe and story in *The Farmer and The Chef*. She is also the owner of her photography business, Katie Cannon Photography.

Bruce Miller was the membership outreach and special projects director for Minnesota Farmers Union, Minnesota Cooks™ director, and also the driving force behind *The Farmer and The Chef* prior to his passing in November 2019. He was a champion for farmers and farm policy. He partnered with Minnesota Public Television on the creation of the Upper Midwest Emmy award–winning television program, *Farm Fresh Road Trip*. He leaves behind a rich legacy in advocacy, fellowship, and local foods.